THE SCALE OF
IMPRISONMENT

Franklin E. Zimring &
Gordon Hawkins

THE SCALE OF IMPRISONMENT

The University of Chicago Press
Chicago and London

FRANKLIN E. ZIMRING is professor of law and director of the Earl Warren Legal Institute at the University of California, Berkeley. GORDON HAWKINS is senior fellow at the Institute. Singly and jointly, their work has had a profound role in shaping the agenda for criminal justice policy and research. Their most recent books include *Capital Punishment and the American Agenda* and *The Citizen's Guide to Gun Control*.

The University of Chicago Press, Chicago 60637
The University of Chicago Press, Ltd., London
© 1991 by The University of Chicago
All rights reserved. Published 1991
Printed in the United States of America
00 99 98 97 96 95 94 93 92 91 5 4 3 2 1

Library of Congress Cataloging-in-Publication Data

Zimring, Franklin E.
    The scale of imprisonment / Franklin E. Zimring & Gordon Hawkins.
        p.   cm.—(Studies in crime and justice)
    Includes bibliographical references and index.
    ISBN 0-226-98353-6
    1. Imprisonment—United States.   2. Prisons—United States.
I. Hawkins, Gordon, 1919–   .   II. Title.   III. Series.
HV9469.Z56   1991
365'.973—dc20   90-44613
                                                                             CIP

∞ The paper used in this publication meets the minimum requirements of the American National Standard for Information Sciences—Permanence of Paper for Printed Library Materials, ANSI Z39.48–1984.

This book is dedicated to the memory of
Molly Dilman Zimring, 1906–1990.

An Earl Warren Legal Institute Study

Contents

Acknowledgments

The research that produced this volume was wholly supported by the Daniel and Florence Guggenheim Foundation through a Guggenheim Foundation grant for a series of seminars in criminal justice policy. For three years running, the Foundation sponsored year-long programs with prison management and crowding as topics. This sustained support was necessary for establishing the scale of imprisonment as a topic in American legal studies. Malcolm Feeley, Sheldon Messinger, and Edward Rubin were the Berkeley colleagues who collaborated in the larger enterprise and thus bear responsibility for helping to launch this volume.

The staff at the Earl Warren Legal Institute performed at its usual high levels in supporting this venture. Karen Chin prepared the manuscript, and made it possible to electronically prepare the book for publication. Since this reduced the price of the book, readers have reason to join us in thanking her. Rod Watanabe of the Center for the Study of Law and Society and Cathleen Hill of the Earl Warren Legal Institute provided administrative support.

Jennifer Pearson served as the principal research assistant on the project. Steven Rein provided additional statistical assistance. Our Berkeley colleagues Messinger, Feeley, and Terence Speed read and reacted to sections of the manuscript as did Richard Harding of the University of Western Australia and Michael Tonry of the University of Minnesota. The dedication reflects a longer-term and larger debt of one of us.

Introduction

Three kinds of question arise in relating a society's use of the criminal law to its prison population. There is first the general justification of the use of imprisonment as a criminal sanction. There is second the justification of the use of imprisonment in particular cases. And finally there is the separate question of the scale of the use of prisons as a penal method.

The first question addresses whether prison should be used as a criminal sanction. The second question concerns whether particular offenders should be sent to prison. The third question, the subject of this book, concerns the size of a society's prison enterprise in relation to other criminal sanctions and to the general population. How many prisoners? How many prisons? What criteria should govern decisions about how large a prison enterprise should be constructed and maintained?

While the institution of the prison is a universal characteristic of industrialized nations, the scale of the prison enterprise varies substantially from place to place and over time. In the United States, the prison population in the state with the highest rate of imprisonment usually exceeds that of the lowest-rate state by a factor of ten. Moreover, in less than two decades, the number of persons imprisoned in the United States has tripled, a substantial change by any measure and one that is not linked to other social or demographic shifts of similar magnitude.

The question of the proper scale of a penal enterprise is distinctive and important but infrequently addressed. Although concern has been intermittently expressed about prison overcrowding throughout the century, little attention has been paid to the factors which determine the extent to which imprisonment is used. Discussions of the purposes of punishment in general, and of imprisonment in particular, have taken precedence over, and have almost entirely precluded consideration of, such questions as how far the use of imprisonment is responsive to social factors and what factors determine the amount of imprisonment imposed. Rarely do we find anything more than oblique reference to such questions.

It might be asked whether such an approach—what we shall call a political economy of imprisonment—is really necessary if an acceptable jurisprudence of imprisonment could be determined. If appropriate principles governing the use of imprisonment have been defined and adopted, would not the application of those principles automatically determine the size of the prison population? Moreover, would not the number of prisoners produced by this calculus axiomatically be an optimum prison population?

In fact, that is not the case. In the first place, the jurisprudence of imprisonment is rarely precise about the number of offenders who must be sent to prison or about the duration of their imprisonment. Aside from mandatory minimum schemes, the law speaks of when offenders *may* rather than *must* be incarcerated. Second, the choice between imprisonment and alternative punishment is a function not only of the application of theoretical jurisprudential notions such as "desert" but also of the nature and extent of alternative punishments available to the system. Third, while "desert theorists" are concerned with what they call "ordinal proportionality," that is, the determination of the rank order of punishments to be used for crimes of different seriousness, the quantum of punishment suitable for a specific type of crime is left an open question.

Indeed, one distinguishing feature of many modern accounts of the jurisprudence of punishment is the leeway that the various schemata allow to prosecutors, judges, and correctional authorities in regard both to the choice between prison and alternative sanctions and to the determination of terms of imprisonment. Thus, there is no necessary concordance between a particular set of jurisprudential principles and the extent of the prison population resulting from the application of those principles.

Empirical demonstrations of the lack of concordance between penal principles and prison populations abound. States with strikingly similar criminal codes have very different levels of prison population. In the United States regional characteristics seem to be more significant determinants of levels of prison population than either substantive criminal law or aggregate crime statistics. Over time, many American states have experienced significant upward and downward variations in prison population without any significant change in either crime rates or penal code provisions which might explain them.

Rusche and Kirchheimer, in discussing "the illusion that a specific penal practice is bound up with a specific penal theory," demonstrated that in "the development of punishment by imprisonment" there were marked differences among European countries in the years following World War I, and considerable fluctuations within those countries, in relation to prison sentencing at a time when formal principles of punishment were both uniform and unvarying. For this was "the period when the reform school was at its height" and "reform theories were officially accepted everywhere" (1939:141–142, 145–165). More recently, Bottomley and Pease have noted the "dramatic differences between countries in their use of imprisonment" evident in Council of Europe data (1986:153), but neither they nor anyone else has identified any marked differences in penal philosophy or principles that would explain the divergent rates of imprisonment.

If the formal structure of the criminal law does not explain the different levels of imprisonment at different times and in different political units, what does? Part I of this book identifies and analyzes four separate traditions for addressing this question. Chapter 1 examines two efforts to think about levels of imprisonment as the outcome of economic and social trends in society. Chapter 2 discusses the work of three social historians whose work on the origins of imprisonment relates to questions about the proper scope of imprisonment. Chapter 3 examines efforts to predict the demand for future prison resources by projecting from past levels of imprisonment, a process called correctional forecasting. These forecasting methods are usually constructed without the benefit of any theory regarding the social forces that influence the decision to imprison. Correctional forecasts were born more from a need to plan than from any belief that variations in prison population can be explained. Correctional forecasters see themselves more as reporting likely future conditions than as finding explanations for them—more like television weatherpersons than meteorologists.

If the correctional forecaster regards levels of imprisonment as similar to natural phenomena, the advocate of the instrumental theories discussed in chapter 4 sees levels of prison population as the outcome of deliberate policy choices related to the manipulations of sentencing policy to influence crime rates. This instrumentalist view was always implicit in the jurisprudence of sentencing but has recently also been formalized in analyses that address the effect of different levels of imprisonment on crime rates. This latter group of studies, while depending on criminological data, most resembles self-conscious political economy in its style and frequently prescriptive approach.

Part II investigates postwar trends in imprisonment in the United

States in some detail. Chapter 5 presents data on trends in U.S. prison population as an aggregate and compares fluctuations in imprisonment with national trends in crime, in unemployment, in demography, and in drug arrests. None of the social factors analyzed vary in a pattern that would explain the prison trends.

Chapter 6 examines regional and state-by-state patterns of imprisonment, showing the wide variation in rates of imprisonment and the significant convergence in trends in recent decades that has occurred despite the decentralized nature of political authority over the scale of imprisonment.

Chapter 7 analyzes the impact of specific criminal justice policies on prison populations, including new penal priorities, mandatory minimum prison sentence legislation, new systems of allocating the authority to set criminal sentences and prison releases, and prison construction policies.

Chapter 8 discusses the potential impact of policy devices that are designed to reduce prison populations, both alternative penal sanction programs and nontreatment devices to reduce population.

Chapter 9 concludes our study with a discussion of the relationship between issues of scale and the usual discussion of prison crowding as well as two elements of what we call the political economy of prison scale.

This project was undertaken not to settle a field of inquiry but to help establish one. It is in that spirit that we offer the book that follows. The end-product is far from a general theory of prison scale. The causes of variation in prison population are not easily specified and not obviously the same in different times and locations. The prescription of appropriate policy responses is not an automatic inference from current data on prison population. But we are confident both of the significance of the topic of scale to criminal justice policy and of the value of further research to scholars and practitioners.

PART I
The Issue of Scale

The occasions for research on the scale of the imprisonment enterprise have been few in number and dispersed throughout the social sciences. This part reviews the principal published work on the subject to provide a background for the analysis in part II. Chapter 1 examines the two attempts to construct criminological theories of prison scale. Chapter 2 discusses the work of the social historians of prison creation who should have, but by and large have not, dealt with questions about what determines the size of a prison system. The two scholarly traditions have different perspectives. The criminologists who are the subject of chapter 1 speak of fixed laws that are expressed in prison population while the historians in chapter 2 address the more particular and contingent circumstances that are the probable causes of the events they describe.

The correctional forecasters profiled in chapter 3 are, at their best, applied social scientists trying to provide practically useful estimates of the need for prison space in a jurisdiction one year and five years forward. To date, they have found little of use from either the historian or the social theorist. The academic social scientists have, in turn, all but ignored the efforts and methods of correctional forecasters. Finally, and unconnected to many of the previously discussed efforts, economists and policy analysts have begun to formulate recommendations of what constitutes a desirable or even optimum prison population from calculations of the cost and functional value of imprisonment, either in dollar savings or in crime avoided. This work is examined in chapter 4.

The primary fact about the literature on what determines the size of a prison system is that there is not much. What is encouraging, however, is that our current lack of knowledge is the product of oversight rather than frustrated scholarly effort. Inattention to this topic has, as we shall see in part II, a sure cure in the policy climate of the United States in the 1990s.

1 Imprisonment as a Social Process: Rusche, Kirchheimer, and Blumstein

This chapter discusses two episodes of scholarly interest in the forces that determine prison population and the lesson these prior efforts hold for contemporary students of the social factors that shape the scale of a prison enterprise. Our researches have identified only these two accounts in all of modern criminology of the forces that influence levels of imprisonment.

In these pages, we develop each theory of the determinants of prison population and describe the reaction of the scholarly community to each of them. A concluding section compares the two explanations as theories of imprisonment and episodes in modern criminological theory.

1.1 PUNISHMENT AND SOCIAL STRUCTURE

The first attempt to study the determinants of prison population was Georg Rusche and Otto Kirchheimer's *Punishment and Social Structure*, published in 1939. In that book the authors note the neglect of such questions as "Why are certain methods of punishment adopted or rejected in a given social situation?" and "To what extent is the development of penal methods determined by the basic social relations?" Moreover, they offer an explanation of that neglect. It can "probably be attributed," they say, "primarily to the fact that the problem is generally approached from the standpoint of penal theory." And they argue that "not only have penal theories made little direct contribution, but they have had a negative influence on the historical-sociological analysis of penal methods" (1939:3–4).

Earlier writers, said Rusche and Kirchheimer, had restricted themselves to such things as "[defending] the ideological integrity of the institution of punishment" or "writing a history of the idea of punishment." "It was also common practice to limit oneself to a mere schema of the succession of historical manifestations, a mass of data supposedly bound together by the notion that they reveal progress." By contrast, they argued that "a more fruitful approach" would consider punishment "in its real relationships . . . in its specific manifestations [and investigate] the causes of its changes and developments, the grounds for the choice or rejection of specific penal methods in specific historical periods . . . the use or avoidance of specific punishments, and the intensity of penal practices as they are determined by social forces, above all by economic and then fiscal forces" (1939:4–5).

The essence of Rusche and Kirchheimer's theory of punishment was that "[e]very system of production tends to discover punishments which correspond to its productive relationships" (1939:5). Their principal thesis was summed up in one sentence by Thorsten Sellin: "In short the demands of the labor market shaped the penal system and determined its transformation over the years, more or less unaffected by theories of punishment in vogue" (1976:vii).

Such broad formulations are, of course, susceptible to a wide range of interpretation and exegesis. But both the virtues and defects of Rusche and Kirchheimer's work and the importance of their contribution to penological theory are largely independent of the minutiae of textual analysis. They are also independent of the various ways in which their work has been construed by interpreters and whether or not it can be properly described as "the landmark Marxist account" (Braithwaite, 1980:192) of the connection between punishment and the economy.

The principal feature of their work which justifies the "landmark" appellation is exemplified in their definition of their approach to the sociology of penal systems. "It is necessary to strip from the social institution of punishment its ideological veils and juristic appearance and to describe it in its real relationships . . . Punishment as such does not exist; only concrete systems of punishment exist. The object of our investigation therefore is punishment in its specific manifestations" (Rusche and Kirchheimer, 1939:5). But insofar as a "landmark" in this context means an idea or insight which may be considered a high point or turning point in the history or development of penological theory, the title is inappropriate. Indeed, their emphasis on the necessity for an empirical approach to the theory of punishment, far from being a turning point, was at that time almost entirely ignored. As Greenberg has noted, "the work of Rusche and Kirchheimer . . . made little impact at the time of publication" (1981:27).

Moreover, it continues to be ignored. One of the most recent discussions of the theory of punishment, in Robert Nozick's *Philosophical Ex-*

planations (1981), provides an apt example. Nozick there discusses the rationale for retributive punishment in precisely the way which Rusche and Kirchheimer condemned in their critique of earlier penal theorists (Nozick, 1981:363–397; Rusche and Kirchheimer, 1939:3–4). As Bernard Williams has observed, Nozick's discussion of punishment "is vastly removed from any actual social institution. There are one or two desultory references to the law, but virtually nothing that focuses on the fact that punishment is inflicted by some actual authority in some actual social circumstances. This characteristic . . . issues in a level of abstraction that is often bewildering" (1982:34).

By contrast, Rusche and Kirchheimer not only focused attention on what occurred in some actual social circumstances but also supported their analysis of the social forces they saw as shaping penal systems with relevant statistical data. In their view, "penal methods [were] determined by basic social relations" (1939:3) and penal theories like those of Beccaria and Bentham merely reflected "the bourgeois desire for security" and the requirements of "the prevailing social order based on private property" (1939:74, 76). Their own view that "specific forms of punishment correspond to a given stage of economic development" was advanced not as another theory of punishment but as the result of "critical historical analysis," the product of which was, they maintained, self-evidently true.
Thus:

It is self-evident that enslavement as a form of punishment is impossible without a slave economy, that prison labor is impossible without manufacture or industry, that monetary fines for all classes of society are impossible without a money economy. On the other hand, the disappearance of a given system of production makes its corresponding punishments inapplicable. Only a specific development of the productive forces permits the introduction or rejection of corresponding penalties. But before these potential methods can be introduced, society must be in a position to incorporate them as integrated parts of the whole social and economic system. Thus, if a slave economy finds the supply of slaves meager and the demand pressing, it cannot neglect penal slavery. In feudalism, on the other hand, not only could this form of punishment no longer be used but no other method was discovered for the proper use of the labor power of the convict. A return to the old methods, capital and corporal

> punishment, was therefore necessary, since the introduction of
> monetary fines for all classes was impossible on economic
> grounds. The house of correction reached a peak under mercan-
> tilism and gave great impetus to the development of the new
> method of production. The economic importance of the houses
> of correction then disappeared with the rise of the factory system
> . . . The transition to modern industrial society, which de-
> mands the freedom of labor as a necessary condition for the
> productive employment of labor power, reduced the economic
> role of convict labor to a minimum. (Rusche and Kirchheimer,
> 1939:6–7)

Nevertheless, despite the declared lack of need for proof or explanation, *Punishment and Social Structure* is devoted for the most part to
providing evidence in support of that summary statement. The history
of penal systems is outlined as a series of "epochs" in which the different
penal systems and their variations are each said to be closely related to
phases of economic development. As far as imprisonment is concerned,
the relevant epoch begins when "methods of punishment begin to undergo a gradual but profound change toward the end of the sixteenth
century" (Rusche and Kirchheimer, 1939:24).

At that time, they argue, the development of mercantilism, which
involved the growth of a financial system and the extension of markets
for mass-consumption goods, led to an increase in demand for labor. In
Europe, however, population growth was either static or as a result of
the Thirty Years' War had sharply declined. This state of the labor market led to the adoption of the exploitation of the labor power of prisoners
by way of such things as galley slavery, transportation to colonies and
military settlements, and "penal servitude at hard labor . . . the hesitant
precursor of an institution [i.e., the prison] which has lasted into the
present" (Rusche and Kirchheimer, 1939:24). The argument is supported by details of birthrates, movements of prices and population,
details of government regulation of labor, and the use of child labor,
public policy toward the poor, and the rise of houses of correction where
the labor power of inmates was utilized either within the institution or
by hiring out to a contractor.

However, the social situation out of which institutions like houses of
correction grew changed.

> The demand for workers was satisfied and a surplus eventually
> developed. The population of England increased by one million

in the first half of the eighteenth century, and by three million in the second half. It was 5.1 million in 1720, 6 in 1750, and 9.18 in 1801. Between 1781 and 1800 the rate of increase was 9 to 11 percent, and between 1801 and 1820, 14 to 18 percent. The population of France was 19 million in 1707, 24 in 1770, and 26 in 1789. What the ruling classes had been seeking for over a century was now an accomplished fact—relative over-population. Factory owners need no longer hunt for men. On the contrary, workers had to search out places of employment. (Rusche and Kirchheimer, 1939:86)

But there remained "a constant shortage of labor in the colonies and . . . the simplest way to supply the needs of the colonies without preju-dice to the interests of the mother country was to send out convicts" (Rusche and Kirchheimer, 1939:58–59). Nevertheless "imprisonment was the most frequent form of punishment even when transportation was at its height . . . In 1937–39, the ratio of transportation to impris-onment [in England] was 23.5 to 100 and in 1844–46 only 15 to 100" (Rusche and Kirchheimer, 1939:103).

At the same time in England "the industrial revolution was making it more and more difficult to obtain any real profit from the demoralized and indiscriminately assembled prisoners" and while "in the mercantil-ist period . . . there was a shortage of labor and prison-made goods were often superior . . . now that it no longer paid to employ prisoners they were frequently left with nothing to do." In America, on the other hand, where there was a shortage of labor and "the price of labor was high," the system which prevailed in prisons "was to make the labor of convicts as productive as possible" (Rusche and Kirchheimer, 1939:110–112). However, even there "the gradual disappearance of the frontier" and "opposition on the part of the free workers" led to "the curtailment of convict labor in the last decades of the nineteenth cen-tury." This curtailment took the form of either the "complete abolition of all forms of prison labor" or its continued utilization under "very considerable limitations, such as work without modern machinery, con-ventional rather than modern types of prison industry, or work for the government instead of for the free market" (Rusche and Kirchheimer, 1939:131–132).

The final epoch in Rusche and Kirchheimer's account of the history of imprisonment extends through the last quarter of the nineteenth and the first quarter of the twentieth century, which is described as a "period of relative prosperity." During this period, they argue,

[t]he value of human labor power was again seen in a different light. It is true that population increased considerably in the nineteenth century and that the period of labor scarcity had disappeared forever; but the immense expansion of industrial production in the era of imperialism provided for a maximum absorption of labor power. The senseless imprisonment of individuals became undesirable and out of step with the times. (1939:139–140)

Thus came the adoption of "the new policy sponsored by the reformers [which] was to keep as many delinquents as possible out of jail by a more extensive use of fines [and] by a probation policy" and by "a decrease in the length and severity of prison sentences" (1939:145, 147). They illustrate this "general tendency toward leniency" with a series of tables giving comparative statistics relating to the use of imprisonment and alternative forms of punishment over the years in European countries. The table reproduced here as table 1.1 shows the decline in prison populations in France between 1884 and 1932, and in England between 1880 and 1931.

Rusche and Kirchheimer illustrate the tendency to substitute other forms of punishment for imprisonment with tables, not reproduced here, showing "the liberal use of suspended sentences and the increase in the use of fines" in France over the years 1900–1934 and the decline in the use of imprisonment and increase in the use of fines and suspended sentences over the years 1905–1933 in Belgium. Other tables illustrate the decrease in the length and severity of prison sentences in Germany over the years 1882–1934 and in France over the years 1932–1933 (1939:147–149).

Rusche and Kirchheimer have been accused of lack of "methodological rigor" and of drawing their data "selectively from modern European history" (Grabosky, 1984:169), but it is notable that they do include a table showing Italy as an exception to the trend toward greater leniency. "Between the years 1893 and 1933 we find a steady increase in the more severe forms of punishment, a decrease in the number of short-term sentences and little change in the number of fines." Regarding this "exceptional development of punishment in Italy," they comment simply that it "coincides with the fact that the number of crimes does not show the same sharp downward trend as elsewhere in Europe" (1939: 148–149).

No attempt is made to explain this "exceptional development" as a

TABLE 1.1 Decline in Prison Population, Late Nineteenth Century and Twentieth Century

A. France: Prison Population, 1884–1932[1]

	Maisons Centrales		Maisons d'Arrêt (as of December 31)	
Year	Men	Women	Men	Women
1884	12,689	1,943	21,257	3,974
1887	11,547	1,635	21,394	3,573
1890	10,540	1,640	20,940	3,440
1891	10,054	1,439	20,336	3,338
1894	9,839	1,294	19,289	3,652
1897	8,434	1,008	15,636	2,790
1900	6,802	801	14,769	2,466
1902	5,906	673	13,941	2,152
1905	5,401	539	13,502	1,902
1909	5,540	507	13,304	1,885
1910	5,612	534	14,518	2,224
1913	6,413	726	14,123	2,219
1920	7,443	863	17,997	3,383
1921	6,247	1,086	13,920	2,911
1922	6,090	935	11,037	2,338
1925	5,529	885	12,278	2,095
1927	5,405	542	14,293	2,316
1929	4,992	573	12,537	2,038
1930	5,085	590	12,575	1,885
1931	4,662	546	11,695	1,756
1932	4,315	469	12,579	1,591

B. England: Persons Sent into Penal Servitude or Imprisoned[2]

Year	Number	Year	Number
1880	32,999	1919	12,732
1890	24,628	1920	15,518
1900	22,432	1921	15,756
1905	28,257	1922	15,520
1910	26,096	1923	14,788
1911	23,758	1924	14,132
1912	23,994	1925	13,580
1913	21,463	1926	14,537
1914	18,195	1927	14,446
1915	11,802	1928	13,726
1916	11,027	1929	13,526
1917	11,930	1930	14,294
1918	11,303	1931	13,838

[1] Compiled from the annual *Statistique pénitentiare*.
[2] From Fox, *Modern English Prison*, pp. 218–219.
SOURCE: Rushe and Kirchheimer, 1939:146–147.

function of the state of the economy or economic forces. But its inclusion does demonstrate their commitment to concrete, historically specific, empirical investigation into penal practice. This rather than their general theory that economic forces wholly determine penal policy constitutes their major contribution to penology. Moreover, there is no doubt that they were correct in their belief that earlier attempts to explain the development of imprisonment "from the standpoint of penal theory" as being shaped wholly by the theories of punishment or penological principles which happened to be in vogue were misconceived (1939:3–4).

It has been said of Durkheim that "many of the studies he inspired . . . have cast doubt on his interpretations" (Grabosky, 1984:166), and the same is true of Rusche and Kirchheimer. Thus, Garland and Young, while noting the "seminal influence" of their work and approving their emphasis on "the need for concrete, historically specific investigations into particular penal practices," are also critical of their "reductionism" and their narrowly "economistic explanations" (Garland and Young, 1983:7, 24). Similarly, David Greenberg says that, "in maintaining that variations in [penal] sanctions are due to the needs of the economy to control the labor force, Rusche and Kirchheimer fall into economic reductionism" (Greenberg, 1980:203).

Again, Melossi and Pavarini, who explicitly claim to be "following in the footsteps of Georg Rusche and Otto Kirchheimer," have criticized their insistence that "religious differences were of no real relevance" in the development of penal institutions (Melossi and Pavarini, [1977] 1981:1, 32). Moreover, Melossi has argued that their conception of "the mode of production" misconceived Marx's ideas, was too restrictive, and was thus unable to accommodate ideological factors or to provide any explanation of that aspect of social relationships (Melossi, 1978:77).

Rusche and Kirchheimer may or may not have misunderstood Marx. But in their attempt to demonstrate what they said was "a truism"—that "specific forms of punishment correspond to a given stage of economic development"—and to emphasize the importance of "above all economic and then fiscal forces" (Rusche and Kirchheimer, 1939:5–6), they either ignored or failed to explain developments that could not be shown to be the product of economic forces or the demands of the labor market.

It is because penal history is full of developments not susceptible to that type of explanation that Hermann Mannheim, in a book published in the same year as *Punishment and Social Structure*, was able to give so many examples of developments in penal methods that show "no connection whatsoever with such [i.e., economic] factors" (Mannheim, 1939:36–53). Perhaps the most notable of these is the Pennsylvania system and its analogues throughout the world.

It is instructive to note how Rusche and Kirchheimer dealt with the Pennsylvania system. The development of the contemporaneous Auburn system which involved "collective labor in the workshops [and] the organization of the prisoners for maximum industrial efficiency" presented them with no problem. It was explained as due to "the state of the American labor market [and] and shortage of workers" in the early nineteenth century. "The prisons become busy factories [and] capitalists became accustomed to contract for the services of such convict labor as they desired" (Rusche and Kirchheimer, 1939:128–131).

By contrast, the Pennsylvania system involved solitary confinement. "The prisoners were isolated in single cells which they never left until their time was up . . . they were not even allowed to work lest it divert them from self-contemplation. The only occupation allowed was Bible-reading" (Rusche and Kirchheimer, 1939:127). It provides a striking example of one of those instances in the history of punishment when, as Max Grunhut put it, "for good or for evil, powerful ideas crossed and even superseded rational and economic considerations" (1948:197). Rusche and Kirchheimer are able to explain the eventual abandonment of the Pennsylvania system as the result of the conditions of the labor market, but that system's widespread adoption (e.g., in Maryland, Massachusetts, Maine, New Jersey, Virginia, and Rhode Island) *at the same time* as the Auburn system was being developed and imitated (Barnes and Teeters, 1943:534–535) is left unexplained. Indeed, a passage in which "the Quaker theory of solitary confinement" is said to represent an abandonment of "the attempt to find a rational policy [which] conceals this fact with a moral ideology" (Rusche and Kirchheimer, 1939:137) suggests that they found it inexplicable in terms of their analysis.

But it was not only in relation to specific penal practices such as solitary confinement that Rusche and Kirchheimer's general theory proved to be inadequate. For what appeared to be a plausible explanation of the Auburn system of imprisonment in a period of labor shortage seemed irrelevant in the 1930s when in almost all capitalist countries there was a substantial surplus of labor. Rusche and Kirchheimer themselves noted that "prison labor . . . has lost its economic significance in countries with a highly developed industrial capitalism" (1939:152). As Ivan Jankovic puts it:

> Rusche and Kirchheimer . . . encountered some difficulties in explaining the continuing use of imprisonment in advanced capitalist countries. The use of imprisonment could be explained by conditions of general labor shortages, when convicts could be profitably exploited. But it defies such explanation in capitalist societies which are not only faced with a permanent oversupply of labor but in which freedom of labor is the essential condition of its productivity, and, therefore, convict labor cannot be profitably exploited. Ultimately, Rusche and Kirchheimer were forced to dismiss imprisonment as an "irrational" penal measure in developed capitalist countries. (1977:18)

In fact, Rusche and Kirchheimer seem to suggest that imprisonment had in the 1930s ceased to correspond to the stage of economic development that had been reached. In their chapter "The Fine in Penal Practice," they note that while "imprisonment remained the central point of the whole system it received increasing competition from the fine, which is today a close rival insofar as frequency of application is concerned." They also present data from a number of different European countries in the form of tables which they argue both "give a clear picture of the progress of the fine" and show that this was "not merely the result of new crimes, like violations of purely police measures regulating traffic, but is also *the consequence of a general policy of substituting the fine for imprisonment*" (1939:166, 167; our emphasis).

In the Introduction to their book, the fine is described as "the typical punishment of modern society." And in their Conclusion, the authors say: "The system of fines, the epitome of rationalized capitalist penal law, is at its height, despite the ideological attacks against it" (Rusche and Kirchheimer, 1939:7, 206). "The fine system," they observed, "helped empty the prisons and reduced the costs and work of administration which would otherwise have increased greatly . . . In general, the fine system contributed to the rationalization of criminal administration" (1939:173).

In discussing the rise of the fine, Rusche and Kirchheimer were drawing attention to something which had until then been largely ignored by penal theorists. In fact, as recently as 1983 it was pointed out that while "one might expect that it would have attracted great attention among penal analysts . . . despite Kirchheimer's pioneering efforts [the chapter on the fine was written by Otto Kirchheimer] the rise of the fine . . . has been almost wholly neglected as a significant penological phenomenon, not only by sociologists of punishment and social control, but even by policy-oriented penologists" (Bottoms, 1983:168).

With the benefit of hindsight—that most powerful of analytic tools—it is clear that Rusche and Kirchheimer were mistaken. The rise of the fine has been an uneven development as between different countries, with considerable fluctuations in some of them (Bottoms, 1983:168). The fine has been "used only sparingly in the United States" (Morris, 1974:74; Carter and Cole, 1979:155), where imprisonment rates have substantially increased since 1939. Moreover, what emerges from any serious examination of the history of imprisonment is that frequently the determining factors are largely if not entirely divorced from economic considerations.

It seems clear also that Rusche and Kirchheimer were well aware of this but unable to accommodate it within their explanatory hypothesis. Thus, they emphasize the significance of the principle of less eligibility, which they refer to as the "notion that the standard of living within the prison must be below the minimum standard outside" and as "the tendency against raising the prisoner's level of existence to that of the outside world." They describe it as *the leitmotiv of all prison administration down to the present time"* and as a principle which "no reform program has been willing to abandon" (Rusche and Kirchheimer, 1939:94, 151, 155, 159, 207; our emphasis). But they make no attempt to show how this leitmotif (whether in the sense of a recurrent theme or a dominant or underlying pattern) could be explained as a function of economic or fiscal forces.

Yet despite the fact that their attempt to explain the history of imprisonment wholly in terms of the demands of the labor market or the rise of the fine as simply a product of fiscal forces now seems jejune and plainly defective, Rusche and Kirchheimer were clearly right about at least two things. In the first place, there is no doubt that "[t]he penal system of any given society is not an isolated phenomenon subject only to its own special laws. It is an integral part of the whole social system, and shares its aspirations and its defects." They were also right in insisting that, in order to understand the history of imprisonment or any other penal method, it is necessary to investigate "punishment in its

specific manifestations, the causes of its change and developments . . .
in specific historical periods" (1939:5, 207). But at that time and for
many years thereafter the message went largely unheard.

1.2 THE CONSTANCY OF PUNISHMENT

As a result, the scale of imprisonment remained relatively un-
charted territory until the 1970s. The work of Dr. Alfred Blumstein and
his associates (Blumstein and Cohen, 1973; Blumstein, Cohen, and
Nagin, 1976; Blumstein and Moitra, 1979), the focus of this chapter,
thus derived from no obvious precursors in empirical criminological
scholarship or social theory. Although these writers linked their hypothesis of the stability of punishment to Emile Durkheim's writings on
crime and punishment (Durkheim, [1893] 1964, [1895] 1938) and also
to Kai Erikson's study of deviance and social control in a Puritan community (Erikson, 1966), by raising and investigating questions about the
stability or constancy of punishment they were in fact breaking new
ground. What they advanced as "an important extension and significant
modification of the perceptions of Durkheim as evolved by Erikson"
(Blumstein and Cohen, 1973:207) appears (at least to us) to have been
largely an inductively derived thesis inspired as much by the shape of
the data as by the theoretical insights of Durkheim and Erikson.

In his analysis of crime, Durkheim argued that some level of crime
is "an integral part of all healthy societies . . . provided that it attains
and does not exceed a certain level for each social type" ([1893]
1964:79). He saw crime as a natural outgrowth of the processes gener-
ating social solidarity. A corollary of this notion that crime is both natural and functional for social life is, as Blumstein and Cohen put it:

> [T]he extent of crime in any particular social group will gener-
> ally be maintained at a specific level. While the optimal level
> may vary with social type, the observed level in any given group
> will rarely fall short of or exceed the relevant optimum. Durk-
> heim even suggests that it may be possible to specify exactly the
> optimum level of crime of the various social types. Further-
> more, Erikson's work includes an attempt to offer some empiri-
> cal evidence for this claim. (1973:198–194)

Blumstein and Cohen questioned Durkheim's theory of a stable level
of crime and posed an alternative position emphasizing the stability of
punishment. Their argument was summarized in the next paper in the
series as follows:

The standards or thresholds that define punishable behavior are adjusted in response to overall shifts in the behavior of the members of a society so that a roughly constant proportion of the population is always undergoing punishment. Thus, if many more individuals engage in behavior defined as punishable, the demarcation between criminal and non-criminal behavior would be adjusted to re-designate at least part of the previously criminal behavior as non-criminal, or the intensity or duration of punishment for those convicted would be reduced. A similar but opposite reassessment would occur when fewer people commit currently punishable acts. [The] principal evidence in support of this hypothesis is the stability of imprisonment rates in the United States over the period 1930–1970 and in Norway over the period 1880–1964. Canadian imprisonment rates over the period 1880–1959 have been obtained subsequently, and these show the same stability behavior. (Blumstein, Cohen, and Nagin, 1977:317)

In that next paper, Blumstein, Cohen, and Nagin extended the theoretical structure and empirical basis of this earlier work and suggested some processes that might generate a stable level of imprisonment. They concluded that

the oscillatory nature of the time series of imprisonment rate per capita cannot be adequately explained by a simple balancing of prison receptions and releases. Rather, a more elaborate model which incorporates a homeostatic shifting in the demarcation between punishable and non-punishable behavior is required to explain these oscillatory patterns. As imprisonment rates increased the threshold of punishable behavior can be expected to rise. When the imprisonment rates decline those thresholds can be expected to drop. (Blumstein and Moitra, 1979:376)

According to this "homeostatic hypothesis," when a nation's prison population begins to fluctuate, pressure is generated to restore the prison population to a stable rate. This process of restoration

would typically be through some form of "adaptation" by the various agencies within the nation's criminal justice system.
    One form of adaptation could result in changes in the manner in which discretion is exercised by the various functionaries within the criminal justice system. If prison populations get too

large, police can choose not to arrest, prosecutors can choose not to press charges, judges can choose not to imprison, or parole boards can choose not to deny requests. This exercise of discretion presumably would be focused on those crimes or offenders that are the most marginally criminal.

Similarly, if the populations drop too far below the stable rate, then pressure would develop to sanction certain kinds of behavior that previously had been tolerated as more annoying than harmful. Alternatively, the level of punishment for a given type of offense could be increased. (Blumstein and Moitra, 1979: 376–377)

The empirical analyses of the homeostatic hypothesis in the Blumstein and Cohen study (1973) and the Blumstein, Cohen, and Nagin study (1977) were based on aggregate rates for three nations: the United States, Norway, and Canada. In the last paper in the series, Blumstein and Moitra sought to explore the applicability of the hypothesis to a larger number of jurisdictions by examining the imprisonment rates of the individual states in the United States.

The basic data for this investigation were the average daily prison population and the total population for each state for each year from 1926 to 1974. In examining the trends in the per capita imprisonment rates in forty-seven states (the imprisonment data from Hawaii and Alaska covered insufficient years and those from Delaware had major gaps; so these three states were excluded from the analysis), Blumstein and Moitra found that almost half (twenty) were trendless, i.e., stationary, and that the trends in the remainder were small, i.e., less than 2 percent of the mean years in all cases. The authors concluded that these findings were consistent with the general homeostatic process in that the phenomenon "appears to hold reasonably well across a wide variety of independent, albeit related jurisdictions" (1979:390).

In a 1974 critique of Blumstein and Cohen's first study, Waller and Chan say that they were "amazed by the number of respected researchers who have quoted these figures and conclusions without question." Their principal criticisms were twofold. First, they argued that Blumstein and Cohen's conclusion that punishment remained at stable levels was achieved "by examining only those imprisoned in State or Federal institutions thus ignoring nearly 160,000 persons held in local jails." Second, they presented data relating to imprisonment trends over time in Canada, England and Wales, Finland, and Norway which they claim "appear to refute the hypothesis that the use of imprisonment remains constant over time" (Waller and Chan, 1974:48, 60). Those data are reproduced here in figure 1.1.

Waller and Chan noted that their data not only illustrated "the lack of consistent pattern" but suggested that fluctuations in imprisonment rates are "usually associated with societal dislocations such as the depression or wars" (1974:60). They did not attempt any interpretation of the data themselves, but David Greenberg, who critically reviewed the second Blumstein study in two articles, offered an interpretation consistent with that suggestion. In the first of these articles, Greenberg argues that although the Blumstein, Cohen, and Nagin model shows an "impressive agreement between prediction and observation" alternative models of the processes that generate imprisonment rates need to be examined. "There are," he says, "many variables that might be expected to influence the rate of prison admissions, such as a community's demographic composition, the amount of resources it can expend on punishment, the prevailing political sentiment, the crime rate, and so on" (1977:644, 648).

Noting that a visual inspection of the annual per capita prison populations suggests a random fluctuation about a sinusoidal oscillation, Greenberg says that "[t]here are two ways such oscillatory behavior can be produced. One is through a self-regulating process of the sort hypothesized by Blumstein, Cohen, and Nagin. Another way is for prison admissions to be driven by a variable that is exogenous to the crime-punishment system, and which oscillates sinusoidally" (1977:647). But he observes that most such exogenous variables change slowly and not necessarily in a sinusoidal fashion so that, whatever contribution they might make to the mean level of a community's incarceration rate, they would not cause that rate to oscillate.

On the other hand, he argues that there are variables, in particular "those variables that characterize the state of the business cycle [which] do show the required behavior, because periods of economic expansion alternate with periods of contraction in capitalist economic systems" (Greenberg, 1977:648). Moreover, he says, there are a number of reasons to expect prison admissions to depend strongly on the phase of the business cycle, including the fact that when the economy is in a period of contraction unemployment rises and persons who are unemployed can be assumed to have a greater incentive to steal than those who are not and may risk less when they engage in crime, for they cannot lose their jobs if they are caught.

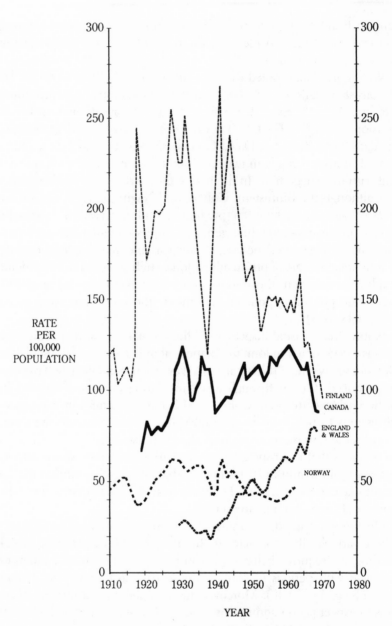

FIG. 1.1. Number of persons in prison per 100,000 population in Canada, England and Wales, Finland, and Norway, 1910–1973. Source: Waller and Chan, 1974.

Greenberg also argues that another reason prison admissions might be expected to vary with the business cycle can be found in Rusche and Kirchheimer's historical survey of punishment practices, which suggests that long-term changes in the form and intensity of state-imposed punishment reflect the supply and demand of labor. "When the supply of labor is high relative to demand, this perspective would suggest that the rate of imprisonment would be increased, with the goal of taking excess labor off the market" (Greenberg, 1977:648).

In support of his argument, Greenberg cites a study showing that, in the United States "for the period 1960–1972, the correlation between the unemployment rate and the rate of first admissions to federal prison was 0.91, and for first admissions to state prison, 0.86 . . . this was not a trend effect; prison admissions rose and fell with the unemployment rate." He also cites Canadian data relating to prison admission rates and unemployment rates for the years 1945–1959 which show a high correlation between unemployment and commitments to prison. "Both rates move up and down, prison commitments following changes in unemployment quite closely, with some evidence of prison admissions lagging a bit behind unemployment. This may be a consequence of court delay" (1977:648–649). Figure 1.2 illustrates the relationship be-

FIG. 1.2. Prison admissions and unemployment rate in Canada, 1945–1959. Source: Greenberg, 1977.

tween prison admissions and unemployment in Canada in the relevant years. Greenberg concludes that

> the analysis of prison admissions presented here does cast doubt on the validity of the assumptions made in the BCN [Blumstein, Cohen, and Nagin] model about the admissions process. We find that whatever effect punishment may have on crime, oscillations in the rate of admissions to prison in Canada in recent years have been governed almost entirely by changes in the unemployment rate. The same relationship appears to hold in the United States as well. (1977:651)

In his second study, Greenberg set out to test the two alternative explanations of the oscillatory behavior of imprisonment rates, i.e., the Blumstein, Cohen, and Nagin hypothesis and the hypothesis that sees prison populations as changing in response to unemployment. The explanations were tested with data on crime and imprisonment in twentieth-century Poland. Neither of the two approaches developed to explain temporal variations in prison populations in Canada, the United States, and Norway proved adequate for Poland. As Greenberg puts it:

> The prewar variations in Polish imprisonment rates rose in a manner that is at least roughly consistent with the proposition that unemployment contributes to imprisonment rates, but the postwar variations do not seem to be due to labor market conditions. The absence of oscillations in the prewar period, along with an increase in the *per capita* prison populations by a factor of 2.5 in a single decade, are inconsistent with any sort of homeostatic model; and the inconsistent relationship between crime rates and imprisonment rates in postwar Poland is also inconsistent with a homeostatic model.
>
> Although the postwar imprisonment rates in Poland do oscillate in a manner that is strikingly similar to the behavior of imprisonment rates in capitalist societies, the reasons for this oscillation appear to be quite different. Changes in conviction and imprisonment rates in this period appear to vary in response to policy decisions made for reasons unrelated to either unemployment or conventional forms of crimes. (1980:202)

Another critic of the stability of punishment hypothesis was Margaret Cahalan, who on the basis of examination of government reports on penal facilities in the United States since 1880 argued that the rate of incarceration in federal, state, local, and juvenile correctional institutions, far from being stable, had actually increased. Specifically, she said:

> Recent studies of the use of incarceration in the United States have tended to focus on the annual reports of state and federal prison populations issued since 1926. Blumstein and Cohen made extensive use of these data in hypothesizing that punishment remains stable, noting that the rate of imprisonment had not varied greatly from 1930 to 1970, except in the period around 1940. However, the inclusion of reports before 1930 and consideration of all levels of incarceration combined indicate that, quite apart from the recent increases in incarceration since 1972, and the rapid increase reported between 1850 and 1880, there is a fluctuating but significant trend toward increased use of incarceration reported from 1880 to 1970. (1979:9)

Her findings are shown in table 1.2.

Blumstein and Moitra responded to this critique by saying that Cahalan's linear-trend model based on nine data points of incarceration rates from 1880 to 1970 was inapposite. "[I]t is difficult to test definitely the model of so complex a process as incarceration from data at only nine data points spaced over 90 years" (Blumstein and Moitra, 1980:91). Moreover, they argued that even those data were better explained by a model consistent with their theory—two constant incarceration rates with a shift from the lower to the higher rate in about 1925 accompanying rapid changes in United States society and in penological thinking.

Finally, in 1981, two papers appeared which addressed the stability of punishment hypothesis with data from California. In one of these, by Richard Berk et al., an attempt is made to reformulate the hypothesis using developments in macroeconomics in which the presence of equilibrating tendencies can be explicitly represented, and to test it with Californian data for the period from the opening of the prison system in 1851 to 1970. The authors conclude that "we can find no evidence of an equilibrating process within the Durkheim-Blumstein perspective" (Berk et al., 1981:826).

They also note that for Blumstein a stable level of punishment was conditional upon a general stability in society and that it might be objected in regard to their conclusion that during the 120 years covered by their study California experienced a number of significant social

TABLE 1.2 Inmates Reported Present: 1850–1972

	Total U.S. Population (in millions)	All Classes (Adults and Juveniles)*		Sentenced Adults and All Juveniles		All Classes (juvenile facilities excluded)		Sentenced (juvenile facilities excluded)	
		Total	Per 100,000 Population	Total	Per 100,000 Population	Total	Per 100,000 Population	Total	Per 100,000 Population
1972	208,234	**	—	**	—	337,692	162.2	274,292	131.7
1970****	203,810	434,021	213.0	350,942	172.2	357,292	175.3	274,213	134.5
1960	179,979	402,531	223.7	+	—	346,015	192.3	+	—
1950	151,868	305,437	201.1	+	—	264,557	174.2	+	—
1940	132,457	317,168	239.4	+	—	+	—	+	—
1933	125,590	++	—	219,929	175.1	++	—	189,433	150.8
1923	111,950	++	—	136,857	122.2	++	—	109,619	97.9
1910	92,407	++	—	136,472	147.7	++	—	111,498	120.7
1890	62,622	95,480	152.5	85,360	136.3	80,634	128.8	70,514	112.6
1880	50,155	69,228	138.0	63,591	126.8	57,760	115.2	52,123	103.9
1870+++	38,558	+++	—	+++	—	32,901	85.3	+++	—
1860+++	31,443	+++	—	+++	—	19,086	60.7	+++	—
1850+++	23,191	+++	—	+++	—	6,737	29.1	+++	—

*The figures include persons incarcerated in state and federal prisons and reformatories, jails, and other local facilities, and juvenile correctional institutions; excluded are persons confined in military prisons and mental hospitals.

**The rate was estimated at 188 per 100,000 in 1972. By 1976, the rate per 100,000 was estimated to be 220 (Florida Clearinghouse on Criminal Justice, *Newsletter* of April 1977).

***The National Jail Survey of 1970, conducted by the Department of Justice, LEAA, listed as confined (detained and under sentence) in the jails 31,674 more persons than did the census report on institutionalized persons for that same year. The LEAA data listed 2,401 fewer persons in state and federal prisons and reformatories. The table uses the LEAA reports because sentenced and unsentenced offenders were classified separately only in the jail survey. The total for all classes reported by the census was 404,749, a rate of 199.7 per 100,000.

+ From 1940 until 1970, the census reports provided no breakdown of adjudication status. The 1940 report counted only those persons fourteen years and older, and did not classify adults and juveniles separately.

++ From 1904 to 1933, the census counted only sentenced offenders. (In addition, the 1904 census excluded those persons incarcerated for nonpayment of a fine.)

+++Census reports from 1850–1870 are unclear as to the definition of institutions used in compiling the data. The classification here is based upon the 1923 census report.

SOURCE: Cahalan, 1979:12–13.

upheavals. To this they offer three rejoinders. First, in none of the stability of punishment statements were they able to find a definition of "what qualifies as a major social upheaval . . . the role of wars, depressions, and demographic shifts is unclear . . . it is not apparent whether social upheavals need be discrete, dramatic events, or whether gradual transitions are also relevant." Second, if social upheavals are defined in terms of wars, depressions, and industrialization, "it may be difficult to find any stable intervals over the past 200 years, at least for Western societies." Third, some of their formulations "explicitly include the potential impact of major social upheavals; one can judge whether the social control ratio is part of an equilibrating process despite social disruptions. We are able to control for dramatic, exogenous shocks to the system and determine if a steady-state target(s) exists nevertheless. Thus, the Durkheim-Blumstein perspective is given the benefit of the doubt and still found wanting" (Berk et al., 1981:826).

In the other 1981 paper to which Blumstein et al. responded, David Rauma reanalyzed one of Blumstein's time series and analyzed several others, including data for California from 1853 to 1970. He argued that these analyses and reanalyses, of both imprisonment and prison admission rates "show no support for the stability of punishment hypothesis" (1981b:1772). What is more, he failed to find any evidence in the California data of either a stable level for imprisonment rates or an upward shift in the 1920s from one stable level to another (1981b:1787–1794).

Much of Rauma's paper is focused on questions of statistical technique and on finding another time-series model that will more adequately represent the available data. He also argues that "actual prison admissions might be a better measure of punishment" than imprisonment rates (1981b:1784). He examines U.S. prison admission rates for the period 1926–1970 and finds "no apparent support for the stability of punishment hypothesis" (1981b:1787).

Blumstein's response to Rauma on the question of time-series models is that Rauma's "competing model is analytically equivalent to ours" and that "in terms of the stability of punishment hypothesis under test, the choice between models is not crucial, as both are consistent with the theory" (Blumstein et al., 1981:1802, 1806). On the question of prison admissions versus imprisonment rates, a reasonable argument is made that "for the United States . . . the ratio of average daily population of prisoners per capita, reflecting not only commitments but also time served [is] the most appropriate measure of punishment." Moreover, using commitments to prison as a measure produces "a time series very similar to that of the incarceration rate" (Blumstein et al., 1981:1804).

Regarding Rauma's analysis of California data over the period 1835–1970, it is said "we are somewhat disappointed that Rauma failed to confirm our hypothesis," but it is also pointed out that "California is only one of the 47 states we analyzed. While the stability hypothesis did not apply universally, the theory did seem to be broadly applicable." On Rauma's failure to find the 1925 "shift" in the California data, it is argued that California might well "fail to mirror an aggregate United States phenomenon, which was more likely to reflect the situation in the Northeast and the Midwest, where the bulk of the United States population was then concentrated" (Blumstein et al., 1981: 1805–1806).

The exchange between Rauma and Blumstein et al., and the lengthy technical discussion produced nothing decisive. In his critique Rauma acknowledged that, while he had found no support for the stability of punishment hypothesis, "Blumstein has other time series that he analyzes, and the sheer mass of evidence may be on his side." However, he says that "competing explanations cannot be ruled out" and cites "the work of Rusche and Kirchheimer" as providing "one promising perspective" (Rauma, 1981b:1796–1797).

In "A Concluding Note on the Stability of Punishment," Rauma returns to this "more general and related concern" (1981b:1809) and raises some questions regarding the nature of the stability of punishment hypothesis considerably more fundamental than the questions of statistical technique and modeling which are his principal focus of interest. The point he raises can best be brought out by quoting his own words:

> Finally, there is some ambiguity, in Blumstein's reply and in his earlier work, concerning the definition of stability. For example, Blumstein and Cohen border on circularity when they describe the United States imprisonment rate series as "reasonably constant" except for the years 1938 to 1945. They explain how those years might be anomalous due to the impact of the Great Depression and World War II. However, why choose those years, except for the reason that imprisonment rates were anomalous? In his reply, Blumstein discusses recent increases in the United States imprisonment rate, and poses several explanations for them. One account is that United States society is "becoming inherently more punitive, and is moving to a new, higher level

of 'stable punishment.'" If United States society is moving to a new level of punishment, it must be changing; yet, Blumstein's only evidence for change is the use of punishment. Without an anchor for determining when and how a society is changing, aside from changes in its use of punishment, the stability of punishment hypothesis becomes, in the extreme, nonfalsifiable. Any aberration in the use of punishment can be explained as resulting from changes in society that, in turn, are identified by changes in the use of punishment. Until a theory of social change is incorporated within the stability of punishment framework, any contrary evidence can be too easily dismissed. (1981a:1811–1812)

The fundamental question raised here concerns the logical status of the stability of punishment hypothesis or the stability of punishment theory. The original formulation of that hypothesis is that, "in a given society, during a relatively stable period, there is a balance of forces that maintains [the rate of punishment] fairly constant" (Blumstein and Cohen, 1973:200). As we have noted above, Rauma, notwithstanding his own doubts, says that "the sheer mass of evidence" (1981b:1796) may support the hypothesis. But the crucial question in this context, as he appears to realize in the passage reproduced above, is not how much evidence supports the hypothesis but rather what would count as evidence against it.

Clearly it is not enough simply to point out instances of inconstancy in the rate of punishment in a given society, because such variations can easily be accounted for. A case in point is what Blumstein and Cohen refer to as "the anomalous points" in the United States imprisonment-rate time series in the years 1938–1945 with the peak from 1938 to 1941. The peak is explained as possibly "a depression aftermath effect" or "a war precursor" (Blumstein and Cohen, 1973:201), the implications presumably being that 1938–1945 was not a relatively stable period. Similarly, in response to David Rauma's demonstration that California imprisonment and admission rates over the time period 1835–1970 had not remained stable (Rauma, 1981b:1787–1794), Blumstein et al. ask "how much of his results, for example, are dictated by the clearly turbulent, Gold Rush period of the 1850s" (1981:1805).

Nor is it enough to point, as Margaret Cahalan did, to "a significant trend toward increased use of incarceration" (Cahalan, 1979:10). For this can also be accommodated in terms "consistent with our theory—two constant incarceration rates with a shift from the lower to the higher rate in about 1925 accompanying rapid changes in United States society and in penological thinking" (Blumstein et al., 1981:1806). Similarly, with regard to "the significant growth of 40 percent in the United States imprisonment rate from 1971 to 1978," it is suggested that "it is entirely possible that American Society is becoming inherently more punitive and is moving to a new, higher level of 'stable punishment' " (Blumstein et al., 1981:1807–1809).

Blumstein et al. enumerate so many suggested explanations of anomalies and counterinstances that it seems as though the "homeo-static process [that] operates within a society to maintain a stable level of punishment" (Blumstein et al., 1977:330) can have very little space in which to operate. Thus, in their brief response to Margaret Cahalan, Blumstein and Moitra mention a variety of "economic, political, social, and cultural factors" that can influence levels of punishment. Thus, "sharp social changes within any particular society may also be reflected by a change in its stable imprisonment rate." "Significant changes" or "important social changes" include such things as an "increase in geographic mobility and urbanization" leading to "higher crime rates and associated imprisonment rates." In addition, "major changes in penological thinking and policy" may result in an "increase in incarceration associated with [that] policy" (Blumstein and Moitra, 1980:92).

The statement of Blumstein et al. that "the weight of evidence in multiple replications in a variety of settings" is "on the side of 'stability of punishment' " (Blumstein et al., 1981:1806) implies that it might be possible to discover findings which would invalidate it. But it is hard to conceive what they might be, for, although the initial formulation of the hypothesis seems to imply that it represents a general theory, it appears that this was not intended. Thus: "We fully acknowledge that the variables we have identified need not be universally appropriate and we expect that examples of jurisdictions can be found which behave in ways contrary to our theoretical construct" (Blumstein et al., 1981:1807).

In the circumstances, it is difficult to know what to make of the reference to "the weight of evidence" that "support(s) our theory." The theory is said to be like "all social theory . . . much too fragile to withstand rigid, mechanical tests of universality. Failings of universality inevitably will occur, and such observations should stimulate modification and revisions, or generalization of the original theoretical construct" (Blumstein et al., 1981:1807). But the crucial question is: What would count as evidence to weigh in the scales against the "theoretical construct?" What would constitute not merely a reason for modification or revision but rather disproof of the hypothesis or sufficient reason for withdrawing it?

Without an answer to that question, the stability of punishment hypothesis is reduced to near meaninglessness. For a hypothesis to be empirically meaningful it must also constitute a denial of whatever would be incompatible with its truth. If there is nothing a hypothesis excludes, it explains nothing. Unless we know what the hypothesis precludes, we cannot know what significance to attach to it; and that is the crucial problem which confronts us in attempting to assess the stability of punishment hypothesis.

Further development of the homeostatic explanation of the stability of punishment might be described as "what didn't happen next." The Blumstein hypothesis was discussed and disputed. National-level aggregate imprisonment statistics had provoked the production of other national-level counterexamples. But there was detailed reanalysis of only one of Blumstein's time series relating to the imprisonment rates of the individual states in the United States. And there the matter seems to have ended.

It seems to have ended just as the nonhomeostatic character of movement in imprisonment rates in recent U.S. history became evident. In that regard, the timing of the flurry of interest in the constancy of punishment is of some significance. American rates of imprisonment per 100,000 reached a postwar low in 1972. They climbed between 1972 and 1980 by about 40 percent. This pattern of growth was consistent with either fluctuation around a constant norm or a sustained upward trend.

Thus in 1980, when a congressionally mandated study of prison overcrowding was published, only eleven of the fifty states reported prison populations that were at an all-time high in rates of incarceration per 100,000 population. Level trends or slight declines after then in prison population would have been consistent with "the dynamics of a homeostatic punishment process" (Blumstein et al., 1977). But rates of imprisonment did not remain stable nor did they decline. Instead, taking the growth achieved in the last seven years of the 1970s as a basis, the escalation of prison population continued. Forty-six of the fifty American states reported all-time highs in prison population rates in either 1986 or 1987.

Apart from the decidability-precluding indeterminacy of the Blumstein hypothesis which emerges from analysis of its authors' response to critics, there are two principal respects in which it is vulnerable to criticism. In the first place, while it may initially appear to have some heuristic value, it incorporates no causal theory and relies for its cogency and plausibility mainly on its descriptive adequacy. Although reference is made to various "economic, political, social, and cultural factors" by which the level of incarceration "is determined" (Blumstein and Moitra, 1980:92), these factors are not comprised in the hypothesis. Second, the hypothesis has no real comparative dimension. The United States, Norway, and Canada are not compared with one another; the imprisonment data for each country are studied retrospectively to demonstrate the operation of the "homeostatic process" severally within each of them. Nor is there any explanation of tendencies for countries of a particular type to have particular, or in some cases similar, levels of punishment over periods of time.

These three characteristics of the Blumstein hypothesis provide a sharp contrast with other functional theories of imprisonment. Indeed, as Greenberg has demonstrated, it is possible from the same point of departure, i.e., Durkheim's hypothesis about a homeostatic or self-regulating punishment process, to arrive at very different conclusions (Greenberg, 1977, 1980). Greenberg has offered an alternative interpretation of changes in the size of prison populations according to which "the oscillatory behavior of imprisonment rates is attributed to oscillations in unemployment." He points out, however, that in singling out unemployment for particular consideration "no claim is made that other variables have no effect on imprisonment rates." Moreover, in his study of penal sanctions in twentieth-century Poland, Greenberg specifically notes that the position taken by Rusche and Kirchheimer, that variations in penal sanctions are due to the needs of the economy to control the labor force, required modification. Nations with different political traditions, he asserts, "may have a different variation in the use of penal sanctions over time . . . even if their economic systems are similar" (Greenberg, 1980:195, 203).

Although Blumstein et al. refer to their hypothesis as "fragile" (1981:1807), its principal weakness, somewhat ironically, is that it is too hardy, a defect that it shares with many "Marxist" explanations. Such explanations are invulnerable to criticism because they can accommodate almost any variations in imprisonment rates. At most, apparently anomalous developments may call for some theoretical refinement. But the findings of empirical research regarding incarceration rates even when those rates rise to historically unprecedented levels never require more than some modification of the fundamental theoretical framework. The trouble with such explanations, however, is that in explaining everything they explain nothing. The difficulty that any trends would have in disconfirming aspects of such theories sets a limit on the contribution they can make to the scientific assessment of trends in imprisonment.

1.3 A COMPARATIVE ASSESSMENT

It is instructive both to compare and to contrast the Rusche and Kirchheimer and the Blumstein hypotheses on a number of dimensions. Such an exercise reveals striking similarities and equally conspicuous dissimilarities.

One of the most notable similarities relates to the derivation of the two hypotheses. Thus, the Blumstein hypothesis is said to be derived from Durkheim: "Building on Durkheim's notion that a society maintains a constant level of crime . . . Blumstein and Cohen have hypothesized that it is not crime that is stable, but rather the level of *punishment*, and imprisonment rate per capita in particular, that society maintains around a constant level" (Blumstein and Moitra, 1979:376; emphasis in the original).

Yet, although this is described as "an alternative position" derived from a reexamination of Durkheim's theory of a stable level of crime (Blumstein et al., 1977:317), it represents a complete inversion of Durkheim's theory. It is as though someone were to take the traditional Marxist metaphor of "base and superstructure" and propose a reversal of the causal relationship between the two, with the superstructure being accorded priority, as an alternative formulation of Marx's theories.

What is more, this reformulation of Durkheim is completely at variance with Durkheim's own theory of punishment, most explicitly stated in his essay "The Evolution of Punishments" (or "Two Laws of Penal Evolution" [Durkheim, [1900] 1973]) where he claims that "the intensity of punishment is greater the more closely society approximate to a less developed type—and the more the central power assumes an absolute character" (Durkheim, [1900] 1983:102–103). In this essay, which is *not* referred to by Blumstein and his associates, Durkheim argues that there is a tendency for the quantity or intensity of punishment to decrease as societies become more developed although this diminishing intensity of punishment may not occur if "the central power assumes an absolute character." This hypothesis regarding the progressive weakening of the intensity of punishment as a consequence of social development and of political organization seems so far from any "theory of the stability of punishment" (Blumstein and Cohen, 1973) that it is difficult to conceive any reconciliation between the two.

But if the relationship between the Blumstein hypothesis and Durkheim's ideas is tenuous, that between Rusche and Kirchheimer and Marx is little more substantial. It is true that Rusche and Kirchheimer's book has been described as "the landmark Marxist account of the nexus between the economy and social control" (Braithwaite, 1980:192). Moreover, its authors have been said to be "the leading Marxist theorists who have dealt with the historical development of penal sanctions" (Greenberg, 1980:203) and "the foremost neo-Marxian theorists of penal severity" (Grabosky, 1984:169). Yet precisely what is meant by referring to Rusche and Kirchheimer as "Marxist" or "neo-Marxian theorists" is unclear.

The entire collected works of Marx and Engels contain only a few brief parenthetic references to penal policy. It has been forcefully argued that "there is no Marxist theory of deviance" (Hirst, 1972:29), and there is certainly "no explicit Marxian theory of penal severity" (Grabosky, 1984:169). In *Punishment and Social Structure*, Marx is referred to only twice and Engels once (Rusche and Kirchheimer, 1939:96, 107–108, 174). Neither reference is relevant to the authors' principal thesis.

Indeed, it is far from clear what the implications of Marxism are, for penological history or theory. Two books which appeared in the 1970s were said to "provide Marxist accounts of the function of imprisonment in capitalist societies in the 20th century": Richard Quinney's *Class, State and Crime: On the Theory and Practice of Criminal Justice* (1977) and Andrew Scull's *Decarceration: Community Treatment and the Deviant—A Radical View* (1977). Both incidentally are said to "draw heavily on Rusche and Kirchheimer's broader historical analysis of the effect of material condition on penal ideas and practices." Yet, as Braithwaite has pointed out, while "both are Marxist analyses" they reach quite contradictory conclusions. "The prediction from Quinney's theorising is that as the crises of capitalism deepen, imprisonment of the surplus population will be increasingly resorted to by the state; while Scull concludes that as the fiscal crisis of the state worsens, imprisonment will be increasingly eschewed in favor of community treatment" (1980:194).

Another respect in which the Blumstein and Rusche and Kirchheimer hypotheses resemble one another is the way in which they were both rendered plausible by contemporaneous developments. Thus, at the time when Blumstein and Cohen originally advanced their hypothesis in 1973, imprisonment rates in several Western nations had been remarkably stable over long periods of time. Moreover, Blumstein et al. noted in 1977 that, while these rates exhibited oscillatory behavior, they rose and fell within fairly narrow limits. It did not follow, of course, that their hypothesis that these oscillations were a manifestation of a homeostatic or self-regulating process was correct. But there was, as David Greenberg noted, "impressive agreement between prediction and observation" (1977:644) with respect to their homeostatic model, which no doubt persuaded some observers that a search for alternative models of the processes that generate imprisonment rates would be otiose.

In the case of Rusche and Kirchheimer, the correspondence between their explanatory thesis and the real world at that time was no less remarkable, insofar as both particular features and general trends are concerned. Thus, their assertion that "the transition to modern industrial society . . . demands the freedom of labor as a necessary condition for the productive employment of labor power [and] reduced the economic role of convict labor to a minimum" (Rusche and Kirchheimer, 1939:6–7) seemed especially plausible because it fitted the industrial situation in prisons at that time.

Furthermore, their view that the use of imprisonment no longer corresponded to the state of economic development that had been reached in "modern industrial society" (Rusche and Kirchheimer, 1939:6) appeared to be borne out by the decline in European prison populations and the increasing use of alternative forms of punishment, which they documented in some detail. During the period with which they were dealing, national prison statistics for several European countries did in fact, as we have noted earlier, reflect diminishing incarceration rates; and their road map seemed to be a reliable guide to an itinerary which was actually being followed.

Another analogous feature of the two explanatory theories is that in neither case did their authors take serious account of evidence which did not accord with their respective theses. Nor did they as a matter of methodology take the essential next step in theory construction of looking for disconfirmatory data or features not in harmony or agreement with their own interpretation of events.

It is true that in the first Blumstein paper reference is made to "anomalous points" in the U.S. prison population time series, in particular, to a peak spreading from 1938 to 1941 that could represent "a depression aftermath effect" or "a war precursor." Moreover, in the same paper it is said that "there should be consideration of the differences in the behavior of different demographic groups and their differing vulnerability to punishment. Further development is needed to identify factors that influence that characteristic punishment rate of a society" (Blumstein and Cohen, 1973:201, 207). But these matters are not pursued in subsequent papers, although in the final paper in the series it is said that the existence of regional similarities in the patterns of imprisonment-rate time series suggests that related socioeconomic and political forces could exert a common regional influence on imprisonment rates; such regional similarities also "suggest the need for further analysis to identify the factors that influence imprisonment rate patterns" (Blumstein and Moitra, 1979:389).

Rusche and Kirchheimer were both less and more accommodating to counterevidence. They were less accommodating in that they believed that their thesis was manifestly true. *"The mere statement* that specific forms of punishment correspond to a given stage of economic development *is a truism"* (Rusche and Kirchheimer, 1939:6; our emphasis). Thus, a search for counterevidence could, by definition, only be inappropriate, irrelevant, and fruitless. The practices and institutions of punishment had only to be examined for it to be obvious that economic needs or fiscal interests determined the creation and shaping of punishments.

At the same time, they did not ignore historical features and events which less scholarly observers might not have mentioned at all. It has been said of them that "Rusche and Kirchheimer focus upon those institutions such as galley slavery, the House of Correction, the early prison, and the modern fine, which can be shown to have direct implications for the state's exploitation of labor power and its 'fiscal interests' " (Garland and Young, 1983:12). But while that is true, it cannot be said that they fail to notice or discuss elements of penal practice which fall outside the terms of their explanation.

It is notable, for example, that they make a number of references to the principle of less eligibility (Rusche and Kirchheimer, 1939:94, 151, 152–153, 155, 159, 207) and indeed emphasize the persistence and potency of this principle throughout the history of imprisonment, particularly in relation to prison labor. At the same time, they nowhere try to explain this principle as a function of a particular set of relations of production or of the needs of the economy to control the labor force. It is not true, however, that "they denigrate the significance of institutions and sanctions" (Garland and Young, 1983:12) which seem inexplicable in terms of their general theory of penal practice. As we have seen in the case of the Pennsylvania system and the use of solitary confinement, they frequently deal with such developments at length (Rusche and Kirchheimer, 1939:127–137). But in the end they leave them without satisfactory explanation.

Finally, a more extrinsic characteristic the two hypotheses we have examined share is that they both appear to have had a relatively short life span and provoked no significant sequential theoretical or empirical development. The Blumstein hypothesis, as we have indicated, seems after a brief flurry of interest to have sunk if not into complete oblivion at least into that limbo where theories which no longer seem relevant to current concerns or contemporary developments have their habitation.

The case of Rusche and Kirchheimer is different but not fundamentally dissimilar. After the appearance of their book, interest in the scale of imprisonment as an issue seems to have disappeared for over three decades. The principal characteristic of the contemporary response to it was the absence of any reaction at all. Far from being "a shot heard round the world" in criminological circles, the authors' emphasis on penal processes as a dependent variable "determined by . . . basic social relations" (Rusche and Kirchheimer, 1939:3) was largely ignored. Their adoption of a macrosocietal perspective was not accordant with the dominant concerns of criminologists in the 1940s and 1950s.

The modest empirical analysis deployed in that book provoked no continuing research or replication in Europe or the United States. The focus of attention in criminological and penological studies and investigations during the 1940s and 1950s was individualistic in bias and treatment oriented. Barnes and Teeters in their influential 1943 text *New Horizons in Criminology* summed up current thought on crime causation in a way which brings out the emphasis on the individual: "In America, we find either the sociological or the psychiatric points of view stressed . . . The psychiatrist speaks of 'the rejected personality' and the sociologist speaks of the 'socially maladjusted' individual." They also wrote of the advent of "the New Penology" involving a "therapeutic program, [a] well rounded plan developed for each prisoner by [a] specialized group of trained personnel" (Barnes and Teeters, 1943:249–251, 737).

Sociologists of crime devised general theories of crime causation—e.g., "differential association" (Sutherland, 1939, 1947) and "conflict theory" (Vold, 1958)—but little attention was paid to the larger "social forces" which Rusche and Kirchheimer saw as ultimately important. Even in the 1960s when yet another sociologist produced a general theory of crime causation—"containment theory" (Reckless, 1961)—only the "radical" criminologists seemed centrally concerned with the political/economic aspects of crime and crime control.

A number of Marxist or neo-Marxist scholars have written on penological topics since 1939, and the emergence of radical criminology in the late 1960s and early 1970s has been said to have led to "a return to . . . partially forgotten texts such as Rusche and Kirchheimer's *Punishment and Social Structure*" (Garland and Young, 1983:7). In 1978 Dario Melossi noted that "*Punishment and Social Structure* has been completely ignored for many years" and wrote of "the rediscovery of a classic" (1978:79, 81). But in 1977 Jacobs observed that "no recent scholars have approached the topic of imprisonment from as broad a comparative macrosociological perspective as . . . Rusche and Kirchheimer" (1977:91). And in 1983 Garland and Young noted that "few Marxist accounts as yet take the penal realm as their specific object of analysis" (1983:24).

The contrast between the Blumstein hypothesis and the Rusche and Kirchheimer approach emerges most clearly in the difference in the nature of their respective explanations of changes in the size of prison populations. The homeostatic hypothesis posits a tendency to maintain stability or equilibrium in imprisonment rates by means of societal responses which automatically compensate for changes in social or economic conditions. The Rusche and Kirchheimer explanation by contrast is dynamic rather than homeostatic and directs attention to those social factors and forces, "above all[,] economic and then fiscal forces," which, it is argued, determine levels of imprisonment over time and within particular countries. Blumstein sometimes appears to regard the level of imprisonment as somehow automatous and self-regulating; as though it were "an isolated phenomenon subject only to its own special laws" (Rusche and Kirchheimer, 1939:207). Rusche and Kirchheimer, on the other hand, see it as governed by "positive conditioning factors" which are present at "a given stage of economic development" or relate to "a specific development of the productive forces" (Rusche and Kirchheimer, 1939:6).

Again, whereas Blumstein and Cohen assert that the process of the stabilization of punishment "reflects the marginal changes resulting from an intricate, continuous process in which a complex of social forces, continually in conflict, win and lose a series of small battles"

(1973:206), the nature of the "social forces" involved is not subjected to any detailed empirical analysis. The "subtle and implicit process of societal adaptation" which is said to occur is described by way of the personification of "society." Thus, we are told, "a society establishes a boundary threshold . . . the society would respond . . . the society can choose . . . the society could accommodate . . . the society may be unwilling" and so on (Blumstein and Cohen, 1973:199–200). Alternatively, reference is made to "pressure." Thus, "if too few are punished," this may lead to "social instability" and consequently "there will be pressures for stricter law enforcement and perhaps more severe punishments" (Blumstein et al., 1977:320). Again, "as a nation's prison population begins to fluctuate, pressure is generated to restore the prison population to [the] stable rate," and "if the populations drop too far below the stable rate then pressure would develop to sanction certain kinds of behavior that previously had been tolerated" (Blumstein and Moitra, 1979:376–377).

Rusche and Kirchheimer, on the other hand, emphasize "the actual structure of modern society with all its differentiations," and throughout their historical analysis they constantly refer to class interest as a significant force. Thus, for example: "Legislation was openly directed against the lower classes"; "The power of the landed gentry was disproportionately great, but they saw in the administration of criminal justice the common interest of all the upper strata"; and "The needs of the politically dominant group in its struggle to maintain power overcame all other considerations and led to an unprecedented degree of repression" (1939:6, 18, 80, 206).

Society is not seen as a homogeneous unit but as an arena of "intense class conflicts." For example: "The constant increase in crime among the ranks of the poverty-stricken proletariat, especially in the big towns, made it necessary for the ruling classes to search for new methods which would make the administration of the criminal law more effective"; "The creation of a law effective in combating offenses against property was one of the chief preoccupations of the rising urban bourgeoisie"; "In the struggle against the lower classes . . . the independence of the judiciary, drawn solely from the upper classes, revealed itself to be not too great an obstacle" (Rusche and Kirchheimer, 1939:14, 15, 142).

Comparative scrutiny also reveals a no less striking contrast between the range of reference and the evidential scope of the two arguments. The Blumstein hypothesis "that a homeostatic process operates within a society to maintain a stable level of punishment" (Blumstein et al.,

1977:330) is supported by evidence relating to imprisonment rates in three countries. The time periods covered are forty-eight years for the United States (1926–1974), seventy-nine years for Canada (1880–1959), and eighty-four years for Norway (1880–1964). The Rusche-Kirchheimer hypothesis that variations in the use of imprisonment are governed by labor market considerations is supported by historical analysis covering the period from the end of the sixteenth century up to the 1930s. The argument embraces developments in such European countries as England, France, Belgium, Germany, Italy, Poland, Hungary, Bulgaria, and Sweden and also those in countries outside Europe such as the United States and Australia. It is also supported by comparative criminal and penal statistics drawn from the countries to which reference is made.

Finally, there is evidently a difference in the policy implications of the two hypotheses. In the last of the Blumstein papers, the conclusion contains some proposals for "future investigation" and "further analysis" which, it is suggested, may "provide the theoretical and operational insights necessary to understand the criminal justice system, as well as to improve it" (Blumstein and Moitra, 1979:389–390). But no particular improvements in the criminal justice system or social policies or programs that might be beneficial seem to be envisaged.

As David Greenberg has remarked, the Blumstein model "projects an air of complacency. On the one hand, we do not need to be excessively alarmed by increases in crime because the normal workings of popular pressure will bring about corrective measures just as in the past; extraordinary steps going beyond what has been done in the past are not needed. On the other hand, in the short run it is primarily through the state's *punishment* policies that the number of criminals in society is regulated" (1977:644).

By contrast, Rusche and Kirchheimer were quite categorical about "the social irrelevance of methods of punishment as a factor in determining the rate of crime." "[T]he policy of punishment and its variations," they said, "have no effective influence on the rate of crime." Indeed, they devoted a chapter to arguing with the aid of statistics drawn from England, France, Germany, and Italy that a "more severe penal policy has had no more effect on crime than a relatively lenient policy." The crime rate, they argued, was "closely dependent upon economic developments" (1939:200, 203, 204, 205).

No one could accuse Rusche and Kirchheimer of projecting an air of complacency or believing in the existence of a self-regulating mechanism governing the number of criminals at large and in prison. And it is clear that they disapproved of "overcrowded prisons, bad conditions among the lower classes generally, and the inefficiency of the administrative apparatus [governing] prison conditions" (Rusche and Kirchheimer, 1939:165). Yet when it came to proposals for reform they were no more specific than Blumstein.

They saw the penal system as "an integral part of the whole social system" and therefore not susceptible to isolated social engineering or discrete programs of reform, so that while they were convinced that "the progress of human knowledge [had] made the problem of penal treatment more comprehensible and more soluble than ever" the only solution they were able to devise seems to have required a prior remodeling of the whole of society. And they concluded that "the question of a fundamental revision in the policy of punishment seems to be further away today than ever before because of its functional dependence on the given social order" (Rusche and Kirchheimer, 1939:207).

2 Imprisonment as Historical Process: Rothman, Foucault, and Ignatieff

In this chapter we consider the work of three social historians who deal with imprisonment in some detail. Social history might seem an unlikely place in which to seek information about the determinants of prison population. For although the discipline involves the historical investigation of every aspect of social life and embraces the whole range of culture, customs, and institutions in society, it is true that few aspects of the use of imprisonment have attracted much attention from social historians, even in what has been called "the pell-mell rush of social historians to open up the crime archives" in the 1970s (Weisser, 1982:x).

There are exceptions, however, and the three whose work we examine here are the notable ones. For them the prison or penitentiary was a focus of attention, although all three were also concerned with the parallel development of other institutions such as the workhouse, the lunatic asylum, and the juvenile reformatory. We shall be arguing later that the adoption of a historical perspective is essential if insight is to be gained into the determinants of movements in prison population. Here by way of introduction we will review three important books published in the 1970s which offered revisionist accounts of the social history of imprisonment.

First, we will discuss the three books, paying particular attention to the relationship between the thesis of each one and its author's treatment of variations in prison population. Second, we will consider the relationship between social history and the study of prison population not only as it appears in the books we review but also with respect to the contribution that future social historians may make to the study of the scale of the prison enterprise in Western society. The first four sections of the chapter lay a foundation, in the particular histories under review, for a broader discussion in the fifth, concluding section.

The first of the three books is David Rothman's *The Discovery of the*

Asylum: Social Order and Disorder in the New Republic (1971), which deals, inter alia, with what he calls "the invention of the penitentiary" in America. The second is Michel Foucault's *Discipline and Punish: The Birth of the Prison* (1977; originally *Surveiller et punir: Naissance de la prison*, 1975), which also is not about imprisonment only but provides an account of the emergence of the penitentiary as the principal punishment for serious crime in France. The third, Michael Ignatieff's *A Just Measure of Pain: The Penitentiary in the Industrial Revolution, 1750–1850* (1978), somewhat narrower in scope, deals with the emergence of the penitentiary in England in the period from 1770 to 1840.

One of the intentions of all three authors was to explain why what Foucault called "the mechanisms of punishment . . . assumed their new way of functioning" at that point in history (1977:15). "Why," asked David Rothman, "in the decades after 1820 did they [the Americans] all at once erect penitentiaries for the criminal?" (Rothman, 1971:xiii). "This book," says Michael Ignatieff, "tries to establish why it came to be considered just, reasonable, and humane to immure prisoners in solitary cells, clothe them in uniforms, regiment their day to the cadence of the clock . . . What new exigencies . . . explain this decisive transformation in the strategy of punishment?" (Ignatieff, 1978:xiii).

All three took the view that the answer to that question could only be derived from an examination of the social context in which the penitentiary system originated. "Institutions," David Rothman said, "whether social, political or economic, cannot be understood apart from the society in which they flourished. The sturdy walls of the asylum were intended to isolate the inmates, not the historian" (1971:xx). Foucault, acknowledging that "Rusche and Kirchheimer's great work *Punishment and Social Structure* provides a number of essential reference points," argued that "we must analyse the 'concrete systems of punishment,' study them as social phenomena . . . we must situate them in their field of operation" (1977:24). Ignatieff maintained that what went on "within the walls obviously must be linked to changes in class relations and social tactics outside the walls" (1978:xiii).

It is not irrelevant to note that the appearance of these three major reexaminations of the history of the penitentiary within one decade was not unrelated to *their* social context, for it was a period of widespread disenchantment with the prison system. When Rothman wrote of "the failure" of the system and declared that "the institutions did not fulfill either the modest or the grandiose hopes of their founders" (1971:xix), the use of imprisonment as a penal method was already the subject of intense critical scrutiny. Foucault remarked that "[i]n recent years prison revolts have occurred throughout the world . . . They were revolts against an entire state of physical misery that is over a century old" (1977:30). And Ignatieff wrote of the "combination of population pressure, public disillusionment, fumbling reform, prisoner militancy, and guard intransigence" that had led to a breakdown from which "there has followed nearly a decade of hostage-takings, demonstrations, and full-scale uprisings" (1978:xii).

In the circumstances, it is perhaps not surprising that all three were extremely, sometimes virulently, critical in their approach. "By what criterion," asked David Rothman, "is a penitentiary an improvement over the stocks or system of fines and whippings?" (1971:xv). Foucault saw prisons as "institutions of repression, rejection, exclusion, marginalization" (1977:308). For Ignatieff they represented "an unprecedented carceral totalitarianism" where "the tyranny of the majority took as its symbol and instrument the silence, the lockstep, and the bullwhip of Auburn penitentiary" (1978:212).

Yet all three were concerned not only to deplore but also to explain. Their explanations like those of most social historians belong to a class of speculations the merits of which are not easy to assess. But all were concerned with what Foucault called "the entire economy of punishment" (1977:7) and with the social forces which influence the use of imprisonment. It is reasonable therefore to ask to what extent their works throw light on the factors which determine the extent to which imprisonment is used. This question can conveniently be approached by dealing with them seriatim, in chronological order of publication.

2.1 THE INVENTION OF THE PENITENTIARY

David Rothman begins by distinguishing his interpretation of the rise and spread of the penitentiary not only from that of what he refers to as "the march-of-progress school" but also from an interpretation which, although he does not refer to them specifically, clearly derives from Rusche and Kirchheimer. "This interpretation," he says,

> insists that coercion and not benevolence was at the heart of the movement, that institutionalization was primarily a method for regulating and disciplining the work force. Society had to keep large numbers of the urban lower classes in line, in a social sense, in order that they would stay on the line, in a factory

sense. If the laborer would not fulfill his task of his own free will, he would be forced to work in an almshouse; should he prefer to live by crime, he would be set to work within prison walls. Thus, institutionalization was a way of making the lower classes work in one setting if not another.

He goes on to say that

> this perspective is too narrow. It makes every spokesman and leader of the movement a tool, conscious or not, of the economic system; rhetoric and perceptions not fitting a production-oriented explanation are ignored . . . Further, this view exaggerates the economic and urban development of the nation in the 1820s and 1830s, when the movement began . . . Perhaps most important of all, it assumes that an urban and industrial society must depend upon caretaker institutions to control the labor force. But later developments amply illustrate that this is by no means so. (Rothman, 1971:xvi)

Instead, as America became increasingly industrialized, he says, new methods replaced institutionalization for dealing with social problems. "When American industrial output surpassed that of every other nation, when the city population outnumbered the rural, and when immigrants flocked to the new world and its factories, then citizens began to . . . experiment with probation and parole systems that would avoid or curtail imprisonment." It is difficult, he argues, in the light of these developments to regard the penitentiary system as "the inevitable concomitant of economic and demographic considerations" (1971:xvii).

According to Rothman's interpretation the invention of the penitentiary represented an attempt to promote the stability of society at a time when traditional ideas and practices appeared outmoded and ineffective: it was "an effort to insure the cohesion of the community in new and changing circumstances. Legislators, philanthropists, and local officials, as well as students of poverty, crime and insanity were convinced that the nation faced unprecedented changes" (1971:xviii). The penitentiary was "designed to join practicality to humanitarianism, reform the criminal, stabilize American society, and demonstrate how to improve the condition of mankind" (1971:79).

Thus in the 1820s Pennsylvania and New York began a movement that soon spread through the Northeast, and then over the next decades to many midwestern states. Nevertheless, although in the first formulation of the penitentiary idea the prospect of improvement both of the individual and of society had priority, after 1850 a "decline from rehabilitation to custodianship" took place and what had been a subsidiary consideration became the primary one. Penitentiaries had been built because of the promise of reform. "The functionalism of custody perpetuated them."

"Urban areas now held populations of unprecedented size, and industrial development had begun to alter the nation's economy: numerous immigrants entered eastern and midwestern cities, and the distinctions among social classes increased. Each change made the traditional mechanisms for maintaining order less relevant. Under these circumstances, incarceration became first and foremost a method for controlling the deviant and dependent population" (Rothman, 1971:79, 239–240).

Rothman supports this interpretation with data drawn from the annual reports of state penitentiaries and those of inspectors of prisons regarding "the social and ethnic composition of the prison population." These show that the overwhelming majority of inmates were at the bottom of the social ladder. There is an "almost complete absence from the prison lists of men of middle or upper-class occupations."

Rothman demonstrates that official statistics also reveal that at least a large minority and often a majority of inmates were not natives to the states in which they were imprisoned. "At first in the Jacksonian period, they were mostly Americans who had moved from one state to another; then in the Civil War era, they became immigrants." Citing figures drawn from the annual reports of inspectors of prisons in New York, Massachusetts, Pennsylvania, and Illinois, he illustrates the way in which during the 1850s the alien or foreign-born came to dominate prison populations and "the state prison population became to a marked degree lower class and immigrant" (Rothman, 1971:252–255).

According to Rothman, America was undergoing a transformation with the passage of colonial society, and "the social and ethnic composition of the penitentiary population represented the most important elements in this transformation." Thus, what had begun "as an attempt to eliminate delinquency ended up as a practical method for getting rid of delinquents." Penitentiaries became places "for restraining the foreign-born and lower classes," and their principal function changed from reformation to incapacitation. The penitentiary "offered the community a measure of security—at least for the period of the convict's confinement. To a society that was only beginning to evolve effective forms of policing, even a temporary respite was welcome" (Rothman, 1971:255, 257, 261).

The relationship between penal function and prison population was a direct one in Rothman's account. The transformation in the function of the penitentiary and in the composition of the prison population was accompanied by an increase in that population. Overcrowding became "another common characteristic of penitentiaries." Institutions like the Philadelphia penitentiary and Sing Sing designed to maintain the solitary isolation of inmates gave way to multiple occupancy of cells. Rothman quotes in this connection from E. C. Wines and Theodore White's 1867 *Report on the Prisons* to the New York legislature their assertion that "at least one third of all convicts did not sleep in individual cells" ((Rothman, 1971:242).

Another factor which contributed to overcrowding in prisons was the sentencing procedure, which was originally formulated in the 1790s but remained in operation for most of the next century. The original plan was that in place of the use of the gallows for a wide range of offenses the severity of punishment would be matched with the seriousness of the act. The procedure involved the passing of a fixed sentence at the close of the trial so that "punishment would become certain and the futility of criminal behaviour obvious." The sentence was predetermined, unalterable, and usually lengthy.

Rothman cites commitment patterns that illustrate how this procedure operated:

> State codes and courts consistently fixed sentences according to the severity of the offense, unhesitatingly meting out lengthy terms for major crimes. The fate of inmates at the Ohio penitentiary illustrated the general condition: the average period of confinement for counterfeiting was four years; for assault, six years; for burglary with larceny, six and one-half years; for rape, twelve and one-half years; and for murder, life. At the Illinois penitentiary, those guilty of larceny served from two to four years; for assault, between five and nine years; and for robbery, between ten and fourteen years. Under these conditions, state prisons, therefore, had the burden of confining murderers for life, rapists for over a decade, and robbers for nearly as long. (1971: 250–251)

In the circumstances, overcrowding was inevitable, but despite over-crowding, penitentiaries continued to dominate the criminal justice landscape and remained central to criminal punishment. "It was not," says Rothman,

> simply a matter of the states being lethargic and economical, and hence unwilling to dismantle the costly structures that they had just erected. Rather, legislators continued to invest in insti-tutions, enlarging existing structures or constructing others. The appropriations were usually not sufficient to prevent overcrowd-ing, but they were adequate for housing an increasing number of inmates. Not until the end of the century was there a marked change in practice and the beginnings of a noninstitutional re-sponse to the problems of poverty, crime and insanity. (1971:238)

It is pertinent to note that Rothman was writing at a time when prison population had been declining. As we shall indicate in chapter 6, the decade 1960–1970 was one in which all regions of the United States experienced a decrease in prison population. In his Introduction Roth-man says "today we steadily abandon a reliance upon institutional treat-ment"; and in the concluding paragraph of his book he says "we have been gradually escaping from institutional responses, and one can fore-see the period when incarceration will be used still more rarely than it is today" (1971:xix, 295).

As with the Rusche and Kirchheimer and the Blumstein hypotheses, Rothman's historical analysis seemed to be rendered plausible by con-temporaneous developments. According to his interpretation of events, the development of the penitentiary system and its perpetuation "long after [its] original promise had faded" were explicable in terms of the "very special needs" of the time (Rothman, 1971:xix, 295); and those needs no longer existed. Over thirty years earlier Rusche and Kirchhei-mer had reached a similar conclusion and had been similarly mistaken.

Rothman was not specifically concerned to define the determinants of prison population, but there is no doubt of the relevance of his analy-sis to that question. Earlier social historians who interpreted the devel-opment of the penitentiary as simply a triumph of humanitarianism, "an inevitable and sure step in the progress of humanity" (Rothman, 1971:xiv), threw no light on it at all. Rothman by placing it in its social and economic context demonstrates that it came to fulfill a very different function from that envisaged by the philanthropists who sponsored it.

He has been justifiably criticized for neglecting "actual trends in crime" during the period because "in the absence of such data, crime becomes a static and empty category in Rothman's analysis" (Ignatieff, 1981:165). But at the same time he drew attention to aspects of the function which imprisonment actually fulfilled at that period that make it clear that to regard the dimensions of prison population as simply a function of crime rates or trends in crime is not only simplistic but grossly misleading.

Moreover, his demonstration of the way in which the extent of prison populations could be influenced not merely by the social situation at the time but by systems of belief and ideological commitments provides a salutary lesson. In drawing attention to the persistent influence on later developments of the ideas and assumptions which lay behind the creation of the penitentiary system, Rothman succeeds in substantiating his claim that the extended use of imprisonment was not simply "the automatic and inevitable response of an industrial and urban society to crime" (Rothman, 1971:xvi).

2.2 THE POLITICAL ECONOMY OF THE BODY

Michel Foucault's *Discipline and Punish* is one of that genre of sociocultural treatise which derives its appeal not from its reliance on empirical research or logical analysis but from its synthesizing power—its ability to fit facts into a coherent and acceptable picture or configuration. If it has seemed compelling, it is not because of the evidence marshaled to support it but rather because it appears to introduce some intelligible order and sequence into an apparently formless confusion of actions and events.

Foucault, as we have mentioned, acknowledges a debt to Rusche and Kirchheimer, but he uses their work as a point of departure rather than a source of insight. Noting that they relate different systems of punishment with the systems of production within which they operate, he says:

> There are no doubt a number of observations to be made about such a strict correlation. But we can surely accept the general proposition that, in our societies, the systems of punishment are to be situated in a certain "political economy" of the body; even if they do not make use of violent or bloody punishment, even

when they use "lenient" methods involving confinement or correction, it is always the body that is at issue—the body and its forces, their utility and their docility, their distribution and their submission. (1971:25)

It seems possible that Rusche and Kirchheimer might not have found *that* general proposition easily acceptable; but they are soon left far behind as Foucault develops his own political economy of punishment in corporeal terms. From the use of "torture as a public spectacle" in the eighteenth century to prison riots in the late twentieth century, the lesson to be learned is "that punishment in general and the prison in particular belong to a political technology of the body." It was in fact, according to Foucault, contemporary prison riots which provided the essential clue which he derived "not so much from history as from the present," and he refers to a series of uprisings in French prisons in the 1970s (Foucault, 1977:7, 30, 268).

"There was," he says of the riots, "certainly something paradoxical about their aims, their slogans and the way they took place," and "one may, if one is so disposed, see them as no more than blind demands or suspect the existence behind them of alien strategies." However, the truth, he maintains, is that "[i]n fact, they were revolts, at the level of the body, against the body of the prison. What was at issue was not whether the prison environment was too harsh or too aseptic, too primitive or too efficient, but its very materiality as an instrument and vector of power; it is this whole technology of power over the body that the technology of the 'soul'—that of the educationalists, psychologists and psychiatrists—fails either to conceal or to compensate, for the simple reason that it is one of its tools" (Foucault, 1977:30).

This is not entirely clear, but it is entirely characteristic of Foucault's mode of argument or method of exposition. The apposition of the human body and "the very body of the prison" has a poetic resonance which transcends logic. In his universe of discourse, the metaphor is an absolute monarch over an enormous domain. The tide of figurative language sweeps over all empirical or logical obstacles in its path as though they did not exist.

Foucault's attitude to contemporary criminological research seems to be one of indifference. He cites historical works by Sellin and Radzinowicz (Foucault, 1977:213, 313, 314) but appears to regard what he calls "the chatter of criminology" (1977:304) as irrelevant. When he does feel the need for evidential support, he adduces historical data which rarely do anything to substantiate his assertions. A case in point is his repeated assertion that imprisonment "causes recidivism" which is backed by statistics establishing no more than the commonplace fact that many prisoners in France in the 1830s (as in all countries, at all times) were recidivists (1977:255, 265–266, 267, 272, 301).

Foucault's principal thesis appears to be that the nineteenth century saw the development of "the carceral archipelago" in which "the penitentiary technique" was transferred "from the penal institution to the entire social body." What is variously referred to as "the carceral network," "the carceral system," "the carceral pyramid," and the "carceral continuum" is said to operate "at every level of the social body" (Foucault, 1977:298, 301–303). "Is it surprising," he asks, "that prisons resemble factories, schools, barracks, hospitals, which all resemble prisons?" (1977:228). The prison "in the central position that it occupies is not alone, but linked to a whole series of carceral mechanisms" which control "the carceral city" (1977:308).

Viewed from this perspective, it hardly seems of much significance whether an individual is in or out of prison, for "the carceral texture of society" is all pervasive (Foucault, 1977:304). And it is not surprising therefore that Foucault has little to say that is more than tangentially relevant to factors which influence levels of imprisonment. Nor is he concerned with differences between countries in their use of imprisonment. He focuses attention on the French penal system only. "Differences in historical developments and institutions would make a detailed comparative examination too burdensome and any attempt to describe the phenomenon as a whole too schematic" (1977:309).

He does, however, draw attention to one feature of modern correctional systems which has at times had some bearing on the extent of imprisonment in this century. He calls it "the Declaration of Carceral Independence." "In it," he says, "is claimed the right to be a power that not only possesses administrative autonomy, but is also part of punitive sovereignty." The prison, he argues, through such means as "release on license" becomes increasingly "an instrument for the modulation of the penalty" (1977:247).

Apart from such parenthetical references Foucault does not discuss the determinants of prison population or demonstrate any interest in such matters. But it is interesting to note that at a time when other contemporary observers were anticipating the diminution of imprisonment and its supersession by alternative methods of punishment Foucault was emphasizing the centrality and "the extreme solidity of the prison." In a passage perhaps less than luminously clear he explains, "If it had been no more than an instrument of rejection or repression in the service of a state apparatus, it would have been easier to alter its more overt forms or to find a more acceptable substitute for it. But, rooted as it was in mechanisms and strategies of power, it could meet any attempt to transform it with a great force of inertia" (1977:305).

2.3 PRISONS, THE STATE, AND THE LABOR MARKET

In A *Just Measure of Pain* Michael Ignatieff appeared to agree with both David Rothman and Michel Foucault. Noting that Rothman had "suggested that the last decade has seen the beginning of the end of the 'total institution,'" he acknowledged that "it is true that there has been a trend under way since the mid-1950s to divert offenders from the 'total institution' by means of probation, early parole, and the expansion of community treatment options."

At the same time he maintained that there had been no fundamental change. "In fact, the proportion of the population sent to the 'carceral archipelago' has not been reduced, since the archipelago has added some new islands, the halfway house, drug treatment centers, restitution centers, and outpatient clinics. In many instances, these supposedly noncarceral alternatives continue to rely on the threat of reimprisonment to maintain discipline and compliance among their 'clients'" (Ignatieff, 1978:216–217).

Although Ignatieff focuses upon the period 1750–1850, his study encompasses the development of the penitentiary system in England from its beginning down to the present day when "the Victorian prisons survive as the most unchanging element in our institutional inheritance" (1978:205). He opens with an account of a convict's day in Pentonville penitentiary, London, in the 1840s—"a model for prison architecture and discipline not only in England but in most of Europe" (1978:3). Near the end of the book he returns to Pentonville as it is today. "In the cells once built for one man's solitude there are now crammed three and sometimes four prisoners, and in the corridors that used to be as silent as catacombs, televisions blare" (Ignatieff, 1978:205–206).

In the intervening pages he gives an account of the history of prisons in which like Rothman and Foucault he repudiates earlier historians' accounts of the development of the prison system as the culmination of a story of progress and reform. Like them he sees the penitentiary as taking "its place within a structure of other institutions so interrelated in function, so similar in design, discipline and language of command

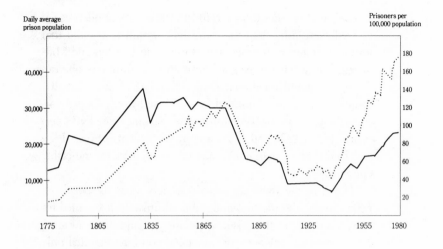

Daily average
prison population

Prisoners per
100,000 population

•••••••••• daily average prison population
———— prison population relative to total population

FIG. 2.1. Daily average prison population and number of persons imprisoned per 100,000 of the total population in England and Wales, 1775–1980. Source: Ramsay, 1982.

. . . It was no accident that penitentiaries, asylums, workhouses, monitorial schools, night refuges, and reformatories looked alike or that their charges marched to the same disciplinary cadence . . . they made up a complementary and interdependent structure of control . . . school-workhouse-asylum-prison, with the pain of the last serving to undergird the pain of the first" (1978:214–215).

Ignatieff seems to have been more sensitive than his predecessors to the need to provide some explanation for such things as "institutional overcrowding" and "the ebb and flow of punishment in the period" (1978:13). Since he was writing about a period in which prison population relative to total population in England reached levels never attained before or since (see figure 2.1), that is perhaps not altogether surprising.

His account of what was happening in the period runs as follows:

> The number of males committed for trial at assize and sessions for serious offenses rose from 170 per 100,000 population in 1824, to 240 by 1828, and to 250 in 1830. After a pause from 1830 to 1835, the rate began to climb again, reaching its peak in 1842, the year Pentonville opened, at 326 per 100,000 population.

The numbers sent to prison for minor summary offenses increased even faster than the numbers committed to stand trial
for major indictable crimes. For example, in London and Middlesex, the number of people committed for summary offenses
more than doubled between 1814–21 and 1822–29, while the
number of persons committed for trial rose by only 28 percent.
Nationally, the numbers committed for vagrancy rose by 34 percent between 1826 and 1829, and by 65 percent between 1829
and 1832—more than double the rate of increase for indictable
committals.

Hence, by the 1840s summary offenders (vagrants, poachers,
petty thieves, disorderlies, and public drunkards) accounted for
more than half of the prison population, while those awaiting
trial or serving sentences for indictable crime represented only
25 percent of the inmates, with deserters and debtors making up
the balance. (Ignatieff, 1978:179)

Although he remarks that, "obviously, labor market conditions are
only one of the factors determining punishment strategy" (1978:12),
conditions in the labor market are at the center of his analysis. Indeed,
he suggests that the magistrates and politicians who formulated penal
policy at that time analyzed the meaning of the rise in criminal committals in the same way.

Crime was interpreted as a sign of an ongoing crisis in labor
market disciplines and class relations, especially in the agricul-
tural districts of the south, but also in the manufacturing districts and in the juvenile labor market of the metropolis. Even
those farmers and industrialists who stood to gain by the whit-
tling away of the vestiges of paternalism, the introduction of la-
bor-saving machinery, and the beating down of wages were
worried about the social costs of these measures [and] were
keenly aware of the contradiction between their interest in social
stability and their desire to transform the economic and tech-
nological basis of their relationship with the classes below them.
The very violence of this transformation threatened the foundations of their hegemony. Their dilemma was to pursue the
capitalist transformation of the social order without somehow
destroying its stability. (Ignatieff, 1978:183–184)

According to Ignatieff, those who are variously identified as "the rulers of English society," "policymakers," the "bourgeoisie," "the proper-

tied and powerful," "the rich and powerful," and the "ruling class" (1978:174, 184, 190, 210, 214) did not resort to mass imprisonment simply because of "its functional capacity to control crime." It represented "a response not merely to crime but to the whole social crisis of the period as part of a larger social strategy . . . designed to reestablish order on a new foundation" (1978:210).

They realized that "in a free labor market the state would have to assume disciplinary functions formerly discharged by 'paternalist' employers." Thus, when the new police were introduced in 1828, their focus of attention was not burglaries, robberies, and other major crimes but the enforcement of laws against vagrancy and public drunkenness. "Eighty-five percent of their arrests in the 1830s were for vagrancy, prostitution, drunkenness, disorderly behavior and common assault, while only 15 percent were for indictable offenses, most of these being petty larceny and pickpocketing" (Ignatieff, 1978:185).

In the case of vagrancy, Ignatieff notes that in Middlesex between 1829 when the police were introduced and 1832 when they reached full strength "vagrancy committals in Middlesex increased by 145 percent." The increase in the volume of petty arrests by the police

> acted to produce severe overcrowding in the London prisons. Two of them doubled their capacity to cope with the pressure. Four hundred new cells were added to the Westminster bridewell, while the capacity of the vast plant at Coldbath Fields grew from 600 inmates in 1825 to 1150 in 1832. The "Steel" became the largest prison in England, a huge machine of cells, workrooms, treadwheels, dormitories and mess halls crammed within the walls built in 1794. More than ten thousand vagrants, beggars, disorderlies, drunks and petty thieves passed through its gates every year. (Ignatieff, 1978:185)

As can be seen from figure 2.1 the daily average prison population in England climbed steadily from the 1830s to reach a peak in the late 1870s. This increase in prison population was evidently a result in part of the decline in the use of transportation of convicts to Australia beginning in the 1830s and its replacement by imprisonment in a national system of convict prisons. The change in policy involved not merely the imprisonment of larger numbers of offenders but also the serving of longer terms by more prisoners. As Ignatieff puts it:

> Between 1848 and 1863, imprisonment, which had once been used for summary offenses and petty felonies, was transformed

into a punishment for all the major crimes, except murder, formerly punished by either public hanging or transportation.

As a result, the authorities were for the first time faced with the task of administering long-term sentences. Until the late 1840s, the longest sentences in English prisons were three years. Most offenders served six months or less. Lord John Russell was only repeating a commonplace when he said in 1837 that a ten-year imprisonment would be "a punishment worse than death." By the mid-1850s sentences of such a length had become common as replacements for the abandoned sentences of transportation. (1978:200–201)

It has to be said, however, that Ignatieff is not much concerned with prison population levels. He describes his book as an attempt "to define where the rich and powerful of English life placed the outer limits of their power over the poor, and how these limits were redrawn during the making of an industrial society" (1978:xiii). He sees the development of the prison system as representing an "extension of a structure of carceral power," as central to "the consolidation of a network of total institutions" (1978:214, 215).

Because of this, although much he describes is relevant to the determination of levels of prison population, he, like Foucault, does not see prison population levels as a matter of great interest or significance. His work was designed to "pierce through the rhetoric that ceaselessly presents the further consolidation of carceral power as a 'reform.'" In a sense his thesis is an irrefutable one, in that even decarceration is interpreted as an extension of the "carceral archipelago." In this connection he cites "a recent study which has concluded that decarceration represents an attempt to meet the growing 'fiscal crisis of the state' and replacing it with cheaper noninstitutional forms of control" (Ignatieff, 1978:216–217; Scull, 1977).

His disinterest is also reflected in his failure to note that prison population reached its all-time peak relative to total population long before the end of transportation. He says,

> By 1877, the major elements of the modern penal system were in place . . . Imprisonment had become established as the punishment for every major crime except murder . . . The last convicts had been sent out to Australia . . . Most of all, the huge glowering presence of the Victorian prison had been placed in the heart of the city, as the new symbolic representation of the state's ultimate power. (Ignatieff, 1978:205)

In fact, as Malcolm Ramsay has pointed out and as is clear from figure 2.1, "relative to the size of the total population of England and Wales, the prison population actually reached its greatest ever extent, at 142 per 100,000 inhabitants, in or around 1832; a long, slow decline set in thereafter, which has not been completely reversed, even in recent years" (Ramsay, 1982:45).

In an essay published three years after the appearance of A *Just Measure of Pain*, Ignatieff provided a critique of recent social histories of imprisonment which covered not only the works of David Rothman and Michel Foucault but also his own book. It is in fact, as he says, "necessarily an exercise in self-criticism" (1981:157), an art not widely practiced in academia; and it is both remarkably vigorous and substantive.

The revisionist historiography of the prison, he says, involved "major misconceptions." He finds the revisionist historians guilty both of "social reductionism" and "Marxist reductionism" and of the mistaken imputation of "conspiratorial rationality to a ruling class." Revisionist accounts that "characterized the penitentiary and other nineteenth century 'asylums' as weapons of class conflict or instruments of 'social control'" are repudiated. He acknowledges that "historical reality is more complex than the revisionists assumed" (Ignatieff, 1981:153, 157, 172, 179).

He disclaims the concept of the "carceral archipelago" and suggests that "the new social history of law and punishment in the seventies exaggerated the centrality of the state, the police, the prison, the workhouse, and the asylum." In his opinion the "distorting misconceptions" which derived from "the grand theoretical tradition" need to be subjected to "empirical examination" (Ignatieff, 1981:153, 184, 185, 187).

But although he remains convinced that "the penitentiary was something new and unprecedented," he has nothing to say about the marked differences in its use between countries or within countries over time. Moreover, in his concluding suggestions about "new areas of research," "new questions," and "empirical fields" that require investigation (1981:186–187), he makes no reference to variations in the scale of imprisonment, as a social enterprise, as being worthy of attention.

2.4 IMPRISONMENT RATES AS NONHISTORY

We will not attempt to catalog the critical reactions of social historians to the works of Rothman, Foucault, and Ignatieff generally. But one aspect of these books, the failure of any of them to deal with variations of rates of imprisonment as an important topic, was not the subject of critical comment, and we think this failure to criticize is worthy of note. Their books have been widely reviewed and much debated by criminologists, sociologists, legal scholars, and historians. Yet, while some other facets of their work have been sharply criticized, this feature has gone completely unremarked.

Thus, David Rothman has been accused of giving an "account of the rise of criminal incarceration that requires significant revision"; of presenting an analysis that is flawed "by a tendency toward idiosyncrasy"; and of providing a treatment that "telescopes the complexity of the social and intellectual landscape on which his thesis rests" (Hirsch, 1982:1194). He has been said to have given a misleading "picture of the thinking and social action of the period" and of "eliminating conflict from his analysis" (Roberts, 1974:305).

Foucault has been much criticized on account of his literary style. "Foucault's thesis is difficult to define with precision, [his] book teems with murky, poetic aphorisms which tend to obscure rather than illuminate" (Singer, 1979:376–377). "Foucault's often opaque language seems difficult to follow" (Milovanovic, 1981:127). He has also been criticized for the inadequacy of his thesis as "an explanatory framework for the analysis of punishment and penal change"; for "its abstruse and philosophical character"; and for its "manifest political weakness" (Garland, 1981:867, 868, 880).

"Foucault," one historian has said, "boldly asserts his ideas as facts [but] if one accepts his analysis . . . it must be more on the basis of faith (and admiration for intellectual brilliance) than on the basis of compelling evidence." His "theory is both ingenious and unprovable" (Wright, 1983:22, 29). Another historian has challenged both the adequacy of his explanation: "the changes in modes of repression are hardly explained at all"; and his account of events: "Foucault's picture . . . is actually far from historical reality" (Spierenburg, 1984:viii).

Ignatieff has been reproached for an unconvincing attempt to "relate the development of the penitentiary to a strategy of social control by his imputing political motivation to evangelical philanthropists." To describe prison reform proposals by such diverse figures as "John Howard, Jeremy Bentham, Elizabeth Fry, and William Crawford, as part of 'social control strategy'" is said "to endow them with a unity of form and conception that would not have been recognized by their contemporaries" (Tomlinson, 1980:75). He has been accused of "insensitivity to empirical detail and complexity," and of the "imposition" on history of a thesis that "the evidence will not bear" leading to a "series of tensions or even inconsistencies" in his work (Young, 1983:91).

It is true that Rothman's history has been said to be "seriously compromised by a curious compass of research that sweeps in all of the United States, yet never strays beyond its bounds" (Hirsch, 1982:1194). And Foucault has been criticized for his "dogmatic mode" of argument and failure to present any "extensive or quantitative evidence" (Garland, 1986:871, 873). Moreover, Ignatieff himself acknowledges that a number of historical "theses and monographs completed within the last couple of years have insisted that the descriptive picture is more complex, contradictory, and inchoate than Foucault, Rothman, or I have suggested" (1981:163).

But for the most part historians have questioned details rather than pointed to lacunae. Thus, Douglas Hay comments that Foucault's argument "scorns chronology" and is oversimplified (1980:56). David Philips in a review of "these 'revisionist' writings on what was happening to law and punishment in the period" mentions "historical inaccuracies" but is mainly concerned to elucidate the nature of the challenge presented to "the standard available" accounts of penal history (1983:53, 65, 69).

None of the critiques, however, have related to the question of incarceration rates. There has been no criticism or commentary directed at the revisionist historians' failure to deal with variations in imprisonment rates over time or across national or cultural boundaries. This is the case even in a work like Stanley Cohen's *Visions of Social Control,* which both reviews the "revisionist history [of] the origins of eighteenth- and nineteenth-century control institutions," with specific reference to Rothman, Foucault, and Ignatieff, and discusses comparative incarceration rates in Britain, Canada, and the United States (1985:13–39, 41–49).

2.5 SOCIAL HISTORY AND PRISON POPULATION

The question with which we are centrally concerned here is the relationship between the existing social history of imprisonment and what is known or thought about the determinants of the scale of the penal enterprise. Our concern thus intersects with the work of social historians at an unconventional angle. In this connection, there arise two separate issues.

First, we can ask whether social historians have addressed questions about what determines the size of the prison population. We can examine their work in search of answers to those questions and note any deficiencies in it when viewed from this particular perspective. Second, and more important, we can consider the interrelationship of the sources and perspectives of social historians of imprisonment and ask how might these sources and perspectives be utilized in future studies of the scale of the penal enterprise. Our argument is not that the social historians have yet to address issues of scale but that the methods and perspective of social history are important tools for future study.

All three of the social historians whose work we have reviewed here regarded the origins and existence of the penitentiary system as a more important phenomenon to explain than the relative use of imprisonment as it has fluctuated over the course of history. Their focus of interest was "The Invention of the Penitentiary" (Rothman), "The Birth of the Prison" (Foucault), or "The Penitentiary in the Industrial Revolution" (Ignatieff). Only infrequently did they make reference to the extent of the use of imprisonment over the years that followed.

It is notable that all of them were writing over a century and a half since the beginning of the penitentiary system. They were dealing with a social institution long established and with a considerable history. Moreover, all of them were concerned with the institution of imprisonment not merely as something of antiquarian interest but as an "enduring institution" (Rothman, 1971:265). Prisons had survived despite an enormous "volume of criticism" directed at their "functional shortcomings" (Ignatieff, 1978:210) and continued to operate and expand "long after their original promise had faded" (Rothman, 1971:xix).

Indeed, none of them confined their attention to the eighteenth and nineteenth centuries. All three made specific reference to the present implications of their studies of the past. Rothman argued that the history of the penitentiary demonstrated that such institutions did not represent "the only possible reaction to social problems" and that "we need not remain trapped in inherited answers" (1971:295). Foucault refers to riots in French prisons and throughout the world. He declares that he is not merely writing "a history of the past" but also "the history of the present." He points out that there is no reason to believe that the prison "cannot be altered, nor that it is once and for all indispensable to our kind of society" (1977: 30, 31, 268, 305).

A reviewer in the *English Historical Review* wrote that Ignatieff's book was "as much a tract for our own times as an authoritative historical study" (Bythell, 1980:432). And Ignatieff himself stated that he was concerned not merely with the history of the penitentiary but also with "how that history continues to constrain the present and define the future." In his later review of the work of the revisionist social historians, he acknowledged that "some, if not all, of the new historiography was avowedly political." He suggested that "the libertarian, populist politics of the 1960s revised historians' attitudes toward the size and intrusiveness of the modern state; the history of the prison, the school, the hospital, the asylum seemed more easily understood as a history of Leviathan than as a history of reform" (Ignatieff, 1978:215; 1981:155).

As Stanley Cohen has pointed out, these discussions of eighteenth- and nineteenth-century structures of punishment "are not just competing versions of what may or may not have happened nearly two hundred years ago." For "all these revisionist histories contain a hidden and sometimes not-so-hidden political agenda for the present." Thus, history provides "an opportunity for a contemporary critique, whether of the liberalism of good intentions or the whole of Western humanist tradition" (Cohen, 1985:15).

Yet, although all three of these historians referred to the apparent diminution in the use of imprisonment at the time of writing (Rothman, 1971:xix, 295; Foucault, 1977:305–306; Ignatieff, 1978:216–217), none of them considered that development in historical perspective, in the light of past fluctuations in imprisonment rates. Nor did they in the body of their works pay any attention to the remarkable variations in the use of imprisonment which are a striking feature of the history of the institution.

In *The Discovery of the Asylum* David Rothman accuses earlier historians of the prison of having "failed to pose the right questions" and thus of being guilty of "bad logic and bad history." He also criticizes earlier accounts of the history of imprisonment for being "long on facts and short on interpretation" (1971:xiv, 303). But there were questions the revisionist historians failed to ask and facts they noted in passing but evidently did not consider required sustained interpretation.

For Foucault this seems to have been because prison is regarded as an almost interchangeable form of social control with so many others in operation that the precise level of prison population could be regarded as a trivial statistic. For Rothman the lack of emphasis on, or interest in, the extent of imprisonment seems to have been due to a preoccupation with the symbolic aspect of the prison in society. The penitentiary was designed "to demonstrate the social blessing of republican political arrangements to the world . . . to demonstrate the fundamentals of proper social organization" (1971:78, 79). Ignatieff too emphasized this aspect, describing the prison as "the new symbolic representation of the state's ultimate power" (1978:205). And viewing social control mechanisms as part of a symbol system is more commonly associated with concern with the qualitative rather than the quantitative aspects of imprisonment.

Because of the qualitative emphasis in existing social histories of imprisonment, two kinds of statistical data are not addressed. First, the movements of prison population over time in the individual countries subject to study are underemphasized in the studies of England and the United States and ignored in France. Second, the differences in levels of imprisonment in different countries with different rates of imprisonment are not exploited as a source of insight into the specific functions of imprisonment in different locales. Little of the social history of imprisonment to date has been self-consciously comparative over national and cultural boundaries. The adoption of such a comparative perspective would seem the logical next step in imprisonment history, and the cross-cultural comparison of rates of imprisonment should play an important role in future inquiries.

In one sense, this would be a step backward rather than forward, for half a century ago this kind of comparative approach to what he referred to as the "fluctuation of extension and severity of punishment in social life" was pioneered by Pitirim Sorokin. In his prodigiously erudite, innovative, and monumental *Social and Cultural Dynamics* he made "the first systematic attempt to measure penal severity and to explain its variation over time and across nations" (Sorokin, 1937:593; Grabosky, 1984:167).

Sorokin sought to elucidate "the dynamics of punishment" by analyzing the criminal codes of five European nations over eight centuries. In his analysis, he used the punishments prescribed in the codes as an index of the movement of punishment. This part of his work is best remembered, or at least most often cited, on account of his refutation of Durkheim's theory of penal evolution, which he described as "internally quite inconsistent" and in addition "factually fallacious" (Sorokin, 1937:612). But for the social historian concerned with the use of imprisonment there is another reason for recalling Sorokin.

Sorokin was well aware that the punishments laid down in criminal codes provided only "a roughly representative indicator of the fluctuation of the intensity and extension of punishment" and that "the problems of increase and decrease of severity of punishment in criminal codes and in social reality are different problems." As to the latter, he said, it was not possible to study it "so far as long periods of time are concerned—because the data are lacking."

But it would be quite possible for a social historian to study, over less extended periods, what Sorokin called the "important and interesting problem of the movement, increase and decrease of quantity (proportion of population upon which punishment is imposed) and of severity of punishment in social life in the course of time." Further, there is no reason why a social historian should not consider Sorokin's suggestion that the validity of hypotheses about "what conditions the amount of and severity of punishment" should be tested by "assembling the relevant historical and statistical evidence" (Sorokin, 1937:581, 594).

The second issue which arises relates to the relevance of the perspectives and methods of social historians to current concerns about prison population. Ever since the eighteenth century, when Voltaire virtually invented social history as a distinctive genre with his *The Age of Louis XIV*, there has been considerable disagreement about its nature and proper scope. But although there have been those who have been content to do little more than recount or describe, for the most part social historians have attempted to answer questions about, and to explain, the processes of change which are the subject matter of all history. And it would seem that the answers they provide must be relevant to those who have to deal with contemporary social problems.

Yet the social historians of imprisonment have signally failed to influence current debate about levels of prison population. Thus, the various lines of inquiry discussed in the rest of the first part of this book have paid no attention to the data or insights of the historians discussed in this chapter. For example, the Rothman history had already appeared before the first of the series of articles by Blumstein et al. dealing with U.S. data was published; and all three histories were available before the series was completed. But although social theory is considered, their work makes no reference to social history. The correctional forecasters discussed in the next chapter have made no use of either the findings or the methods of social history. The prescriptive theorists reviewed in chapter 4 make no mention of the historians' work.

The relevance of the historian to the tasks of either the social theorist or the correctional planner should be obvious. Any theory of the constancy of the scale of imprisonment, for instance, either is consistent with a social theory of the function of prisons or stands in opposition to such a theory. If, as Rothman and Ignatieff appear to think, prison is a largely symbolic institution, this symbolic function may allow prison populations to remain stable because precise numbers are not of decisive importance. If, on the other hand, prison populations vary widely, this would suggest a more than symbolic function for prison and changing social functions of imprisonment.

For the correctional forecaster, the existence of long-term data on trends is important and so is its interpretation. How frequently do trends in prison population change and why? How much of a change up or down takes place before pressures in the opposite direction take hold? Do different patterns of emphasis on the function of imprisonment lead to different trends in rates of imprisonment? These questions should concern the prescriptive theorist, too. Have those periods when there was domination by one or another purpose of imprisonment been associated with different trends in prison population? If so, with what effect on crime?

Yet the promise of social historical methodology has not been recognized or exploited by those professionals concerned with the determination of prison population. The uses of that methodology could include the testing of hypotheses that prison is used for particular purposes by analyzing contemporary documents, examining the background of those incarcerated, reviewing public debate, and relating trends in imprisonment to trends in contemporaneous social and governmental processes. The multiple use of such varied and often qualitative material and sources would seem essential for any policy analysis attempting to interpret past trends in correctional population or for predicting future levels.

3 Imprisonment as a Natural Outcome: The Art or Craft of Correctional Forecasting

The focus of this chapter is something quite different from the investigations of Rusche and Kirchheimer and Blumstein and his associates into the forces which are said to either produce or stabilize prison populations. Correctional forecasting is neither systematic nor exact. It is closer to weather forecasting as practiced on television than to the meteorologist's study of the science of atmospheric phenomena. It is also a relatively recent development.

In section 3.1.1 of the chapter, we deal with the beginning of empirically based correctional forecasting as it evolved during the rise of criminal justice planning as an activity and as a profession. In section 3.1.2, we consider linear extrapolation, that is, simple inference from known facts to projected future developments, as a correctional forecasting tool. In section 3.1.3, we examine more sophisticated forms of empirically based projection as exemplified in a study commissioned by the U.S. Department of Justice, Law Enforcement Assistance Administration, in 1977. In section 3.1.4, we consider demographically based forecasting systems, which exemplify what is essentially demographic determinism.

In section 3.2.1 of the chapter, we deal with two types of projection, which from empirically identical sets of facts or observations reach very different theoretical conclusions. On one hand, it is argued that the creation of prison capacity generates prisoners to fill it; on the other, that limited prison capacity acts as a constraint on prison population which, if removed, would be subject to no effective control. Both these hypotheses are self-fulfilling prophecies, but they are self-fulfilling for importantly different reasons.

In section 3.2.2, we consider a particular example of demographic determinism which suggests that the size of prison populations is simply a function of the size of the population at risk. We also examine the limited utility of hypothesizing from particular indices without any causal model of the underlying forces which determine the variables selected as significant.

The history of correctional forecasting is a parallel development to other approaches to imprisonment, but it never mingled with academic social science or formal theoretical exercises. Correctional forecasting grew from the culture of correctional administration and criminal justice planning. Its practitioners were part of the closed loop that links state and local government, state legislatures, public planning agencies, and consultants. By contrast, the cultural setting for sociological theories of imprisonment was the academic world concerned with ideas that might have no direct practical application.

In our view, to ask which of these milieus is parochial is to miss the point. Both approaches remained confined to a particular perspective apparently unaware of alternative ways of considering imprisonment. The correctional planners commonly viewed prison population as though it were a natural phenomenon like rainfall totally beyond the control of policy agencies. "We take what the courts send us" was the response of a New England state to a request for information about their projection methods in 1977 (U.S. Department of Justice, National Institute of Justice, 1980:II.45). Academic theorists for the most part remained unaware of substantial increases in imprisonment rates into and almost through the 1980s. It is because a separate culture generated the practice of correctional forecasting that how that culture came to exist becomes a major key to understanding the uses and limits of prison population projections.

3.1 VARIETIES OF PROJECTION

3.1.1 The Beginning of Correctional Forecasting

On October 15, 1976, the Crime Control Act of 1976 was enacted into law. It was passed by Congress just at the beginning of a period of largely unanticipated growth in prison populations throughout America. In response to concern about prison crowding, the act assigned to the National Institute of Law Enforcement and Criminal Justice, within the Law Enforcement Assistance Administration, the responsibility for executing a survey of "existing and future needs in correctional facilities in the nation."

Accordingly, the institute set up a research project which ultimately produced five final report volumes making up a wide-ranging study, *American Prisons and Jails*. Volume II of that study, entitled *Population Trends and Projections*, deals with both historical prison population flows and their implications for anticipated future correctional needs. It includes detailed projections for federal and state inmate populations. This exercise was itself as unprecedented as the prison population explosion that prompted its initiation and development.

That this was so is clear from the brief section headed "Previous Research" in the final report. There, specific reference is made to only two previous attempts at prison population projection. The first was a series of projections for the Federal Bureau of Prisons prepared by the Congressional Research Service in connection with a 1974 appropriation debate. The projection anticipated only limited growth in prison population (U.S. Congressional Research Service, 1974). But in fact federal prison population went on to increase beyond all recent precedent.

The second exercise was one carried out by the National Planning Association in 1976. It consisted of a series of projected manpower needs for each component of the criminal justice system. The report, released in November 1976, projected a gradual increase in prison population over a ten-year forecast period (U.S. Department of Justice, Law Enforcement Assistance Administration, 1978). By 1980 the projected maximum had already been exceeded.

Reference is also made in the final report to various projections of inmate populations prepared for state and local jurisdictions. "For the most part," it said, "projection of prison population has been a preliminary step in projecting the year's operating budget for state prison systems. Depending on the degree of controversy associated with the budgeting process, any number of projections from zero growth and up may be prepared . . . The projections were intended to serve diverse purposes, were made to meet different standards of accuracy, and were based on data of widely varying scope and quality." It could also be said that for the most part they reflected "the generally inchoate state of the projection art" (U.S. Department of Justice, National Institute of Justice, 1980:II.44–45, 46, 60).

The absence of reference to predictions or forecasts of future prison population prior to the 1970s does not so much reflect disinterest in earlier attempts at prison population projection as it does the absence of interest in such matters in earlier years, even at times of sustained increase in population. Thus, when the National Commission on Law Observance and Enforcement (the Wickersham Commission) published its *Report on Penal Institutions, Probation and Parole* in 1931, it asserted that overcrowding in prisons was "probably worse than it has ever been, taking the country as a whole." The report of an advisory committee appended to the main report also dealt at some length with "the enormous overcrowding that at present exists" and noted that "at no time in the history of the country has it been so serious as at present" (National Commission, 1931b:211, 231–232).

Yet neither in the main report nor in that of the advisory committee is the discussion of overcrowding followed by any review of past trends or estimates of future possibilities in population growth. Overcrowding, said the advisory committee, "is one of the things which the warden or superintendent is least able to control. He cannot say to a prisoner committed by the courts, 'You may not enter; we have no room.' He is bound to receive him. There is no escape. The warden must take the offender who presents himself with the properly executed papers of sentence."

It was "of the utmost importance, therefore," the committee went on to say, "that the responsible government authorities not only try to avoid overcrowding but, when planning new buildings or alterations have in mind the future of the prison population, and try to build for the needs of several years in advance and not only for the immediate current needs." But the committee refrained from any speculation about the future of the prison population or what the needs of several years in advance might be. Moreover, in the discussion "Some Aspects of Prison Building" which immediately follows, it is "the type of housing accommodations" required that is the focus of attention rather than the need for capacity changes to adjust to likely future population changes (National Commission, 1931b:231–232, 234–238).

The Wickersham Commission's investigation was the most important inquiry into prisons in the first half of the twentieth century. It was not until 1965 when President Johnson established the President's Commission on Law Enforcement and Administration of Justice that another comprehensive nationwide survey of correctional operations was carried out. At that time, overcrowding was not seen as a serious problem and the commission's Task Force on Corrections only mentioned it in passing as a feature of a few facilities. The task force report noted that "[t]he number of inmates in State and Federal prisons for adults has decreased about 1 percent per year in the past few years, despite increases in the total population of the country and in serious crime" (President's Commission, 1967b:45).

In the circumstances, it is not altogether surprising that the task force was not preoccupied with the possibility of future overcrowding in prisons. Unlike the Wickersham Commission, however, it did consider the

TABLE 3.1 Average Daily Population in Correctional
Institutions, 1965, and Projections for 1975

Type of Institution	1965 (actual)	1975 (projected)
Misdemeanant	141,303	178,000
Juvenile	62,773	108,000
Adult felon	221,597	237,000
Total	425,673	523,000

SOURCES: 1965 data from National Survey of Corrections
and special tabulation provided by the Federal Bureau of
Prisons; 1975 projections by R. Christensen of the Commission's Task Force on Science and Technology, "using
methods described in appendix B of this report." President's
Commission, 1967:45.

likely growth of various correctional populations in the years ahead.
Table 3.1 shows the projected growth of institutional populations based
on population increases and on the assumption that current trends in
arrest, conviction, and release rates would continue.

The task force report noted that "[t]he population projection for the
prison system shows the smallest aggregate increase of any of the correctional activities." It also anticipated that special community programs
and the increased use of probation and parole would in practice "curtail
the projected institutional growth" (President's Commission,
1967b:4–5).

In a brief appendix to the task force report, by Ronald Christensen,
the assumptions on which the projections shown in table 3.1 were
based, and the manner in which they were computed, are discussed
(President's Commission, 1967b:213–215). Unfortunately, the appendix is terse to the point of ellipsis and neither from the account given
there nor anywhere else in the report itself is it possible to determine
precisely how the estimates were arrived at. Nevertheless, the attention
paid to population projections represents a significant development.

By 1973 when the National Advisory Commission on Criminal
Justice Standards and Goals reported, the national prison population
had stopped declining and started rising. The population increase, however, did not lead the commission to anticipate a need for more prisons.
Indeed, the commission's *Task Force Report on Corrections* said: "The
facts lead logically to the conclusion that no new institutions for adults
should be built and existing institutions for juveniles should be closed."
Moreover, it said that except in rare instances public policy should be

"a 10-year moratorium on construction of institutions" (National Advisory Commission, 1973:358, 597). From what facts did these policy recommendations "logically" flow?

The answer to that question turns out to have nothing to do with correctional forecasting. It can be found in the final chapter of the task force report under the heading "Priorities and Implementation Strategies." It is asserted there that "[t]he prison, the reformatory and the jail have achieved only a shocking record of failure. There is overwhelming evidence that these institutions create crime rather than prevent it . . . In view of the bankruptcy of penal institutions, it would be a grave mistake to continue to provide new settings for the traditional approach in corrections" (National Advisory Commission, 1973:597). As to the overwhelming evidence that prisons create crime, no references are cited.

Elsewhere in the task force report, under the heading "The Future of Institutions," it is said that "the need for some type of institutions for adults cannot be denied [because] there will always be a hard core of intractable, possibly unsalvageable offenders who must be managed in secure facilities." But it is also said in regard to such facilities that "there are already more than enough to meet the needs of the foreseeable future." It seems clear that the policy recommendations of the commission were not derived logically from any set of facts regarding prison population trends but rather from the commission's commitment to "the position that more offenders should be diverted from adult institutions [and] that much of their present populations should be transferred to community-based programs" (National Advisory Commission, 1973:349). The art or craft of correctional forecasting was not advanced by anything the National Advisory Commission said or did.

3.1.2 The Uses of Rulers: Straight-Line Trend Projection

Corrections administrators and planners, however, faced with increasing prison populations, cannot operate effectively without estimates of the number of prisoners for whom housing will be needed in future years. This is especially the case because of the time required to plan and build new prison facilities. Accordingly, many state correction departments prepare and publish prison population projections using a variety of methods. In the era when the need for criminal justice planning became the dominant theme for system management and the need for forecasting at the state level received wide recognition, the new emphasis on population projection was usually met with statistics based on linear extrapolation.

When in the 1970s the Florida Department of Offender Rehabilitation surveyed state corrections departments, it found that, of thirty-two states publishing projections, two-thirds (twenty-one) based their projections on simple linear extrapolation (Florida Department of Rehabilitation, 1977). This most widely used method involves graphing data on prison populations or admissions against time and projecting present trends into the future. Although it lacks logical or theoretical justification, it may provide satisfactory results over short periods of time.

Linear extrapolation is based on the assumption that present prison population trends, whether of growth or decline, will continue into the future at a uniform rate and can therefore be reflected in a straight line ruled on a graph. The reason why it may work well over short periods of time is that historically prison populations have been marked by long periods of increase or decrease and as long as the projection period is contained within one of those periods linear extrapolation will produce acceptable results.

Thus, the study reported in *American Prisons and Jails* identified about six episodes of sustained increase or decrease in U.S. prison population over the previous fifty years, with the average length of an episode eight or nine years. This means that linear extrapolations done in the first or last years of an episode will be falsified in one year but that short-term extrapolations will indicate the right direction of population changes more often than not.

In the long term, however, because of the occurrence of changes in trend and "since elapsed time is not the real cause of change, we can be confident that sooner or later linear extrapolations will produce absurdities." Thus, "[i]ntermediate-term (five-year) projections which rely on linear extrapolation would have called the right direction [only] 11 of the last 50 years (22%)" (U.S. Department of Justice, National Institute of Justice, 1980:I.95, II.59). The trouble with the use of rulers is that periods of growth or decrease in prison population do not continue forever in straight lines.

3.1.3 Modified Rulers

A relatively more sophisticated type of projection taking into account trends in factors thought to influence arrivals and departures in the correctional system was used by Ronald Christensen in the projections he developed for the 1967 President's Commission Task Force on Corrections. Christensen's population projections were derived from computations which took account of such factors as the total population in relevant age groups, the arrest rate for the relevant age group, the ratio of convictions per arrest, and the fraction of those convicted sentenced to prison (President's Commission, 1967b:213).

Christensen also tried to take account of sentencing trends, but data on these were not available on a nationwide basis. However, on the ground that, as reported by the commission, "[m]ost correctional officials believe that probation is being used increasingly across the Nation" he used data from California. This was because "[i]t is the largest state; it has a variety of probation agencies; it has had a definite increase in the use of probation; and its records in this regard are quite complete."

Because of lack of adequate data to determine trends in all factors which could influence the number of arrivals and departures in correctional institutions, it was assumed, "lacking justification for doing anything else," that those factors held constant for purposes of the computation. Where there were sufficient data to establish a trend, it was assumed that current trends in such things as arrest, conviction, and release rates would continue (President's Commission, 1967b:6, 214).

It is clear that Christensen did not, and could not, take account of all the factors that might influence the size of future inmate populations. Many highly speculative and imponderable factors are involved, which always makes the projection of prison populations extremely speculative. Nevertheless, in taking account of some of the relevant factors not covered by a linear extrapolation model, Christensen's estimates represented a significant technical advance in prison population projection methods.

A far more comprehensive exercise in forecasting prison population for the federal prison system was undertaken by the U.S. Sentencing Commission when it was directed by Congress to estimate the impact of the commission's federal sentencing guidelines on future prison populations. Working with the Federal Bureau of Prisons, the commission developed a computer simulation model, designed to project future demand, incorporating a considerable variety of factors and assumptions. As this is the most sophisticated simulation exercise attempted to date, it merits detailed examination here.

The factors of which account was taken included time served under current sentencing practices; anticipated prosecution trends; the Anti–Drug Abuse Act of 1986; the career-offender provision of the comprehensive Crime Control Act of 1984; and the commission's guidelines. Then, using alternative assumptions regarding such unknown factors as future prosecution and conviction rates, plea negotiation

TABLE 3.2 Sentencing Commission Projections of Federal Prison Population

	1987*	1992	1997	2002
High	42,000	79,000	118,000	156,000
Low	42,000	72,000	92,000	105,000

*Actual.
SOURCE: U.S. Sentencing Commission, 1987:71, 73.

practices, and levels of departure from the guidelines, prison population forecasts were derived from almost twenty possible scenarios. The results under these scenarios provided upper and lower bounds on the estimates of prison populations. By this method, the study projected the prison capacity demand for 1992, 1997, and 2002 shown in table 3.2.

It is notable that both the low and the high estimates projected unprecedented numerical growth of the federal prison system over the next fifteen years. Under the low projections, the prison population in fifteen years in federal institutions would be two-and-a-half times the 1987 level, with the most significant growth spurt occurring between 1987 and 1992, when the population was projected to increase from 42,000 to 72,000, or 71 percent. Under the high projections, the prison population would climb 86 percent over the following five years but then continue the sharp increase so that the total expansion in the fifteen-year period would reach a population of 156,000, 275 percent of the 1987 total.

The commission's original research core for the projection exercise was a survey of 10,500 convicted federal offenders in 1985. The analysis of these data was combined with historical data on trends in conviction for federal crime, and the literal provisions of the new drug laws, the career criminal legislation, and the guidelines. To derive prison populations, the commission used extrapolated trends in the numbers of individuals convicted for federal crimes derived from aggregate historical trends and combined them with sentence estimates based on the factual circumstances of the 10,500 1985 convictions and the legal provisions governing sentencing length of the drug laws, the 1984 Crime Control Act, and the postsentencing guidelines. The commission thus estimated prison population by stacking new sentences each future year on the then-existing prison population.

There were four stages in building the estimated population levels reported in table 3.2. The first stage was to estimate what would happen to the federal prison population in the next five and fifteen years if there

TABLE 3.3 Projected Federal Prison Population Based
on Changes in Conviction Only

	1992	1997	2002
High	62,000	78,000	95,000
Low	57,000	61,000	65,000

SOURCE: U.S. Sentencing Commission, 1987:71, 73.

were no changes in the sentencing patterns given conviction. The commission then assumed two growth rates for convictions in federal court, the high and low scenarios reflected in table 3.3.

Under the low-growth scenario, it was assumed that the annual growth in convictions in federal court would continue for the next three years at the rate at which it had expanded for the previous five years (as a policy impact of the Reagan presidency) and then fall off with an annual growth rate of 1 percent for all the other years in the model. Under the high-growth-rate projections, 1992 figures were derived by assuming that the next five years would have the same amount of total growth as the previous five years, and the fifteen-year estimates were derived by assuming the growth rate in persons convicted over the next fifteen years would be the same as the rate experienced during the period from 1971 through 1986.

The prison population projections directly reflect those assumptions. Both the high and the low scenarios have sharp growth in the first period but differ after that. Under the low-growth scenario, there would be twice the increase in prison population in the next five years as there would be over the following decade, 1992–2002. Under high growth, the total prison population would more than double over the next fifteen years even if no changes in sentencing were projected, solely as a function of the increase in the number of individuals convicted in federal court.

Table 3.4, which extends the projections by factoring in changes in drug law sentences provided in the 1986 anti–drug abuse legislation, shows the same relative contrast between high projections and low projections as table 3.3 because the same assumptions about conviction rates are used. The estimates for drug law sentencing were derived in the following manner. The mix of drug law violations was estimated by studying the facts of the sample of 10,500 cases and determining the "real offense" committed by the defendants in the 1985 sample. The estimated sentences were then obtained, for those convicted by jury or at bench trial, by matching the real offense with the sentence provided for that offense in the 1986 legislation.

For guilty pleas, it was assumed that the same percentage of persons who pleaded guilty in the 1985 sample would plead guilty in the future, and their sentence was derived by taking the same percentage discount observed in the contrast between guilty pleaders and those convicted by trial in 1985 and applying that as a discount from the 1986 law penalties. The fifteen-year prison population projections cum drug laws then reflected more than a doubling in the low estimate and growth of about 225 percent under projected high growth conditions.

The independent contributions of career criminal provisions in federal legislation and of the guidelines then appears relatively modest when added on top of the drug law and conviction growth projections. This is shown in table 3.5. The career criminal effects accumulate over time as the number of individuals with life sentences increases. The guideline effects were estimated by taking random midguideline values (excluding the highest and lowest allowed) as the sentence given in each case but used different techniques when probation was allowed by a guideline. The guidelines never have an aggregate impact as great as 10 percent on top of the inflated projected populations. Their highest percentage impact is on five-year projections: 7 percent of the nonguideline projected total.

TABLE 3.4 Federal Prison Population under Drug Assumption

	1992	1997	2002
High	73,000	108,000	138,000
Low	67,000	85,000	93,000

SOURCE: U.S. Sentencing Commission, 1987:71, 73.

TABLE 3.5 Federal Prison Population with Impact of Career Criminal and Guideline Provisions

	1992	2002
High projection	73,000	138,000
With career criminals	+1,000	+12,000
With guidelines	+5,000	+6,000
Low projection	67,000	93,000
With career criminals	+1,000	+9,000
With guidelines	+4,000	+3,000

SOURCE: U.S. Sentencing Commission, 1987:71, 73.

The detailed population estimates that are derived from use of this research to simulate the policy impact of the 1986 drug legislation, career criminal provision, in recent federal law and the guidelines themselves are necessarily speculative, and the commission acknowledged that the fifteen-year projections were "very speculative" (U.S. Sentencing Commission, 1987:56). Nevertheless, by using alternative assumptions regarding such unknown factors as future crime rates, expenditures, and policy (as reflected in prosecution rates), the study made a genuine attempt to take account of them. And the provision of both low-growth and high-growth projections demonstrates recognition of the essentially conjectural character of all future prison population projections.

The federal projections also show the arbitrariness of the assumptions used to make projections. With respect to future trends, the commission both assumes that historical trends will hold (for other than drug offenders and habitual felons) and that sharp discontinuities will occur for

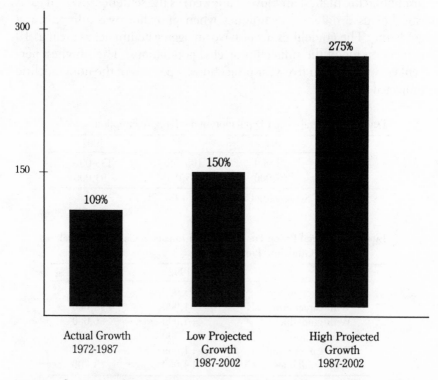

FIG. 3.1. Sentencing Commission projections of federal prison populations. Source: U.S. Sentencing Commission, 1987.

these two categories of offenders. No "system dynamic" reactions are forecast in which increases in prison population will reduce the rate of new prison commitments or the length of sentences, nor is there any provision for a downward impact on prison commitments for non–drug offenders to compensate for the new drug priorities. The result is a much sharper projected increase than has ever occurred previously, as shown in figure 3.1.

3.1.4 Demographic Determinism

Demographic data relating to the age, sex, and race of prisoners provide details of some external variables which are claimed to bear some relation to future prison populations. Because female incarceration rates are so low (96 percent of prisoners are male), the sex ratio in prisons is of little use as an indicator in predicting prison populations. But "population" defined as referring to groups stratified on race and/or age is sometimes seen as a leading indicator.

Thus, as the *American Prisons and Jails* researchers noted, "[a] popular hypothesis relates the most recent growth in prison populations to the fact that the fraction of the U.S. population in the most incarceration-prone ages (just over eighteen) grew significantly during the 1970s" (U.S. Department of Justice, National Institute of Justice, 1980:II.46). At the same time, there is gross disproportionality between blacks and whites in the composition of prison populations, for although blacks constitute only one-eighth of the population they represent about one-half of the prison population.

When incarceration rates are considered in relation to the demographic variables of age and race, it emerges that the group with the highest incarceration rate in the population consists of black males in their twenties. Alfred Blumstein in a study of racial disproportionality in United States prison populations found that this group suffered an incarceration rate twenty-five times that of the total population. His findings are reflected in table 3.6, which shows demographic-specific incarceration rates (in units of prisoners per 100,00 persons within each indicated demographic group) in state prisons (not including federal prisons or local jails) for blacks and whites and their total.

Blumstein further found that the severe disproportionality between black and white incarceration rates, which stood at a ratio of more than seven to one, held throughout the decade of the 1970s although there was a slight downward trend in the black fraction in prison, which "might be an artifact of changes in the arrest reporting process" made

TABLE 3.6 Demographic-Specific Incarceration Rates[a] in U.S. State Prisons[b]

Demographic Group	Total[c]	White	Black	Black/White Ratio
Total population	124	72	493	6.9
Males	233	142	1,012	7.1
Males, 20–29	755	425	3,068	7.2

[a] The "demographic-specific incarceration rate" is the ratio of prisoners in the indicated demographic groups to the population within that demographic group, in prisoners per 100,000 population.

[b] The estimates of state prisoners within each demographic group are derived from a survey of state prisoners conducted in 1979 by the Bureau of Justice Statistics. The estimates of the population within each demographic group are obtained from the U.S. Bureau of the Census.

[c] The totals for both prisoners and population are based only on black and white groups. Other races are omitted from the calculations.

SOURCE: Blumstein, 1982:1260.

during the decade (Blumstein, 1982: 1271–1272). It might seem in the light of such findings that prison population was largely a function of demographic distribution and that race and age-at-risk would provide reliable predictors of prison populations.

This possibility was considered by the National Institute of Justice researchers who investigated how age-at-risk had performed as a predictor of prison populations in the past and how it compared to other correlated time series, such as a simple straight-line fit or the total population of the state. They reported that:

> [w]e tested these models in two exploratory studies using the 20-
> to 29-year-old segment of the total population and the 20- to 29-
> year-old black population as candidate leading indicators in se-
> lected states where detailed data were available. Both studies had
> disappointing results. Over the comparatively short time span of
> the last decade, the changes in prison population have been too
> rapid and abrupt to fit any simple function of the demographic
> distributions. Since 1960, the ratio of inmates to population at
> risk declined steadily in Iowa, increased in South Carolina, and
> fluctuated in Illinois. Using the post-war Iowa time series, a
> statistically significant correlation between the number of in-
> mates and the population at risk is found. Unfortunately, for
> both variables, the simple correlations are negative. If a regres-
> sion model is used to remove the common effect of a simple

linear growth trend from the two series, the correlations vanish. Moreover, the imprisonment rates are statistically less stable than the prison populations per se. The coefficient of variation of the rates is roughly twice as high as for the number of inmates. (U.S. Department of Justice, National Institute of Justice, 1980:II.47)

Projections based on demographic data appear to assume the truth of a version of determinism—demographic determinism. The implicit assumption is that there is a necessary connection between demographic characteristics and imprisonment: a chain of causation leading from those characteristics to criminal behavior and to imprisonment. Furthermore, the underlying deterministic model appears to ignore the fact that systems change with time and are not static but rather dynamic.

As the National Institute of Justice study points out, projections relating to subgroups stratified on race and age "are invariably based on the assumption that imprisonment rates will remain constant within strata throughout the future of the projection period, often despite evidence that the rates have not remained constant in the very district for which the projection is being prepared" (U.S. Department of Justice, National Institute of Justice, 1980:II.46).

The assumption of constancy implies that demographic-specific incarceration rates reflect aspects of society which are sui generis and unaffected by any extrinsic factor. It involves ignoring such things as the kinds of disadvantage flowing from socioeconomic status that are correlated with race and the influence of racial discrimination in the criminal justice process. In fact, it treats as irrelevant all those fundamental conditions of social life which the social and behavioral sciences have shown to be relevant to the incidence of crime.

3.2 Some Issues
3.2.1 Self-Fulfilling Prophecies

In this section, we examine two hypotheses about the relationship between prison population and prison capacity which reflect contrasting views about the potential dangers and benefits involved in projections of correctional populations as part of the policy and planning process. Both derive very different conclusions from the same empirical base. Both may become self-fulfilling prophecies but for importantly different reasons. The first hypothesis is that additional prison capacity will generate an increased number of prisoners. The second is that the limitation of prison capacity will result in fewer offenders being imprisoned.

3.2.1.1 Build and Fill

The first hypothesis, that capacity drives population or that "new space finds its own occupants" (U.S. Department of Justice, National Institute of Justice, 1980:I.138), was the subject of heated debate in the 1970s when the National Moratorium on Prison Construction was launched (National Moratorium, 1978; see also Nagel, 1977). As early as 1971, when the decline in the national prison population had slowed, the American Friends Service Committee, with what looks like remarkable prescience, had argued that the result of providing new cell space was "inevitable: the coercive net of the justice system will be spread over a larger number of people, entrapping them for longer periods of time" (American Friends, 1971:172).

Support for this position was not slow to develop. In 1972 the National Council on Crime and Delinquency (NCCD) declared that "no new detention or penal institution should be built before alternatives to incarceration are fully achieved" (NCCD, 1972). A report of the American Assembly adopted a similar view (American Assembly, 1973); and in 1973, as noted earlier, the National Advisory Commission on Criminal Justice Standards and Goals recommended a ten-year moratorium on prison construction (National Advisory Commission, 1973:352, 357). Then in 1975 the National Moratorium on Prison Construction was organized by the Unitarian Universalist Service Committee with the assistance of the NCCD.

One of the principal arguments advanced by those opposing more correctional construction rested on the hypothesis that prison capacity inevitably generated prison population. The argument is somewhat analogous to Parkinson's law, which holds that work expands to fill the time available for its completion (Parkinson, 1957:2). This form of capacity-population hypothesis holds that prison population expands to fill available buildings. Thus, as the NCCD policy statement on prison construction put it: "To allocate funds for institutions will increase rather than decrease institution populations" (NCCD, 1972).

Harold Confer of the American Friends Committee on National Legislation drew an analogy with firearms and violent crime. "Just as the availability of guns facilitates armed robbery," he said, "the construction of new prisons tends to strengthen policies of incarceration." It would do so, he suggested, because "the taxpayers are going to say . . . why have you spent so many million dollars in constructing new facilities if you do not really intend to use them" (1975:11, 19). Milton Rector, the director of NCCD, suggested another reason. "Would not judges who were once reluctant to commit, because of the conditions of the old prisons," he asked, "now send throngs of inmates to the sparkling new ones?" (1977:20).

Although some of those opposed to prison construction seemed to treat this capacity-population hypothesis as self-evidently true, there is some evidence which appears to support it. The National Institute of Justice study, for example, reported in 1980: "As a matter of history, this study has found that state prison populations were more likely to increase in years immediately following construction than at any other time, and that the increases in the numbers of inmates closely approximate the change in capacity." But the report went on to say that although they had found data consistent with the hypothesis "these data are suggestive, not conclusive" (U.S. Department of Justice, National Institute of Justice, 1980:I.138–139).

The National Institute of Justice study also pointed out the implications of this hypothesized capacity-population relationship for prison population projections. It drew attention to "the possibility, indeed the likelihood," that a high projection might be given too much weight and that "the false confidence may become the self-fulfilling prophecy." Thus, "there is evidence in at least some jurisdictions that the supply of prison space is among the factors that influence the demand for that space. Where this is the case, an unwarranted confidence in high population projections can prove accurate merely because there are enough potential prisoners waiting in the wings so that any newly created capacity is 'automatically' used" (U.S. Department of Justice, National Institute of Justice, 1980:I.92).

3.2.1.2 Limit Space/Limit Population

An alternative view of the population-capacity relation also emerged during the prison construction debate. This involved a different model of the dynamics of correctional capacity and rates of incarceration. The emphasis in this case was on mechanisms that limit prison populations. On this view, capacity—in this case, limited capacity—serves to limit the prison population.

One of the ways in which this could happen was exemplified in the refusal of federal judges in the 1970s to tolerate traditionally high levels of crowding in prisons. Another way was noted by James Q. Wilson in his essay "The Political Feasibility of Punishment." He referred there to the reaction of sentencing judges to prison overcrowding and the unsatisfactory conditions resulting from it. He argued that many existing facilities were "too lacking in amenity to enable many judges in good conscience to send offenders there" (1977b:120).

As to the federal courts, the National Institute of Justice study noted that since "the Attica tragedy of 1971 . . . no region in the country has been unaffected by federal, and occasionally state, court orders to eliminate substandard conditions of confinement . . . The courts have repeatedly characterized crowding as the condition of confinement that exposes inmates to the most harmful physical and mental consequences" (U.S. Department of Justice, National Institute of Justice, 1980:I.34). As a result, while no clear set of standards for determining constitutionally acceptable prison population levels emerged from the substantial body of litigation challenging overcrowded confinement conditions, there is no doubt that in some cases the state's ability to use imprisonment as a sanction was significantly curtailed.

The courts' action to remedy unlawful crowding took a variety of forms. Some judges enjoined corrections officials from receiving any new prisoners. Some ordered individual facilities to be closed. In many cases accelerated release programs or reclassification and the transfer of inmates from prisons to community treatment centers and halfway houses were used to achieve compliance with court-ordered prison population reductions.

In these and other ways it is clear that judicial activism operated in such a way that the supply of prison space was a major factor in limiting the size of prison populations. It is also clear that low prison population projections if taken seriously by correctional authorities might also act as population-control mechanisms by limiting the construction of new correctional facilities and thus available prison capacity.

In other words, low population projections could also become self-fulfilling prophecies. Viewed in this light, space limitation is seen as a constraint on prison population which otherwise would be subject to no effective control. James Q. Wilson argued the case for more prison construction on the ground that "[s]ince society clearly wishes its criminal laws more effectively enforced . . . this means rising prison populations, perhaps for a long period" (1977a:22). The alternative view of the population-capacity relation we are considering reflects the obverse of Wilson's position. As the National Institute of Justice study put it: "Excessive confidence in low population projections . . . may mean that society's desire to respond with proportionately more stringent incarceration will be thwarted in the absence of sufficient prison capacity" (U.S. Department of Justice, National Institute of Justice, 1980:I.92).

On this view, the significance of this aspect of the population-capacity relation is that it is unlikely that there has ever been a period when society did not wish to have "its criminal laws more effectively enforced." So it is argued that there is no level of prison capacity that would meet society's "desire to respond with proportionately more stringent incarceration." In short, the limitation of prison capacity represents a necessary restriction, without which prison population would increase in a totally uncontrolled fashion. As long as there is a crime rate, one can consider the public demand for additional capacity to be unlimited. The fact that crime continues to exist is evidence that the problem prisons are designed to solve has not been solved. So the limitation of capacity becomes an artificial constraint where there are no natural restraining factors.

Two further points relating to the political setting in which the prison construction debate takes place complicate matters. The first is the way in which prison construction issues seem to polarize participants as either wanting to combat crime or being opposed to crime control measures. Spending on prisons is never presented as one of several crime control options which might be chosen. The debate becomes a referendum on whether more should be spent to combat crime. As a result, political expediency may force individuals to vote for more spending on prison construction than they would otherwise regard as necessary or justified.

The second point is that there commonly is a time lag between those periods when pressures for stiffer sentences are at their maximum and the point at which decisions about prison construction and the provision of the necessary funds are made. Additional prisons must be built years before crimes are committed if extra prison capacity is really to function as a sentence enhancer. But if the anger and frustration which animated the public demand for more prisons are moderated or qualified in the more abstracted atmosphere in which prison building decisions are made, an apparent shortage of prison capacity may always appear to exist, although this actually only reflects the different emotional context in which sentencing decisions and spending decisions are made.

The number of cells we decide to build in the cool and abstract process of correctional planning may well be far fewer than the number of cells felt to be necessary in the middle of an emotional public reaction to particular crimes or series of crimes. But the difference may simply reflect a difference in mood and the smaller amount of space could just as easily be as socially optimal as the larger. If the insulation between public reaction to crime and decisions about prison building were removed, it could well lead to overinvestment in prisons. Most of us would recognize that decisions made in the heat of passion would not represent a considered judgment of what was in our best interest. There may be an analogy here in the politics of prison capacity.

There is an interesting parallelism in these two accounts of the population-capacity relation. In the first place, both of them are derived from observation of the same set of empirical facts. They represent different interpretations of a single body of data. Thus, there is little doubt that in some states building more prisons has been a factor in increasing prison population, that building more prisons has in fact helped to make the difference between having a stable or an expanding population. At the same time, the notion that capacity may limit rather than lead population is also supported by some of the evidence relating to federal court intervention in prison administration noted above.

Nevertheless, in neither case is the inference that there is some kind of necessary relationship between capacity and population justified. If there were, then in the case of the hypothesis that capacity drives or leads population there would never—except for very short periods—be any unfilled prison space. In fact, many jurisdictions have in the past had—and some still do have—an excess of capacity over population. On the other hand, in the case of the capacity-limits-population hypothesis the truth is that court-ordered prison population reductions have often resulted not in the reduction of incarceration but simply in the crowding of other facilities such as jails. Thus, the National Institute of Justice study reported that in the period following court orders affecting state facilities "it has often been the case that the prison crowding problem has shifted to county and city jails where state officials have housed thousands of prisoners awaiting transfer to state facilities" (U.S. Department of Justice, National Institute of Justice, 1980:I.37). There is, however, a more fundamental similarity between these two hypotheses, for not only do both involve overstatement or overgeneralization but also they ignore the fact that physical capacity is only one of a multitude of factors which influence imprisonment rates. To nominate one item from the mass of independent random and systematic sources of change in prison populations as of paramount importance is contrary to reason.

Additions to prison capacity may sometimes be a factor in increasing prison population just as existing capacities can function as a limiting factor on the use of imprisonment. But in neither case is there any evidence to suggest that these relationships between capacity and population are necessary or inevitable ones. As the National Institute of Justice study said in relation to the capacity-drives-population hypothesis, "Since any number of circumstances may influence both decisions to build and decisions to incarcerate we cannot suggest that new space will always find new occupants independent of these circumstances" (U.S. Department of Justice, National Institute of Justice, 1980:I.94). Nor is it any more reasonable to suggest that capacity limitations will always act as a curb on incarceration rates.

3.2.2 The Absence of Theory
3.2.2.1 Causal Vacuum

The fact that simple linear extrapolation involving no more than drawing a line through points on a graph and extrapolating the line into the future is not merely unreliable but leads to obviously absurd conclusions (U.S. Department of Justice, National Institute of Justice, 1980:I.95) is now widely recognized. As Blumstein puts it, "If the points follow a downward trend, even the most naive extrapolator would know not to draw that line so far that it took on negative values for prison" (1984:213).

It is also widely recognized that to select only one variable, time, as the leading indicator of future prison population and ignore all the other factors that influence imprisonment is singularly simplistic. However, a more fundamental defect involved in this type of projection is shared by the other models we have considered. The National Institute of Justice study referred to this defect when it noted the weakness of the theoretical justification for the extrapolation model and in particular the fact that "elapsed time is not the real cause of change" (U.S. Department of Justice, National Institute of Justice, 1980:I.95).

This criticism is more fundamental and is also widely applicable. It applies, for example, to the use of demographic-specific incarceration rates in estimating future prison populations. The finding that black males in their twenties have the highest incarceration rate in the U.S. population makes it possible to extrapolate that incarceration rate as an aid to the generation of estimates of future prison populations. But the assumption that incarceration rates within a demographic group remain constant over time and will continue to do so in the future can lead to erroneous forecasts. Moreover, as with the linear extrapolation of population trends over time, it involves ignoring all other political and socio-economic factors that are relevant to changes in incarceration rates.

More important, the use of demographic-specific incarceration rates as the leading indicator in projecting prison populations shares with the simple linear extrapolation model the theoretical weakness that the variables selected—age and race—are "not the real cause of change." Such projections may appear to "rely on a chain of causation leading from demographic characteristics to criminal behavior to criminal sanctions" (U.S. Department of Justice, National Institute of Justice, 1980:II.47). In fact, however, no causal hypothesis linking age and/or race with crime is offered. Indeed, what is striking is the absence of any etiological hypothesis whatever.

This is also true of both forms of the population-capacity hypothesis we have considered. In neither case is it said explicitly that the relationship between population and facility capacity is a causal one. Moreover, suggesting this would lead to conclusions no less absurd than those which follow from simple linear extrapolation. Thus, the capacity-creates-population hypotheses would imply that building decisions were the ultimate determinants of prison population and that, however extensive a prison building program was launched, there would always be potential prisoners available to fill it. By contrast, it would follow from the hypothesis that capacity provides an inflexible limit on prison population, and in fact determines the size of the population, that the problem of prison overcrowding could be solved by the simple expedient of pulling down prisons.

Although models that use only a single variable may be faulted for ignoring a variety of other variables related to prison populations, models which invoke a number of variables can be no less defective when they rely on no more than observed correlations, for they provide no insight into the significance of the statistical patterns they record and use. They serve no heuristic function whatever, and the demand for explanation in this context is not merely a reflection of idle curiosity but an essential condition of realistic, veridical projection.

3.2.2.2 The Limited Use of Blind Models

The use of models which include any number of exogenous variables for projecting future prison populations may in this respect be no better than simple linear extrapolation. The National Institute of Justice study remarked of linear extrapolation: "The problem is that it provides no hint of when a change in growth will occur, or of how large such a change might be" (U.S. Department of Justice, National Institute of Justice, 1980:II.59). But the inclusion of more variables in more sophisticated forms of extrapolation is little more helpful.

Thus, the addition of demographic variables might appear to represent a substantial advance. As Blumstein has said, "The number of men in a particular high-imprisonment group (for example, ages twenty to twenty-nine) is relatively easy to project for at least twenty years into the future. All individuals in that age group are already born; therefore the only uncertainty is associated with death and migration. Death rates are . . . reasonably predictable. Migration can be a major distorting factor . . . and must certainly be taken into account." But as Blumstein also noted, the use of such variables in projecting prison populations involves considerably more uncertainty, for the crucial assumption in this approach is that "the incarceration rates remain fairly constant within any demographic group over time." In fact such an assumption may be totally unjustified. Indeed, there was, as he points out, over the period of 1974 and 1979 "significant growth in incarceration rates" (1984:214–215, 216–217).

The truth is that the use of more indicators without any model of the underlying forces which may generate change really does not represent a great advance on simple linear extrapolation of the time series of prison population. For however strong a correlation may be found between two sets of data, unless the reason for that relative correspondence is known there is no reason to believe that it will remain strong. Indeed, without some explanation of past patterns one cannot go beyond the use of rulers. If one cannot explain why the past took the shape or form that it did, then it is impossible to generalize from past experience. One cannot predict what one cannot explain, and blindness to theory is a disability which in this context ultimately renders the most sophisticated and complex projection techniques inadequate and unreliable.

3.2.3 Margins of Error

If television weather forecasters had to be correct to be listened to, television program schedules would be filled with gaps. Instead, we listen to the weather forecasters because their predictions are right more often than could be attributed to chance, and because we regard their reliance on meteorological theory regarding atmospheric phenomena such as clouds and wind direction as plausible. We listen to them because we accept the theory—about such things as the causation of the condensation of moisture in the atmosphere which then falls to the earth in the form of rain—which underlies the predictions about specific events that they make.

Correctional projections, because they involve what we call "blind models," are persuasive or plausible predictors if at all only because they have worked in the past. The blind model lives or dies by its empirical track record because there is no other reason to suppose that the model will accurately predict future events. Yet a systematic assessment of the accuracy of past correctional predictions has never been attempted. We do not know whether a particular method works better than another, under what circumstances it works, or even whether it works at all. The paucity of validation or assessment of correctional forecasting is partly due to the absence of retrospective assessment by those agencies of government that generate and use such forecasts. But it is also the consequence of lack of attention by criminological or sociological theorists who could act as external evaluators.

4 Imprisonment as a Policy Tool: Prescriptive Approaches

4.1 INTRODUCTION

4.1.1 Prescriptive Rationales versus Prescriptive Programs

Ever since the eighteenth century, when the prison or penitentiary began to take over the function earlier fulfilled by a variety of
different penal methods such as corporal punishment, transportation,
and the death penalty, attempts have been made to answer questions
about the justification of imprisonment. In that the prison system is a
part of the penal system, discussion of these questions has largely been
a reflection of a more general debate on the ethics of punishment and
has usually been couched in the same terms.

As in that more general debate, much of the discussion has taken the
form of argument about various prescriptive rationales offered as justifications for the practice or institution of punishment and for particular
methods of punishment such as imprisonment. In fact, the theory of
punishment has traditionally been largely made up of recommendations
or prescriptions. As H. L. A. Hart put it, "Those major positions concerning punishment which are called deterrent or retributive or reformative 'theories' of punishment are moral *claims* as to what justifies the
practice of punishment—claims as to why, morally, it *should* or *may*
be used" (1957:446–447).

For the most part, these prescriptions regarding what should be done
were ex post facto justifications for what was already being done. The
use of imprisonment, in one form or another, as a punishment long
predated most of the literature dealing with punishment theory. When
Beccaria wrote about "the political intent of punishments" ([1764]
1963:30) and Bentham about "the several *objects* or *ends* of penal justice" (1802:IV.174), they were offering what they saw as a rational basis
for the employment of a penal method which was already being exten-
sively used.

The penitentiary, as the name implies, was originally designed as an institution where offenders were to submit to punishment as an expression of penitence. By undergoing penitential discipline, they were expiating or making atonement for their crimes and extinguishing their guilt. The central purposive justification of the institution was moral or spiritual reform, an objective two of the earliest and shrewdest outside observers of the system, Beaumont and Tocqueville, regarded as quite unrealistic (Beaumont and Tocqueville, 1964:89).

Bentham, by contrast with the pioneers of the penitentiary system, saw the worth or value of the system as being determined by its utility, primarily as a means of crime control. He was prepared to acknowledge that it might have multiple ends or objectives including Example (i.e., Deterrence), Reformation, Incapacitation, and Compensation or Satisfaction (i.e., Retribution). But of these he maintained that Example (i.e., Deterrence) was "beyond comparison the most important" (1802:IV.174).

He defined deterrence simply in terms of "intimidation or terror of the law." And he distinguished between what later came to be called individual deterrence and general deterrence: "*Particular prevention* which applies to the delinquent himself; and *general prevention* which is applicable to all members of the community without exception" (Bentham, 1789:I.396). But although he gave the subject of "pecuniary economy" some attention in his "Panopticon; or, The Inspection House" (1791:IV.47) and again in "Panopticon versus New South Wales" (1802:201–211), he did not enter into any consideration of how much prison space might be required to achieve a particular level of crime control. He went no further than observing that "Economy" was something that "ought not to be departed from to any greater distance, than the pursuit of the direct ends [of penal justice] shall be found to render unavoidable" (1802:IV.174).

The kind of prescriptive rationale for imprisonment offered by Bentham has until comparatively recently made up most of the substance of debate about the purpose of and justification for imprisonment. A great variety of terms, almost invariably capitalized, have been used to denote what have been seen, in addition to Deterrence, as the principal tasks or goals of the prison system: Reform or Rehabilitation, Prevention or Incapacitation, Just Deserts or Retribution, Custody or Control, and so on. Much of the discussion has been concerned with which of these purposes should be regarded as the primary task of the system or what should be seen as the proper hierarchy of aims. What has been absent from almost all these discussions has been any consideration of how many commitments to prison would be required to achieve these multiple purposes; how much prison space would be required to put these defining principles into practice.

Prescriptive programs as opposed to prescriptive rationales are a relatively recent development and have arisen largely as a result of prison population pressures and recognition that prison is a scarce political and economic resource. Thus, in the course of the correctional construction debate, the NCCD in 1972 and 1973 issued policy statements in which the function of imprisonment was defined as incapacitation and the amount of prison space required to perform that function was precisely defined.

"Confinement," it said, "is necessary only for the offender who, if not confined, would be a serious danger to the public. For all others, who are not dangerous and who constitute the great majority of offenders, the sentence of choice should be one or another of the wide variety of noninstitutional disposition." By its standard of dangerousness, the NCCD drew the conclusion that "only a small percentage of offenders in penal institutions today" really required incarceration. Indeed, "in any state no more than one hundred persons would have to be confined in a single maximum security institution." On that basis, the NCCD concluded that "we have vastly more institutional space than we need" (NCCD, 1972:382; 1973:449, 456).

James Q. Wilson also adopted a prescriptive approach with a similar emphasis on incapacitation. "We would view the correctional system as having [this] function—namely, to isolate and to punish . . . The purpose of isolating—or more accurately closely supervising—offenders is obvious: Whatever they may do when they are released, they cannot harm society while confined or closely supervised. The gains from merely incapacitating convicted criminals may be very large" ([1975] 1977:193–194). Unlike the NCCD, however, Wilson, as noted in chapter 3, envisaged an expanded use of imprisonment and "rising prison populations perhaps for a longer period" (1977a:22).

The implementation of the NCCD program would have resulted in a national prison population total of about 5,000. Possibly because of realization either that this was unrealistic or that it would be politically unacceptable, the NCCD subsequently abandoned attempts to specify a numerical limit on population size. James Q. Wilson offered no precise estimates. Indeed, he stated specifically that, before adopting "such a policy, one would first want to know the costs in additional prison space and judicial resources, of greater use of incapacitation" ([1975] 1977:226). He did not, however, offer any estimates—although since then, as we shall see, more precise attention to these topics has been paid.

4.1.2 Crime Control, Sentencing, and Prison Space

Historically the relationship between sentencing policy and the issue of prison capacity requirements has received little consideration. Such questions as how much imprisonment would be required for prisons to fulfill their proper function have not been answered because they have not in the past been raised. This has been due in part to the fact that what we have called prescriptive rationales have never embodied any conception of a distinctive function for prisons; prisons have been seen, rather, as performing a variety of tasks. It was simply assumed that prison space would be, or would somehow be made, available to accommodate all those consigned to them by the courts.

Prescriptive programs, however, have necessarily involved some focus on what distinctive contribution to crime control prisons can make. What is it that prisons can do that other punishments cannot? The most obvious answer to that question is almost a matter of definition. To sentence a person to imprisonment means to order them to be deprived of their liberty by confinement in a prison. As J. E. Thomas puts it: "Society has defined the need for removal of the criminal and the prison system, as an organization, has come into being to achieve this task" (1972:5). And there is no doubt that viewed in historical perspective what Thomas variously calls control, custody, or containment has been the principal function of the prison whatever else it may or may not have achieved. Moreover, one of the principal measures of the success or failure of the prison system is, in the eyes of the public, the degree to which it is effective in achieving simple containment.

Implicit in the custodial process or function is prevention or incapacitation. While the offender is in custody he cannot offend again; incapacitation is achieved for so long as the sentence lasts. This incapacitative function was in fact recognized early in this century and made explicit in sentences of "preventive detention" imposed on persistent offenders who were judged to be committed to a life of crime. It is only in recent years, however, that incapacitation has been advocated as providing the dominant justifying aim of all incarceration and moreover as imposing some kind of rational limit on the use of imprisonment. In this way, the linkage between sentencing policy and prison population size is made clearly evident.

4.1.3 Prison: Crime Control Function

Recognition that imprisonment's distinctive feature as a penal method is its incapacitative effect has implications for criminal justice policy. The contribution of prisons to crime control by way of rehabilitation programs or individual and general deterrence is problematic. But there can be no doubt that an offender cannot commit crimes in the general community while incarcerated.

Evaluative research on the rehabilitative effects of prison programs has not established any method that effectively reduces subsequent criminal behavior. Such research as has been carried out on deterrence has been equally nondefinitive. With regard to incapacitation, however, no research at all is necessary to establish that imprisonment has incapacitative effects. Indeed, those effects would be achieved even if no prisoners at all were reformed or rehabilitated and, as James Q. Wilson puts it, "even if the prospect of going to prison deterred no one from committing a crime" ([1975] 1977:194).

It is not altogether surprising therefore that some scholars have concluded that a rational crime control policy would focus on the use of imprisonment as a means of incapacitation and exploit the incapacitative potential of imprisonment to the fullest extent. This strategy, which is known as collective or general incapacitation, might take the form of an increase in all prison sentences, with the object of maximizing the amount of crime prevented in the community by removing offenders from society.

In view of the fact that imprisonment is not only the most serious sanction available in almost all cases but also the most expensive, the question which immediately arises is whether the social costs averted by the use of increasing levels of imprisonment are great enough to outweigh the very considerable expenditure involved in expanding prison capacity to accommodate the extra prisoners who would be incarcerated under such a policy. And as we shall see, it has been argued that, when the probable costs of crime committed by offenders if released from prison are compared with confinement costs, the former so far outweigh the latter that an increased use of imprisonment would evidently produce massive economic savings.

Others have arrived at rather more modest estimates of the amount of crime reduction likely to be achieved by increasing the total level of incarceration. They have urged the adoption of a policy of what David Greenberg called "selective incapacitation," as opposed to "collective incapacitation" (1975:542), under which prison capacity would not be expanded but rather reallocated to confine those most likely to offend again or those presenting the greatest risk of future crime in terms of both frequency and seriousness. On this view, imprisonment should not be regarded, as it is now, as an appropriate punishment for all types of offense and offender but simply as one among several methods of crime control. It should be used to do what it clearly can do, immobilize high-risk offenders; and other nonincarcerative sanctions should be employed to deal with those for whom incapacitation is not necessary.

One of the most significant effects of the substitution of prescriptive programs for prescriptive rationales has been the change in the character of contemporary debate about penal policy. In the case of prescriptive rationales, the emphasis was on the moral justification for punishment. Discussion centered on ethical concerns, and questions about the cost or effectiveness of penal methods were largely ignored. In regard to prescriptive programs, however, such questions cannot be passed over. The debate about incapacitation has been principally concerned with the incapacitative effectiveness of incarceration. That is not to say that ethical questions about the legitimacy of imprisoning individuals because of possible future crimes rather than those already committed have not been raised. It is simply that the principal emphasis has been on empirical questions regarding the differential outcomes of particular policies and the cost effectiveness of alternative programs.

4.2 OF COST AND BENEFIT

When Gary S. Becker published his seminal article "Crime and Punishment: An Economic Approach" in 1968, he referred to "the almost total neglect by economists" of crime and also to the possibility that "the reader [might] be repelled by the apparent novelty of an 'economic' framework for illegal behavior." But he noted that two pioneer contributors to criminology during the eighteenth and nineteenth centuries, Beccaria and Bentham, had "explicitly applied an economic calculus" and he expressed the hope that his work could be viewed "as a resurrection, modernization and thereby I hope improvement on these much earlier pioneering studies" (Becker, 1968:170, 209).

Becker thought that the neglect of crime as an economic activity probably resulted from an attitude that illegal activity was "too immoral to merit any systematic scientific attention." However that may be, it is true that only in the last two decades has serious attention been paid by economists and other scholars to questions regarding the costs of crime and the cost effectiveness of punishments. The approach adopted in Becker's article was soon followed and developed by other scholars (e.g., Stigler [1970], Ehrlich [1972], Posner [1970 and 1972], and Landes [1971 and 1973]), and there is now a substantial literature on the economics of crime and punishment; but his essay remains the clearest exposition of the basic theory.

4.2.1 The Theory of Optimal Levels of Crime Control Spending

One significant respect in which Becker's approach differs from that of Bentham is that, whereas Bentham regarded economic considerations as "indirect or collateral" aspects of punishment which might be disregarded if necessary in the pursuit of deterrence, reform, incapacitation, or retribution (Bentham, 1802:IV.174), Becker treats the economic aspect as central and calls such things as deterrence, rehabilitation, and retribution "these catchy and dramatic but inflexible desiderata" (1968:208).

Becker's analysis is based on a model of criminal behavior according to which a criminal is a person who chooses to engage in criminal activity because the expected utility of that activity to him, less anticipated costs, is greater than that of any available legitimate activity. Using this model, he says, enables one to "dispense with special theories of anomie, psychological inadequacies, or inheritance of special traits and simply extend the economist's usual analysis of choice" (1968:170).

Thus, the potential criminal's calculation of advantages and his choice can be altered by changing factors that affect the anticipated utilities and costs of crime. Expected punishment is one of these costs, and increasing punishment cost therefore offers a means of combating crime by diminishing the attractiveness of criminal behavior. This analysis clearly has significant implications for criminal law enforcement, for imposing costs on offenders of the level necessary to reduce the incidence of crime involves the expenditure of resources on apprehending, convicting, and punishing offenders. It follows that the control of crime is principally a matter of allocating the appropriate amount and type of resources and punishments which will minimize the social loss from offenses.

Becker uses economic analysis to demonstrate that optimal policies to combat criminal behavior are part of an optimal allocation of resources. The optimal amount of enforcement is arrived at by formulating a measure of the social loss from offenses and determining those expenditures of resources and punishments that minimize that loss. According to this analysis:

> The public's decision variables are its expenditures on police, courts, etc., which help determine the probability (p) that an offense is discovered and the offender apprehended and convicted, the size of the punishment for those convicted (f), and the form of the punishment: imprisonment, probation, fine, etc. Optimal values of these variables can be chosen subject to, among other things, the constraints imposed by three behavioral relations. One shows the damages caused by a given number of illegal actions, called offenses (O), another the cost of achieving a given p, and the third the effect of changes in p and f on O. (Becker, 1968:207)

Becker's essay concentrates on determining optimal policies and does not pay much attention to actual policies. But he claims that

> the small amount of evidence on actual policies that I have examined certainly suggests a positive correspondence with optimal policies. For example, it is found for seven major felonies in the United States that more damaging ones are penalized more severely, that the elasticity of response of offenses to changes in p exceeds the response to f, and that both are usually less than unity, all as predicted by the optimality analysis. (1968:208)

He concludes that while "many more studies of actual policies are needed they are seriously hampered on the empirical side by grave limitations in the quantity and quality of data on offenses, convictions, costs, etc." (1968:209). Since that time, there has been some improvement in both the quantity and the quality of the relevant data. Moreover, a recent example of optimality analysis deals specifically with the use of imprisonment as a means of incapacitation.

4.2.2 The Theory Applied

The example of optimality analysis in question is a research paper entitled "Making Confinement Decisions" by Dr. Edwin W. Zedlewski, published by the National Institute of Justice in 1987. In it, Dr.

Zedlewski presents an assessment of the costs and benefits of increasing levels of imprisonment which concludes that communities are paying far more by releasing offenders from prison than by expanding prison capacity. In fact, the bottom-line estimates presented in his analysis are arresting. One year's imprisonment is said to involve total social costs of $25,000 whereas the social costs averted by that imprisonment through incapacitation alone are estimated to be $430,000, or over seventeen times as great.

Zedlewski's conclusion is derived from an estimate of the cost of crime based on "every published expenditure on crime that could be found" (Zedlewski, 1987:3). He contrasts this with an estimate of confinement costs arrived at by adding to custodial costs (according to the American Correctional Association) the amortized costs of constructing a prison facility (according to a 1984 General Accounting Office report) and his estimate of the indirect costs incurred by removing an offender from the community such as welfare payments to offenders' families.

Direct expenditures due to crime and crime prevention are given as approximately $100 billion in 1983. These expenditures were divided among victim losses ($35 billion), private security goods and services ($31 billion), and the operation of the criminal justice system, including prisons, jails, police, and the courts ($42.6 billion). It is noted that prison and jail operations consume only $8.6 billion, less than 10 percent of the total, and that a year in prison implies "total social costs of about $25,000" (Zedlewski, 1987:3).

The next step in the analysis is to weigh the social cost of an imprisonment decision—about $25,000 per year—against the social cost incurred by releasing offenders. What are called "release costs" are approximated by estimating the number of crimes per year an offender is likely to commit if released and multiplying that number by an estimate of the average social cost of a crime.

The first of these two figures is derived from a National Institute of Justice–sponsored survey by the Rand Corporation of inmates confined in jails and prisons in California, Michigan, and Texas (Greenwood and Abrahamse, 1982). The survey found that inmates said they were committing crimes at what would be an annual rate of between 187 and 287 exclusive of drug deals just prior to their most recent incarceration.

To compute the cost of an average offense, total expenditures on crime in the United States, estimated at $99.8 billion in 1983, were then divided by the total number of crimes (as reported in Bureau of Justice statistics and estimated in the last reported National Crime Survey), estimated as totaling $42.5 million. Dollars spent divided by crimes resulted in a figure of $2,300 per crime.

By combining crime costs and offense rates (at 187 crimes per year), it was calculated that a typical inmate was responsible for $430,000 in crime costs (187 × 2,300 = $430,100). The conclusion derived from this analysis was that sentencing 1,000 more offenders to prison would cost an additional $25 million per year. By contrast, about 187,000 felonies would be averted through the incapacitation of these offenders, representing about $430 million in social costs. Ten thousand extra prisoners would save slightly over $4 billion, and 100,000 extra prisoners would generate $40 billion in additional savings.

Zedlewski acknowledges that the dollar estimates used in his analysis are only "approximated crudely" and that his estimates reflect "substantial imprecision." But he argues that variations in cost estimates due to imprecision are of little consequence. "The conclusion holds even if there are large errors in the estimates" (1987:3, 4). And it might seem that it would make no great difference if a marginal investment in prison space of $1 would generate only a $10 savings in social costs rather than $17.

Zedlewski's paper is an example of the prescriptive approach which recommends a strategy of collective or general incapacitation. It merits examination, however, not merely as an example of a particular approach but also because of what careful review of his analysis can teach us about the difficulties encountered with uncritical use of statistics; about the intractable problems we confront when trying to calculate the social costs of both crime and imprisonment; and about a debate in which the same arguments for and against prison expansion can be and are made at almost any level of current imprisonment.

4.2.3 Objections to Cost and Benefit

One insight into the significance and validity of Zedlewski's cost-benefit calculations may be gained by considering some of the statistical relations implied by his analysis and seeing how closely our recent history conforms to the predictions his confinement study produces.

The first such set of predictions concerns crimes prevented through incapacitation. If the rate per offender is stable, as the study estimates, at 187 per offender, the total crime cost of $42.5 million is attributable to just 227,800 street criminals (42.5m/187) of the kind we imprison. Thus, a 35 percent decrease in the population behind bars should double the crime rate by releasing about 225,000 of the 700,000 persons in U.S. prisons and jails. And a 33 percent increase in the prison and jail population from 700,000 to about 930,000 should reduce crime to zero in the United States (230,000 × 187 = 43,010,000).

Since 230,000 persons is about one-eighth of the number of adults on probation in the United States, such a shift could be achieved by changes in sentencing policy without changes in apprehensions. And the total social cost would amount to less than $6 billion according to the study (230,000 × $25,000 = $5,750,000,000). In short, expenditures of about 6 percent more than what we currently spend on criminal justice and crime would solve the crime problem.

But there are indications that these estimates are far from accurate. First, the normal turnover in the prison and jail population provides one natural test of the criminal propensities of the incarcerated population. Almost all of the more than 200,000 U.S. jail inmates are released each year as well as more than 200,000 of the more than 500,000 in the prison population. Even if all these persons were back behind bars after one year, at an annual rate of 187 crimes per subject, the 221,768 offenders released from prison in 1984 should have been responsible for just under 100 percent of all crime in the United States in 1986.

One problem with this estimate is that it leaves no room for juveniles, new recruits, a dark figure of adult offenders, the almost 2 million on probation, or even ex-inmates who were released from confinement during the previous year. Even then, the hundreds of thousands of jail releasees who should at 187 crimes per person account for almost 100 percent of crime themselves must instead be assumed to be crime-free in 1985, or we have explained 200 percent of the crime rate with jail and prison releases alone. So these estimates seem not merely wrong but ludicrously wrong.

There is, moreover, another straightforward test of these crime-imprisonment ratios, a natural experiment we have been running in the United States since the early 1970s. Since then, the U.S. prison population has been rising substantially. Thus, we can use the methods of analysis employed in "Making Confinement Decisions" to test the study's conclusions against our recent history.

We start with 1977, needing two numbers to match the analysis in "Making Confinement Decisions," an estimated number of crimes per criminal, and a total volume of crime. The estimated number of crimes per criminal can be taken at 187. Indeed, this figure was derived from inmate self-reports of their offenses during the late 1970s rather than at later dates. The total volume of crime estimated by the methods used

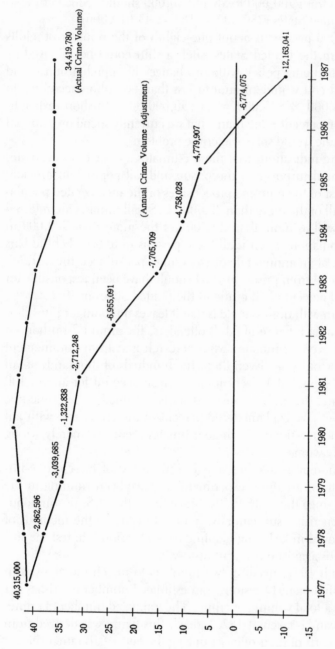

FIG. 4.1. Actual and projected volume of crime in the United States, 1977–1987. Net increases in crime volume. Population increases: 1977—15,308; 1978—16,255; 1979—7,074; 1980—14,504; 1981—37,193; 1982—41,207; 1983—25,444; 1984—25,561; 1985—36,225; 1986—65,043. Sources: U.S. Department of Justice, Bureau of Justice Statistics, 1986b, at table 1, p. 1; 1987b; and 1987c, at table 6.22, p. 400.

by "Making Confinement Decisions" was about 40 million in 1977. At 187 crimes per criminal, the incarceration of about 230,000 extra offenders should reduce crime to zero on incapacitation effects alone. The problem is that on this account, crime disappeared some years ago because the U.S. prison population expanded by a total of 237,000 from 1977 through mid-1986.

Figure 4.1 presents two trend lines for the volume of crime in the United States. The lower line begins with 1976 crime levels and subtracts 187 crimes per year for each net increase of one imprisoned offender. The upper line shows crime estimates from successive crime surveys, using the figures for crimes reported by householders only.

A similar point can be made about the costs of crime saved by imprisonment. In the reported calculus, each crime prevented by incapacitation saved $2,300 in social costs and 34 percent of those savings are in public expenditures on criminal justice. This criminal justice saving of $782 per crime adds up to just over $146,000 that will be saved each year an offender spends in prison.

These estimates yield predictions about patterns of public expenditures that can be tested on the recent experiment in prison population expansion. Between 1977 and 1987, the prison population in the United States grew by 237,000. At 146,000 1983 dollars per prison year, this growth should have reduced criminal justice expenditures by a net figure of about $34.6 billion per year by the end of the ten-year period 1977–1987. But, in fact, the criminal justice budget increased from about 15 billion current dollars in fiscal 1975 to 45 billion current dollars in 1985, with no sign that prison-based incapacitation reduced police, court, or correctional budgets.

One final statistical grace note relates to the negative marginal cost of imprisonment in this study. According to this calculus, each person sent to prison for a year saves almost $37,000 in prison and jail expenditures during that year (.086 × $2,300 = $197.80 × 187 = $36,988.60), or more than the estimated cost of imprisoning the inmate ($15,000). Taken literally, this predicts that aggregate expenditures for prisons should decrease as the number of inmates increases.

Estimates of this character raise questions not only about the methods used to generate them but also about the nature of the whole enterprise. When a set of estimates suggests that crime can be abolished for $6 billion, it is clear that something is wrong with them. When, if those estimates were correct, criminal justice expenditures would have decreased and crime rates would have declined toward zero as the U.S.

prison population has doubled, it is even clearer that some mistake has been made. When a study argues that locking up 230,000 additional offenders should reduce nondrug crime by 40 million units, at a time when we have just finished running that experiment with no such results, it is evident some kind of fundamental error must be involved.

The foregoing analysis of the statistical implications of the study suggests that the conclusions advanced in "Making Confinement Decisions" are not simply wrong, but rather that they are a case study in compound catastrophic error. How did this happen? What factors conspired to produce such extraordinary overestimates of the incapacitative potential of expanding imprisonment?

Six features of the study which contribute to the magnitude of error deserve mention: the high estimate of incapacitation effects; disregard of the diminishing marginal returns of predictive imprisonment; the problematic allocation of public expenditures such as police budgets as costs of crime; the "average cost" treatment in which all offenses (other than drug crimes) are represented as having equal social costs; the assumption that the costs of crime prevention and law enforcement are marginally proportional to crime rates; and the imprecision and uncertainty associated with the concept of the social cost of crime and thus of any cost-benefit comparison. Each problem raises issues of substantial importance to serious students of criminal justice.

The study takes its 187 crimes per offender from a 1982 Rand Corporation survey of inmates sponsored by the National Institute of Justice (Greenwood and Abrahamse, 1982). There are a variety of ways of estimating the average number of crimes that would have been committed by a group of individuals had they not been incarcerated. The estimate cited by Zedlewski (1987) is the highest that he could have found, in National Institute of Justice–sponsored research, on which to base an assessment of the extent of incapacitative effects.

Much well-regarded research would place crime prevention volume at less than one-tenth of the 187 crimes per offender figure (Cohen, 1986:352). Indeed, some of the studies cited in "Making Confinement Decisions" give much more modest levels of the crime that is potentially preventable by imprisonment. Yet this is not mentioned in the study and neither the controversy over the correct levels of criminal incapacitation effects nor the 1986 National Academy of Sciences panel study on this issue (Blumstein et al. 1986) is referred to.

Not only are the criminal propensities of those currently incarcerated overestimated but the problem of diminishing marginal returns in crime prevention as a larger number of individuals are sent to prison is ignored in the computations. Yet that problem is clearly evident in the Rand Corporation study principally relied on in "Making Confinement Decisions." It is graphically illustrated in the Table of Inmate Annual Offense Rates from the Rand Corporation study, reproduced in Zedlewski's (1987) paper and as table 4.1 below.

The table shows that robbers and burglars in California prisons report robbery rates four times as high, and rates of burglary more than twice as high, as robbers and burglars in Texas prisons. The reason for this difference is that Texas has a much higher rate of imprisonment so that high-rate offenders make up a larger proportion of the California prison population than of the Texas prison population. This relatively large proportion of high-rate offenders (as of 1982) is the reason why the overall estimates in the Rand Corporation study are so high in California. It is a function of a relatively low level of imprisonment.

Texas had already watered down its prison stock when the survey was taken by mixing in a greater number of low-rate offenders. This explains why, whereas the California prisoners report a robbery rate of fifty, the corresponding number for Texas prison inmates is only twelve. But this does not mean that the incarceration of the next Texas prisoner at the margin will prevent as many as twelve robberies that would otherwise have been committed. As long as most high-rate offenders are already in prison, offenders at the margin of imprisonment will have much

TABLE 4.1 Inmate Annual Offense Rates (Varieties of Criminal Behavior, Rand Corporation, 1982)

Crime Committed	Prisons			Jails	
	California	Michigan	Texas	California	Michigan
Robbery	50	35	12	33	25
Burglary	102	115	46	85	102
Assault	8	4	3	6	6
Motor vehicle theft	30	118	31	19	94
Miscellaneous theft	222	88	166	221	165
Forgery	78	135	40	123	111
Fraud	151	47	110	264	100
Drug deals	1,318	1,378	718	1,352	1,009

SOURCE: Zedlewski, 1987:3.

lower average crime rates than those already in prison. Thus the phenomenon of diminishing marginal returns.

The author of "Making Confinement Decisions" seems to be schizophrenic about this feature of the research results. On one hand, he acknowledges the highly skewed distribution of individual offense rates in the Rand Corporation study (half of the inmates surveyed reporting individual crime rates that were less than one-tenth of the 187 crimes figure). Moreover, in relation to current sentencing practice, he acknowledges that "on average, we would expect those released to be somewhat less criminal than those incarcerated" (Zedlewski, 1987:3). On the other hand, the 187 annual crimes estimate is used without amendment and without explanation.

The problems associated with estimating the number of crimes prevented by incapacitation are compounded by the difficulties involved in calculating the cost of crime. The method employed for measuring the cost of crime is artless in its simplicity. In the case of public expenditure on crime and crime prevention, the entire budget of all the agencies of criminal justice is assumed to be part of the cost of crime. Yet, with regard to the police, by far the largest public expenditure item, that allocation is ludicrous.

As Egon Bittner has demonstrated, "the majority of police actions are unrelated to criminal law enforcement" (1982:6; 1974). It has been estimated by the research division of the International Association of Chiefs of Police that "the percentage of the police effort devoted to the traditional criminal law matters probably does not exceed ten percent" (Niederhoffer, 1969:75). Crime prevention is one of many general police functions. The police also maintain public order, control traffic, provide a range of citizen services, and respond to a wide variety of public needs not related to the FBI "part one" crime rate or to the size of the prison population. Most police expenditures would continue even if crime rates decreased dramatically. They are not in this sense costs of crime.

Not only are all the costs of law enforcement assumed to be costs of crime in this analysis, but it is also assumed that the correct way to express the cost of a crime is by dividing total costs by the total number of crimes committed. Allocating this average figure to each crime seems wrong both in theory and in practice, obscuring the need for priority decisions as well as being inconsistent with any known economic theory of crime. If both a single robbery and a single theft have cost estimates of $2,300, we should be indifferent as to which offense our policies would prevent. This $2,300 estimate in the text is only unobjectionable if it is meaningless. Since no rationale for this procedure can be found in "Making Confinement Decisions," it is impossible to determine what justification for the practice the author of the study may have had in mind.

The study's estimate about how much money would be saved if the crime rate dropped is based on the assumption that the cost of an individual crime is that act's proportional share of the total cost of all crime. Thus, if the total number of robberies is 100 and the total police budget for robbery is $200,000, the report assumes that reducing the volume of robbery from 100 to 90 will reduce police expenditure for robbery by $20,000—from $200,000 down to $180,000. Yet there is no reason to suppose that reducing the volume of robbery from 100 to 90 will reduce police expenditure in the same proportion, nor is any reason given to support this assumption of marginal proportionality.

In fact, there is good reason to suppose that reductions in crime rates of this magnitude would generate cost savings at a considerable lower level. If $200,000 of police resources are invested in the prevention of robbery when the robbery rate is 100, it may well be thought prudent not to disturb that investment at all if the rate drops to 90. The productivity of prevention programs is based on the number of potential robberies, not the actual crime rate.

As to the resources devoted to the apprehension of robbery offenders, it is unlikely that any of those engaged in that task would be reassigned simply because of a 10 percent drop in the offense rate. It is more likely that the police establishment would view the decline as providing an opportunity to do a more effective job with a stable level of police resources.

With regard to some other public sector costs of crime, a reduction in the crime rate achieved by increasing the number of offenders sent to prison or by increasing the length of sentences imposed could actually increase rather than decrease total criminal justice system costs. By raising the stakes in so many criminal prosecutions, the total costs of prosecution, defense, trial, and appeal will increase for the "get tough" group of cases. Even a smaller number of cases could lead to a greater aggregate expenditure of resources if the penal stakes of the average criminal prosecution increase (see Polinsky and Rubinfeld, 1986).

With respect to private expenditures for crime prevention, there is also no evidence to suggest that reductions in crime rates will lead to proportional reductions in crime prevention expenditure. If the chances of being burglarized fall from 10 in 100 to 9 in 100 in a particular neighborhood, is it plausible to assume that the number of dogs purchased and fed on account of the fear of burglary will decline by 10 percent? Why? Yet that is precisely the assumption made in this study's estimates of the costs of crime and the benefits of imprisonment.

There has been experience in recent years of the consequences for public expenditure on criminal justice during periods of decline in the rates of some types of crime. Yet the study marshals no evidence from this experience to support its claims. And we are aware of no jurisdiction in which a decline in the incidence of a particular category of crime has led to a proportional drop in private or public expenditure.

One reason why crime prevention expenditures are not responsive to crime rates on a strictly proportional basis is that the fear and anxiety generated by crime is unlikely to be reduced by a corresponding degree when a crime rate falls. If robbery rates are reduced by 25 percent, there is little likelihood that the fear of robbery will undergo an equivalent reduction. It seems more probable that fear and anxiety are responsive only to sustained shifts in perceived personal risk, so that even if the total abolition of robbery would yield public savings of $50 million, it does not follow that cutting robbery by 50 percent would reduce the cost of that crime to the community by $25 million.

The foregoing analysis suggests that "Making Confinement Decisions" contains a number of specific errors in the computation of the costs of crime and the costs and benefits of prison as crime prevention; and the list compiled here could be considerably lengthened. But an emphasis on the avoidable errors in such an exercise may leave the mistaken impression that it is feasible to perform an analysis of the social costs of crime on which a reliable and precise cost-benefit estimate could be based in dollar terms.

Yet the history of efforts to quantify the social costs of crime counsels against the assumption that this can be achieved. Over half a century ago, the Wickersham Commission reported at length (657 pages) on *The Cost of Crime*. The Commission concluded that

> [i]t is wholly impossible to make an accurate estimate of the total economic cost of crime to the United States. This is true whether we look at the immediate cost of crime to the tax-paying and property-owning public and the individuals composing it, or whether we consider the net ultimate cost to the community as a whole. Many "estimates" of total cost have been made, but

they, in our opinion, have only been guesses; and we do not feel
that any useful purpose would be served by still another guess.
(National Commission, 1931a, 12:442)

Over thirty years later in the early 1960s, two researchers at the Cambridge University Institute of Criminology in England noted that "the
only major study of the cost of crime in an English-speaking country
was that made in the USA by the Wickersham Commission in 1931."
The researchers acknowledged its "considerable virtues" but also noted
its limitations and opined that "thanks to the development of social accounting and survey techniques it is now possible both to make a more
refined analysis of some topics covered by the Wickersham Commission
and to tackle questions beyond the power of the methods available in
1930" (Martin and Bradley, 1963–1964:591–592).

Subsequently, however, one of them, J. P. Martin, reported that "an
apparently simple subject is in fact one of great complexity." He set out
at length some of the general methodological and conceptual problems
involved in computing the cost of crime. He noted that "the concept of
public cost . . . depends on the making of various assumptions and, if
these become too numerous or too cosmic, the value of the resulting
figures may be minimal; [it] tends to involve guesswork on such a grandiose scale that the result might as effectively be obtained from the study
of a crystal ball" (Martin, 1965:57–58, 63).

In 1965 when another presidential commission considered the question of the cost of crime it abstained from analysis under that rubric in
favor of simply investigating what it called "the economic impact of
crime." "The information available about the economic cost of crime,"
it reported, "is most usefully presented not as an overall figure, but as a
series of public and private costs." Accordingly, it presented some figures
relating to "six different categories of economic impact both private and
public," but warned that in arriving at the figures "estimates of doubtful
reliability were used [and] the totals should be taken to indicate rough
orders of magnitude rather than precise details" (President's Commission, 1967a:31–33).

One difference between the concepts of the "cost" and the "economic
impact" of crime is that a study restricted to economic impact does not
attempt to monetarize such essentially nonpecuniary losses as pain,
fear, shock, and diminished social interaction and sense of security. Nor
does the economic impact approach provide a direct guide to action—for example, gambling has a much larger economic impact than

homicide ($7 billion as opposed to $750 million according to the 1967 commission [President's Commission, 1967a:33])—but it avoids the inherent difficulties that confront attempts to assess the social cost of crime comprehensively.

There may be many different ways to measure the harm attributable to crime. But even if we confine ourselves to trying to estimate costs in dollars, the attempt to aggregate guard-dog food expenditures with victim dollar losses with variations in police pension levels into a single monetary total seems misconceived. Those who invest resources in pursuing this goal may be barking up the wrong tree; and in relation to "Making Confinement Decisions," the level of error in the exercise suggests that it was a case of the wrong dog barking up the wrong tree.

There is one final aspect in which both the argument and the context of "Making Confinement Decisions" are instructive. Possibly one of the most significant features of the study is the fact of its appearance in 1987. It appeared at a time when prison populations in the United States had increased by almost 150 percent in fifteen years. Even after this degree of expansion, what Dr. Zedlewski calls "a popular sentiment for more prison space" 1987:1) persists. This publication is not alone. Many argue with conviction that substantial further expansion in prison population will produce benefits far exceeding its costs and that lenient treatment of offenders is a central problem.

This suggests that there is no natural level of prison accommodation or rate of imprisonment that would significantly reduce the need felt by many citizens for more prisons. Moreover, as statistics change, the arguments made for expanding prison capacity do not change much. The same arguments are propounded with the same force when the prison population is 500,000 as when it was 217,000; and will probably also be made when it reaches 750,000.

As long as levels of crime are high enough to generate substantial anxiety, those who view increased imprisonment as a solution will continue to demand more prisons and will do so in terms that do not change markedly at any level of incarceration. Indeed, the more attenuated the link between the malady and the proposed remedy, the more insatiable will be the demand for more of the remedial measure.

4.3 THE SAGA OF SELECTIVE INCAPACITATION

As noted above, incapacitation as a crime control strategy need not take the form of general incapacitation but may involve only the incapacitation of selected high-rate offenders. This would involve imprisoning particular individuals not simply for the crimes they have committed but because of the crimes they would commit if they were allowed to go free. A policy of selective incapacitation therefore depends on the ability to make predictions of the future criminality of particular individuals. Insofar as such predictive capability exists, a policy of selective incapacitation would clearly do better in preventing crime than one of collective incapacitation based on the average consequences of a sentencing strategy.

One of the earliest attempts to estimate the potential gains in increased incapacitation if such a policy were adopted, and one regarded in 1978 as "the best approach to estimating the incapacitative effect available to date" (Cohen, 1978:230), is a 1975 study by Shinnar and Shinnar. Using data for New York state as a base for their analysis, they attempted to show by means of "simple quantitative arguments" that a policy of uniform prison sentences for selected types of convicted criminals could substantially reduce crime.

Their study focused on what they referred to as *safety* crime, by which they meant the violent index crimes and burglary. Their conclusion was:

> We submit that a policy of uniform prison sentences for convicted criminals could under present conditions reduce *safety* crime by a factor of four to five. This would require net prison stays of five years for muggers and robbers and other violent crimes, and three years for burglars. (As we have pointed out, it is only net prison stay which is important and not sentence length.) (Shinnar and Shinnar, 1975:607)

The achievement of such a fivefold decrease in crime would, they acknowledged, involve a "substantial but not extreme" effect on prison population. It would mean "that we need a prison system [in New York state] that can accommodate 40,000–60,000 people for criminals convicted of safety crimes. Its institutions presently accommodate somewhat less than 35,000 so that larger facilities would be needed . . . but their cost would be negligible compared to the present cost of crime" (Shinnar and Shinnar, 1975:606–607).

If the good news was that the rate of violent crimes would be reduced by as much as 80 percent, the bad news was somewhat obscured by the reference to the "substantial but not extreme" increase in prison population required to achieve the reduction in crime. For as Jacqueline Cohen observed:

In fact, they are talking about accommodating 40,000 to 60,000 prisoners in New York State for "safety" crimes (the violent index crimes and burglary) alone, compared with an average daily prison population in 1970 of only 9,000 for safety crimes and 12,500 for all felonies. The anticipated prison population for safety crimes in New York State would thus be about 25 percent of the total current prison population of the entire United States and represents an increase of 355 to 567 percent in the New York prison population. (1978:218)

A later study which confirmed the finding that incapacitative sentences for serious violent offenses have a significant effect only at the price of enormous prison population increases was carried out by Petersilia and Greenwood in 1978. In their study, an attempt was made to estimate the effect mandatory minimum prison sentences would have on adult crime rates by analyzing data on a random sample of defendants convicted of serious offenses over a two-year period in the Denver, Colorado, district courts. The technique they employed involved using career histories to estimate the probable incapacitation effects if offenders had been sentenced differently in the past. The procedure involved taking a cohort of arrested or convicted offenders, examining their past convictions, and determining whether each offender would have been imprisoned at the time of his current offense if a particular sentencing policy had been applied at the time of his last conviction.

Petersilia and Greenwood dealt with the crime reduction potential of different mandatory minimum sentences on three cohorts of offenders: those charged with violent crimes; those charged with burglary; and those charged with other felonies. They estimated the extent to which the violent cohort's crimes (violent criminals being defined as offenders charged with robbery, rape, aggravated assault, homicide, and kidnapping) would have been prevented by the imposition of mandatory prison sentences for their preceding adult felony conviction under a variety of different sentencing policies.

They found that only a severely stringent policy, under which every offender convicted of any adult felony, violent or not, regardless of prior record, were sentenced to a mandatory prison term of five years, might lessen violent crime by one-third. This policy incidentally would increase prison population by close to 450 percent. A sentencing policy which would impose a five-year sentence for any person previously convicted of at least one adult felony would have prevented 16 percent of violent crimes and increase the prison population by 190 percent. A sentencing policy requiring offenders to have prior convictions for violent offenses would have reduced violent crime by less than 7 percent even with mandatory five-year sentences (Petersilia and Greenwood, 1978:607–608, 610, 613–614).

At that stage, research into the potential of selective incapacitation as a sentencing policy had been limited to officially recorded data on past offending. In the late 1970s Greenwood, employing inmate self-reports as well as official records as the source of data, attempted to develop a scale for prospectively identifying offenders who would commit crimes at high rates in the future. Using data from a self-report study of 2,190 incarcerated offenders in California, Michigan, and Texas, he selected seven variables (see table 4.2) that individually classified inmates into high, medium, and low rates of offending for robbery and burglary. Greenwood estimated that incapacitation policy could reduce robbery rates by 20 percent without increasing the prison population in California (Greenwood with Abrahamse, 1982:79). The variables were each scored either 0 or 1 to form an additive scale that produced a prediction score between 0 and 7 for each inmate. Inmates were then classified as committing crimes at a low rate (score 0 or 1), medium rate (score 2 or 3), or high rate (score 4 or over).

But no validation of the scale on future offending was carried out, and without that its utility for prospectively identifying future high-rate offenders could only be surmised. In 1983, however, the Panel on Re-

TABLE 4.2 Variables Used to Distinguish Inmates by Individual Crime Rates

Variable[a]	Source
1. Prior conviction for same charge (robbery or burglary)	Official criminal records[b]
2. Incarcerated more than 50 percent of two years	Self-report
3. Convicted before age sixteen	Self-report
4. Served time in state juvenile facility	Self-report
5. Drug use in preceding two years	Self-report
6. Drug use as a juvenile	Self-report
7. Employed less than 50 percent of preceding two years	Self-report

[a] All variables are scored as 0 or 1 depending on the presence or absence of the attribute.
[b] Data available only for prison, not jail, inmates.
SOURCE: Greenwood with Abrahamse, 1982:50.

search on Criminal Careers was convened by the National Academy of Sciences' National Research Council "to evaluate the feasibility of predicting the future course of criminal careers, to assess the effects of prediction instruments in reducing crime through incapacitation (usually by incarceration), and to review the contribution of research on criminal careers to the development of fundamental knowledge about crime and criminals" (Blumstein et al., 1986:I.x). The panel undertook an intensive review and reanalysis of the Greenwood study, which had received extensive public attention.

Among other things the retrospective accuracy of the seven-variable classification was tested. It was found that even within the sample used to construct the scale "55 percent of the classified high-rate group (27 percent of the total sample) were false positives who did not commit crimes at high rates" (Blumstein et al., 1986:I.179). Moreover, further examination of the scale's accuracy revealed significant cross-state variation in its predictive power. Thus, "False-positive rates for high-rate robbers were 60 percent in California and Michigan and 48 percent in Texas. Focusing on high-rate offenders, especially robbery, these false-positive rates reflect a 57 percent relative improvement over chance in California but only 21 percent and 38 percent in Michigan and Texas, respectively" (Blumstein et al., 1986:I.180).

Other classification scales have shown greater accuracy in identifying worst-risk offenders (Hoffman and Beck, 1974; Hoffman, 1983; Fischer, 1983, 1984; Rhodes et al., 1982). These other scales were also reviewed by the panel, but the panel concluded that

> with available statistical scales, gains in crime control efficiency through selective incapacitation would be modest at best—a 5–10 percent reduction in robberies by adults, for example, with an increase of 10–20 percent in the number of convicted robbers who are incarcerated. Similar crime control through general increases in incarceration would require substantially higher increases in prison populations. (Blumstein et al., 1986:I.195–196)

One reason why excessive claims about potential offense reductions from selective incapacitation are illusory is that we already selectively incapacitate substantial numbers of high-risk offenders. Many of the characteristics that figure in the scales are already taken into account in making criminal justice decisions about the disposal of offenders. Moreover, there is in practice considerable doubt about the operational availability of some of the variables used in the prediction scales. In the case of Greenwood's scale, for example, all the variables except prior conviction for the same charge are, as shown in table 4.2, based on inmate self-reports.

But at sentencing only official records would be available and, as the National Academy of Sciences panel reported, "For some of the scale variables, especially those relating to juvenile record, drug use, and employment, this requirement may be more than record systems can routinely deliver." Furthermore, the panel found that elimination of variables from the Greenwood scales "does significantly reduce the accuracy of the scale in identifying high-rate offenders; the percent of true high-rate offenders who are missed by the scale increases from 50 to 87 percent when the scale is limited to only adult criminal record variables" (Blumstein et al., 1986:I.180, 181).

There have been ethical objections regarding the possible use of measures of the juvenile record, drug use, and recent employment in this way. Indeed, much of the debate about the use of prediction-based classifications in criminal justice decisions has centered around ethical concerns regarding not only the choice of variables that can be used in prediction-based classification but also the legitimacy of imposing different punishments for the same crime. Many of these are addressed in a paper dealing with normative issues relating to the use of prediction in the criminal justice system by Mark Moore which was commissioned by the National Academy of Sciences panel. Moore is critical of "the technocratic enthusiasm for prediction" (Moore, 1986:352).

Yet the truth is that throughout history, and long before there was any technocratic enthusiasm for it, informal predictions about future behavior have been (and from day to day still are) made whenever decisions are taken about the secure confinement of offenders. It is ironical that in this context concern about ethical principles has developed only in response to proposals to make use of improved prediction techniques and to introduce some rational order into what Moore himself calls the current "crazy-quilt pattern of discretionary decision making that leaves great room for injustice" (1986:351).

Some years ago, in relation to the deterrent efficacy of penal sanctions, we noted that "[d]iscussion of what we are justified in doing not only takes precedence over, but even precludes consideration of, what in practice we can do" (Zimring and Hawkins, 1973:2). In the early 1990s research is being directed to empirical questions about whether and to what extent criminal sanctions can produce significantly reduced crime rates by way of both deterrence and incapacitation. And this represents an important step forward not least because it addresses one of the most pervasive and fundamental *moral* deficiencies in the administration of criminal justice: the fact that throughout the system we act in a state of ignorance.

4.3.1 Criminal Careers

The implementation of explicit selective incapacitation policies depends on the development of systems for the classification of offenders on the basis of assessments of their criminal careers. In practice, as noted above, criminal justice decisions are constantly made on the basis of informal criminal career assessments, that is, estimates of offenders' propensities to commit crimes in the future. The concept of "career" in this context refers simply to an individual's crime-committing propensity and does not mean that crime is necessarily his only employment or primary source of income. And there is no doubt that a multitude of criminal justice decisions from arrest to sentencing do take into account the potential risk that offenders are thought to pose in the future.

Clearly, however, the adoption of official policy of selective incarceration requires more than the kind of intuitive judgment on the basis of individual experience on which those decisions are commonly based. Specifically what is required is some analysis of the nature of criminal careers, in this sense of the term, and of the features characterizing them, for the objective of selective incarceration is the imprisonment of those whose removal from the community would maximize the incapacitative effect. For this purpose it is necessary to be able to identify those with high serious crime rates who are most likely to persist in criminal careers; in short, the focus is on the frequency, seriousness, and duration of criminal careers.

Thus, the most important features of criminal careers in this context are individual crime rates in terms of crimes per year, the seriousness of offense types, and criminal career length or duration. The existence of statistical relationships between frequency, duration, and offense seriousness on one hand and offender characteristics on the other is what provides the basis of the classification scales designed for use in making criminal justice decisions.

The National Academy of Sciences panel reviewed the available research on criminal careers and found that some of the most important conclusions related to factors well known to be associated with aggregate crime rates or aggregate arrest rates such as age, race, and sex. However, it found that although these demographic variables were associated with participation in crime they were only weakly related to individual frequency.

The panel found that at virtually all stages of criminal careers the known factors that distinguished the highest-rate offender included the following:

1. high frequency of prior offending;
2. early onset of delinquency as a juvenile;
3. drug use, measured either currently or over time; and
4. unstable employment in the recent past.

It also found that

> [o]ffenders engage in a great diversity of crime types, with a somewhat greater tendency for offenders to repeat the same crime or to repeat within the group of property crimes or the group of violent crimes. For samples of juvenile offenders, later arrests tend to be far more serious offenses than earlier arrests, but it is difficult to determine how much of that tendency is a consequence of more serious offenders committing a larger number of offenses or of the same individuals escalating the seriousness of their offenses as their careers progress. Adult offenders who are arrested more than once do not, on average, escalate to more serious crimes as their criminal careers progress.

As to the length of criminal careers, research indicates that

> careers are reasonably short, averaging about 5 years for offenders who are active in index offenses as young adults. In the first 10 to 12 years of adult careers, residual careers (i.e., the time still remaining in careers) increase from 5 years for 18-year-olds who commit FBI index offenses to an expected 10 years for index offenders still active in their 30s. This increase probably occurs because of early career termination in the early years by many offenders, leaving the offender group more densely populated with offenders who have longer average career lengths. Offenders with the longest residual career length are those who were active in careers at age 18 and who are still active in their 30s. Career length does not begin to decline rapidly until active offenders reach their 40s. (Blumstein et al., 1986:I.94–95)

The crucial question in this context relates to the degree to which this body of data and research, as reflected in prediction-based classifications, can improve attempts to reduce crime through incapacitation of offenders. Does it promise significant improvement, or does it merely confirm decision makers' current belief and practices? The panel concluded that it was "still unclear how much better than current practice statistically-assisted prediction can be. One can expect currently available scales to produce only limited improvement to existing decision practices in terms of crime control" (Blumstein et al., 1986:I.197)

In the history of the development of classification systems for the purpose of selective incapacitation on the basis of criminal career data, there is an almost classic progression. It begins with dramatic initial claims, is followed by modified claims, and ends in chilly realism tempered by the hope that future research may uncover some opportunities for improvement in current practice.

This development is exemplified here in an almost paradigmatic fashion. It begins with the Shinnar and Shinnar promise of a 75 to 80 percent reduction in violent crime at a "negligible" cost in terms of expanded prison facilities (Shinnar and Shinnar, 1975:606–607). This is followed by the substantially modified claim that a policy involving an increase in prison population close to 450 percent might lessen violent crime by one-third (Petersilia and Greenwood, 1978:610, 613).

Thereafter Greenwood and a number of others develop classification scales for identifying worst-risk offenders. Then the National Academy of Sciences panel after reviewing all the available evidence concludes that "it is still unclear how much better than current practice statistically assisted predictions can be." Certainly, "gains in crime control efficiency through selective incapacitation would be modest at best—a 5–10 percent reduction in robberies by adults, for example, with an increase in 10–20 percent in the number of convicted robbers who are incarcerated." Finally, the chastened hope is expressed "that future research will improve criminal justice decisions by highlighting additional salient predictor variables and by pointing to variables that are often used but are indeed weak" (Blumstein et al., 1986:I.195–196, 197).

Two further points relating to research programs in this field. The first relates to the fragmented, compartmentalized, and uncoordinated way in which research proceeds. The various areas of research such as deterrence, incapacitation, and the economics of crime and punishment are studied in isolation from one another with no apparent communication between them. Thus, the Zedlewski paper was published nearly two years after the National Academy of Sciences Panel Report on Criminal Careers (Blumstein et al., 1986) and his research was funded by the same agency—the National Institute of Justice. Yet the two efforts seem totally unrelated. There is no reference in the Zed-lewski paper to the panel's report, and the analysis seems heedless of any of the data and insights in that report. Thus, large prescriptive claims can be made, which unless met with specific refutation using the identical vocabulary enjoy remarkable immunity to criticism.

The second point relates to the way in which the different prescriptive programs and research projects remain encapsulated in their own prescribed contexts. By the time the National Academy of Sciences report appeared, America had experienced a massive upward swing in prison population. Indeed, as the panel noted, it was the rapid growth in the U.S. prison population, which had more than doubled in the previous decade, which led to the convening of the panel to review research on criminal careers (Blumstein et al., 1986:I.ix). Yet the report contains no linked discussion of criminal career research and prison population studies. For the most part, however, the connection between these issues has been recently made by Professor Barnett (1987). Study of the incapacitation effect is pursued as though it belonged to a different universe of discourse from study of prison population, and the question of the effects of the escalation of imprisonment on criminal careers is not considered anywhere in the report.

4.4 CONCLUSION

An important distinction between prescriptive rationales and prescriptive programs relates to the question what *should* determine prison population levels, and those social, political, and economic factors that in fact *do* exercise a determinative influence. It is clear that the pursuit of particular crime control goals and also particular changes in criminal justice policy are likely to have effects on prison populations. But although the connection between criminal justice and crime control policy and prison population seems logical, it has been little studied and no obvious examples spring to mind.

There are two contrasting ways in which it might be possible to study the way in which particular policies or principles could have influenced prison populations. In the first place, it might be possible to identify an isolated policy change and attempt to determine what impact it had on prison population and how long that influence persisted. In the second place, it would be possible to take two different jurisdictions with substantially different imprisonment rates and seek to determine whether that difference reflected different patterns of emphasis in crime control policies and goals.

As to the first of these approaches, such things as the introduction of a vigorous campaign against drunk driving, the election of a "law and order" state governor, the introduction of a new penal code, or the adoption of a mandatory minimum sentencing scheme could provide suitable opportunities. For while there have been a number of studies of the impact of "get tough" initiatives and their impact on the criminal justice system, the purview has rarely extended to include impact on prison population and when it has, such impact has never occupied a central place in their analyses. Such data as are available on sentencing outcomes suggest that even dramatic mandates for change have had only incremental effects on sentencing practice and very modest consequences for prison population.

Nevertheless, while specific policy initiatives seem rarely to have any major impact on prison population, it is conceivable that the changes in mood that lead to those initiatives may have pervasive effects. Thus, a "get tough" executive attitude with an emphasis on accountability may lead to more diligent and efficient performance on the part of criminal justice and law enforcement agencies. Such diffuse effects, however, are hard to define and not easily susceptible to measurement.

With regard to the second type of approach, the object would be to select jurisdictions with very different imprisonment rates, for example, Texas and Pennsylvania, and to attempt to determine whether the difference was due, as it might conceivably be, to a difference in emphasis on the need to incapacitate offenders or alternatively to something like a different social definition or perception of the "cost" of crimes such as robbery and burglary. In the present state of knowledge there are no answers to questions of this kind and we can only speculate because the necessary research has not yet been done.

The rhetoric of sentencing is strikingly similar in states as dissimilar as Texas, Florida, and Pennsylvania, and may obscure substantial differences in policy. As Blumstein et al. pointed out, "predictive considerations have long played an implicit though informal role in criminal justice decision making" (1986:I.165) and a lot of decisions based on incapacitative considerations are made in the ordinary course of sentencing in both high- and low-imprisonment states. Low-imprisonment states can achieve the most dramatic incapacitative effects on a case-by-case basis by confining imprisonment to high-rate offenders.

But just as there is no convincing evidence that particular prescriptive rationales are associated with large increases or decreases in prison population, it is by no means clear that states and localities that differ in their emphasis on particular principles of imprisonment also differ in the proportion of their population that they imprison. We are skeptical about the existence of a direct connection. But to raise the question is to identify an important field of study.

What emerges clearly from our examination of the literature dealing with the social determinants of prison population, correctional forecasting, and prescriptive rationales and programs is that they all represent important strands in the same fabric. The potential for error in correctional forecasting can be diminished by paying attention to the social, political, and economic factors that influence imprisonment rates. Examination of the empirical data on prison population movements derived for the purpose of forecasting can provide a useful corrective in the formulation of general theories of imprisonment. And those who espouse prescriptive approaches can learn from a study of both the social process material and the empirical data on prison populations.

This is not to say that some synthetic combination of these three perspectives or elements is possible or even necessary. What is necessary and possible is that those who study the determinants of prison population should be aware of the complexity of the problem and the wide range of reference necessary for understanding its nature. The only method or system likely to produce useful results in this area is eclecticism.

PART II
The American Experience

This section brings into focus the extraordinary increase in prison population in the United States in recent years, and discusses the lessons that can be drawn from this development, regarding the relationship between legal policy and prison population. Chapter 5 begins the analysis by exploring the relationship between fluctuations in prison population and movements in social and demographic variables which are thought to influence levels of imprisonment.

Chapter 6 shifts the discussion from trends in national aggregates of prison population to variations in rates of imprisonment at the state level. Analysis of patterns of imprisonment since the 1960s suggests that there are nationwide trends that influence the majority of state systems.

Chapter 7 examines recent history for evidence on the relation between variations in state correctional and criminal justice policy and subsequent variations in rates of imprisonment. None of the specific policies we examine appear to have been a major influence on movements in prison population in recent years.

Chapter 8 discusses a variety of policies that have been proposed to reduce growth in prison population, ranging from alternative treatment programs for prison-eligible offenders to restructuring of sentencing authority.

Chapter 9 provides an economic context for discussion of some of the forces that determine prison population and summarizes the conclusions of this study about the pattern of growth in prison population in the United States since mid-century.

Our coverage of topics related to prison scale is necessarily incomplete since almost any issue concerning correctional institutions is influenced by substantial growth in prison population. Thus, questions regarding privatization of some aspects of corrections, the growth of litigation about prison conditions, and the changing federal role in criminal justice policy have all been influenced by changes in prison population levels. But we must leave to others the task of charting in detail the relationship between these policy shifts and questions about the scale of the prison enterprise.

5 Five Theories in Search of the Facts

This chapter is an attempt to match common theories regarding what influences rates of imprisonment to the specific patterns experienced in the United States since 1950. In contrast with part I of this book, we are not primarily interested here in theories of what drives prison population generally, although the better a theory predicted general movements in prison population the more likely it would be that the theory's prediction would fit the facts of the period under study.

In this chapter, we examine mechanical theories of prison population, explanations that posit uncomplicated causal relationships between factors such as crime rates, unemployment, or drug abuse, and rates of imprisonment.

Selecting a particular historical period as a testing ground for alternative theories of causation is a frequently employed method of investigation. The four decades of experience with imprisonment in the United States beginning with the 1950s commend themselves as a focus of study in this context for three reasons. First, the period encompasses substantial variation in prison population both upward and downward. Theories designed to explain variations in prison population will thus have a great deal of variance to explain.

Second, the patterns observed in the United States during this period do not parallel trends in prison population in other Western nations. Thus, to the extent that theories regarding prison population trends require cross-sectional differences in outcome to test their predictive power, there is ample difference in patterns available to test them.

The third argument for regarding the recent American experience as a test case concerns policy significance. Explanations of why prison populations have varied over time are of particular importance because a large majority of American states are currently considering substantial expansion of prison holding facilities. Theories that can persuasively explain the dynamics of prison population movement in the United

States over the forty years from 1950 to 1990 should also help to predict what is likely to happen in the 1990s.

The decade of the 1990s is of special significance. However flexible one's definition of the capacity of a particular facility to hold prisoners, a prison population of 1 million in the United States prior to the year 2000 would either imply considerable expansion of facilities or generate conditions of crowding excessive by almost any measure. The period 1950 to 1990 leading to this juncture is thus both interesting and significant. In this chapter we will first describe changing rates of imprisonment over the study period and then compare trends in imprisonment with variations in the crime rates, in political sentiment, in demography, in economic performance, and in narcotics abuse.

5.1 FLUCTUATIONS IN AMERICAN IMPRISONMENT

Figure 5.1 shows movements in total prison population and in rates of imprisonment for the United States as an aggregate for the period 1950 to 1988.

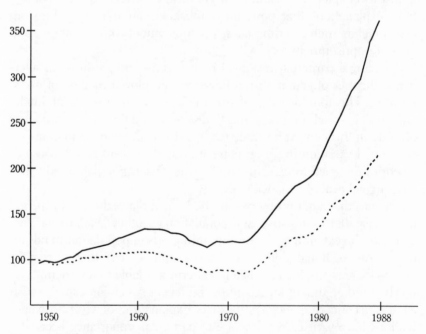

FIG. 5.1. Total prison population and rate of imprisonment per 100,000 in the United States, 1949–1988. Solid line: total prison population. Dashed line: imprisonment rate. 1950 = 100 (total population = 166,123; imprisonment rate = 109). Source: U.S. Department of Justice, Bureau of Justice Statistics, 1988c:486 and 1989:2.

Two different measures of imprisonment are reported because each conveys significant information that the other omits. Numbers of offenders in prison provide a more accurate picture of the actual scale of the prison enterprise and of the extent to which existing prison facilities, which may not change much over time, are being used. Rates of imprisonment provide better information regarding the relative importance of the prison enterprise to the general society. What are trends in imprisonment relative to the growth or stability of the general population? What fraction of society's population is being brought under this form of social control?

The two measures of imprisonment trends show similar patterns throughout the period under scrutiny. Rates of imprisonment are relatively flat through the 1950s; decrease substantially through the 1960s; and begin a long and uninterrupted ascent after 1973. Shifting the measure to total prison population produces some increase during the 1950s; a less striking but still substantial decrease in the 1960s; and a more pronounced expansion since the late 1970s than the rate trend. The question we now address concerns the extent to which those factors thought to determine fluctuations in rates of imprisonment can explain this specific recent history of imprisonment in America.

5.2 FIVE THEORIES

In this section we state a series of hypotheses of direct causation regarding the relationship between a measurable social indicator and variations in rates of imprisonment and test each hypothesis against aggregate American experience over the four decades from 1950 to 1990.

5.2.1 Crime

The hypothesized relationship between levels of crime and prison population is that prison populations increase or decrease as a function of increases and decreases in crime rates. A modified version of this hypothesis would be that prison population increases or decreases as a function of fluctuations in the rate of serious crime. The theory behind this hypothesis is straightforward. Imprisonment is a criminal sanction: its use will therefore fluctuate in direct proportion to changes in the level of the behavior to which it is designed to respond.

Figure 5.2 compares fluctuations in the reported FBI index crime rates with annual fluctuations in rates of imprisonment per 100,000 population for the four decades under study.

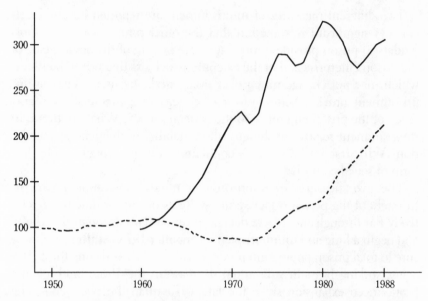

FIG. 5.2. Rate of index crime per 100,000 and rate of imprisonment per 100,000 in the United States, 1949–1988. Solid line: index crime rate. Dashed line: imprisonment rate. 1960 index crime rate (1887.2) = 100. 1950 imprisonment rate (109) = 100. Sources: U.S. Department of Justice, Bureau of Justice Statistics, 1988c:319, 486; and U.S. Department of Justice, 1950–1989.

Visual inspection of figure 5.2 reveals what further statistical analysis will confirm: the lack of a close relationship between crime rates measured in this way and trends in imprisonment. Major discontinuities between the two trends are clearly evident. Most notable is the fact that the steepest increase in index crime occurred during the 1960s when rates of imprisonment were decreasing. Moreover, index crime rates decreased during the early 1980s as rates of imprisonment increased.

Even the years after 1972 when both crime and prison population were increasing do not provide good evidence of cause and effect. The salient feature of the crime index during the entire period under examination here is its tendency to increase over time. In fact, index crime increased at no greater rate during these periods of increase in rates of imprisonment. The correlation between the degree of increase in index crime in one year during the period and changes in the rates of imprisonment during the next calendar year is in fact negative: −.29.

The comparison made in figure 5.2 may be misleading because aggregate statistics on crime are dominated by offenses at the lower end of the scale of seriousness, such as theft, which are so frequently reported that variations in rates of more serious offenses may be hidden. Yet it is the more serious forms of index criminality that account for the bulk of prison commitments. Thus, it seems reasonable to assume that fluctuations in the rates of serious crime should best predict changes in prison population.

Figure 5.3 puts this modified hypothesis to the test by comparing rates of imprisonment from figure 5.1 with fluctuations in the rates of the four violent index felonies.

Inspection of the figure reveals that trends in serious crime, as measured by this index, track fluctuations in the rates of imprisonment even less consistently than the overall index. A threefold expansion in the violent crime rate occurred before 1975. The period of great growth in prison population during the early 1980s parallels a declining rate of violent crime. The association between rates of growth in this crime measure and fluctuations in prison population is also small and negative: −.28.

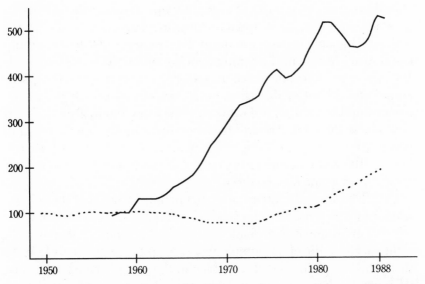

FIG. 5.3. Rate of four violent crimes (murder, forcible rape, robbery, and aggravated assault) per 100,000 and rate of imprisonment per 100,000 in the United States, 1949–1988. Solid line: violent crime rate. Dashed line: imprisonment rate. 1957 violent crime rate (116.6) = 100. 1950 imprisonment rate (109) = 100. Sources: U.S. Department of Justice, 1950–1989; and U.S. Department of Justice, Bureau of Justice Statistics, 1988c:486 and 1989:2.

Why are not variations in crime rates major factors in explaining fluctuations in American imprisonment rates? One set of problems concerns the measurement of crime. The statistics of "index" crime include only offenses known to the police, and the index may vary independently of underlying crime rates. The crime index also reports an amalgam of serious and not so serious offenses, with only the former likely to result in prison sentences. This problem persists even when only the violent crime index is reported because of the large numbers of assaults and classified robbery incidents there included that are neither life threatening nor inevitably treated seriously by law enforcement authorities.

Another reason why variations in index crime are not mirrored by fluctuations in rates of imprisonment is that many offenses are committed by juveniles too young to be eligible for prison, or very young adult offenders who are not likely to be sent to prison for most felony offenses. During periods when the rate of crime increases, these very young offenders may be a disproportionate part of the increase and not reflected in prison statistics.

In this connection, a fact of overriding importance is that imprisonment is not the statistically usual response to felony crime in the United States. Some studies have estimated that, of every 100 felony crimes committed, less than 1 commitment to prison will result (Zeisel, 1982:17–18). This attenuated relationship explains why changes in crime rates do not predict changes in rates of imprisonment. Let the rate of imprisonment drift downward from 1 per 100 to 1 per 125 and increases in the crime rate will have no impact on the numbers sent to prison. And an increase in the prison commitment ratio from 1 per 100 to 2 per 100 will result in a substantial increase in the rate of imprisonment even if crime rates go down.

Do all these qualifications and attenuations mean that there is no relationship between the rates at which offenses are committed and the use of imprisonment? Not at all. What figures 5.2 and 5.3 demonstrate is the lack of a direct and simple relationship that would enable us to successfully explain most fluctuations in the rate of imprisonment by reference to changes in crime rates. Special measures of crime, time lags, and multivariate statistical investigations relating crime and imprisonment might illuminate the nature of a complex relationship. But the central lesson of figures 5.2 and 5.3 is that fluctuating rates of criminality do not provide a short cut to understanding the fundamental changes in rates of imprisonment that occurred in the United States from 1950 to 1990.

5.2.2 Politics and Public Opinion

If modest changes in the ratio of prison commitments to crime can produce substantial changes in imprisonment, is there a direct observable relationship between public opinion expressed through the political process and the fluctuations in rates of imprisonment reflected in figure 5.1? The simple explanation would be that decreases in rates of imprisonment reflect trends toward liberalism, while the most likely cause of increases in rates of imprisonment is a crackdown in sentencing policy associated with punitive public opinion and conservative turns in governmental policy. This kind of explanation is quite popular in the United States. Observers note that public fear of crime has led to tougher attitudes toward sentencing, which has increased imprisonment.

At one level, the relationship between public attitudes and corresponding rates of imprisonment should be self-evident in a democracy. Yet a review of rates of imprisonment over time in the United States shows that changing rates of imprisonment do not closely parallel national political trends, and analysis of the processes that produce changing imprisonment rates in the United States reveals why fluctuations in public mood cannot be directly tied to shifts in the imprisonment rate. The eventual influence of public opinion on criminal justice policy is inevitable under democratic government. But the relationship in recent history has been neither simple nor automatic.

Most "conservative crackdown" explanations see recent trends in American imprisonment rates as a "get tough" reaction or conservative "backlash" that not only has increased rates of imprisonment but threatens to increase them even further. The principal problem faced by a proponent of this explanation is the difficulty of explaining lower rates of imprisonment during earlier periods, and particularly the declining rates of imprisonment reported in figure 5.1; for public attitudes toward offenders are invariably supportive of punitive approaches.

Some might argue that the declining rates of imprisonment were associated with a public mood supportive of civil rights during the 1960s and that a sort of consensus liberalism was the baseline policy against which the more recent backlash was a reaction. But the problems associated with this account of the matter provide a good insight into the principal weaknesses of this type of simple "public opinion" explanation.

In the first place, nine-tenths of American imprisonment policy is made at the state level, as we will demonstrate in the next chapter. Rates of imprisonment declined during the 1960s in a number of southern states which were at the time far out of sympathy with political liberalism and the civil rights movement. States like Arkansas and North Carolina are much more attuned to civil rights in the late 1980s with extremely high prison populations than they were in the 1960s with declining populations in their prisons.

No less striking is the fact that the national election that most prominently featured a conservative backlash specific to crime and leniency in the treatment of offenders was conducted in 1968. Yet, despite the victory of Richard Nixon's "law and order" campaign, the considerable decline in rates of imprisonment in the United States continued throughout Nixon's first term in office. Clearly such a result belies any direct referendum model that ties movements in prison population to shifts in public mood.

Why isn't the relationship between public attitudes to the treatment of offenders and prison populations simple and direct? Taking the example of the 1968 presidential election in the United States, there are four important reasons why rates of imprisonment are insulated from variations in public opinion in America. First, the most significant element of public attitudes toward crime and criminals may operate principally at the symbolic level, so that what the public wants from participants in political debate is symbolic denunciations of criminals rather than concrete plans for action in the criminal justice system. If disapproval is the principal currency in the politics of crime and punishment, it need not have any fixed rate of exchange with factors like prison population.

The emphasis in political debate on the symbolic aspects of criminal justice fits in well with that feature of American government which is the second reason why national law and order campaigns have little direct impact on prison populations. In the United States the federal government plays a minor role in determining prison population. As chapter 6 will demonstrate, fewer than 10 percent of all prison inmates are the responsibility of the national government. In the aftermath of a national political campaign concerned with the symbolic aspect of criminal justice policy, the lack of direct responsibility could serve as an excuse for the lack of dramatic action on the part of the government—if such an excuse were needed.

But this sort of excuse is rarely required in the aftermath of political campaigns. It is much more likely that successful law and order candidates can delegate power to determine criminal sentences outside the most responsive political channels in government. Thus, the third reason for the insulation of imprisonment rates from public opinion is a division of labor that is maintained between political actors charged with denouncing crimes and criminal justice system professionals given authority to carry out sentencing and correctional policies. So even after four years of continued decarceration, the Nixon administration's National Advisory Commission on Criminal Justice Standards and Goals did not feel constrained by their president's law and order credentials to argue for either larger prison populations or longer prison sentences.

Many of the features that insulate national government in the United States from the pressure of public opinion to expand prison population might make state and local governments more vulnerable to political pressure, but a fourth aspect of governmental organization in America has protected all levels of government from strict accountability for the level of criminal sanctions delivered by the system. The responsibility for the administration of criminal sanctions is so diffusely distributed throughout the system that it is difficult to hold particular actors responsible for particular results.

If the level of criminal convictions is low, the police can blame prosecutors for laziness or ineptitude and judges for undue preoccupation with the rights of the accused. Prosecutors in turn can blame unprofessional police work and a weak and sentimental judiciary. Judges can impugn prosecutors and the police. No single agency need take the blame. What looks like a high level of chronic backbiting and buckpassing in the system is really a particular ecology of nonaccountability that works to shield the system from political responsibility on a more direct basis.

Linked to this is the fact that aggregate statistical measures like clearance rates, conviction rates, and prison population data do not play an important role in public perceptions of the performance of the criminal justice system. So politically sensitive actors within that system are not traditionally held accountable with a statistical scorecard stressing aggregates like clearance and conviction rates or prison population figures.

None of this is to deny the importance of public opinion in the formation and implementation of criminal justice policy at every level of government in a democracy. But for present purposes it is sufficient to note that the relationship involved is not a simple and direct one. Certainly public opinion cannot account for such significant fluctuations in imprisonment rates as are the particular concern of this chapter.

It seems likely that one of the reasons why simple "crackdown" explanations of rising prison populations are so persistent is that this type of explanation is only referred to in apparently appropriate cases. Just as no one remarks that "only the good die young" when a good man dies at a great age or a bad man dies young, the only context in which "crackdown" explanations are put forward is one in which prison populations are increasing. This produces a strong relationship between increasing prison populations and a noted public willingness to crack down on criminals because public antipathy to criminals is a constant feature in all Western democratic societies.

What remains to be tested is whether and to what extent variations in public attitudes may explain variations in rates of imprisonment. There are two different effects to be tested. First, there is the effect of variations in public antipathy toward criminal offenders. Thus, for example, we could attempt to test the effect of changes in the average response to a question like "Do you feel that most criminals are treated too leniently?" The issue here is whether rates of imprisonment would change as variations in public opinion fluctuated in the narrow band between "agree" and "agree strongly."

Figure 5.4 shows the percentage of the public that believed the courts were dealing "not harshly enough" with criminals when responding to the question, "In general, do you think the courts in this area deal too harshly or not harshly enough with criminals?" over the years 1972 through 1989, as reported by NORC (National Opinion Research Center). This is contrasted with the trend in rates of imprisonment over the same period as reported in figure 5.3.

Over the years from 1972 through 1988 the percentage of the public that believed the courts were too lenient was never less than two-thirds of the total sample polled, and it exceeded 75 percent in each year after 1973. With majorities that substantial at the beginning of the time series, there is little room for further dramatic upward trends. Peak rates of public discontent with the leniency of the courts were achieved in 1978 and then from 1982 to 1986.

Three things can be said about the relationship between these public opinion poll responses and rates of imprisonment. First, if one wanted to attribute the upward movement in imprisonment rates, as the U.S. Department of Justice did in 1983, to "stiffened public attitudes toward crime and criminals" (U.S. Department of Justice, Bureau of Justice Statistics, 1983:1), then the public opinion poll data would support that conclusion at any point. The same is true of Time magazine's explanation of what it called "the imprisonment spree" in 1982. "The public

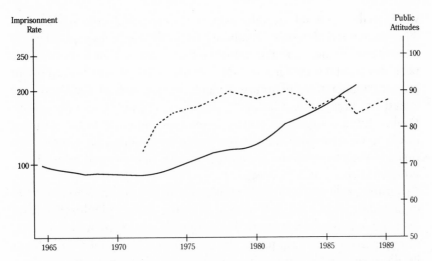

FIG. 5.4. Public attitudes and rates of imprisonment, 1972–1989. Solid line: imprisonment rate. Dashed line: percentage of public opinion "not harshly enough." Sources: U.S. Department of Justice, Bureau of Justice Statistics, 1988c:142–143, 487; and NORC, 1972–1989:346–347.

wants to 'get tough' with criminals, and legislators, prosecutors and judges are obeying that diffuse mandate by sending more people away for longer stretches . . . U.S. citizens [have] reached a critical level of panic and anger at what they feel is a constantly lurking threat" (Anderson, 1982:38, 40). However, since dissatisfaction with the leniency of the courts appears to be a chronic condition, if negative public views caused increases in prison population, that population would be ceaselessly spiraling upward.

Second, a striking phenomenon illustrated by figure 5.4 is that public opinion regarding the leniency of sentencing has not responded to variations in criminal justice policy during the 1970s and 1980s. As rates of imprisonment have increased, both per 100,000 population and per 1,000 reported crimes (U.S. Department of Justice, Bureau of Justice Statistics, 1988c:319, 486), public judgment that the courts are too lenient has either remained stable or increased. Moreover, it is unlikely that this simply reflects a time lag in public perceptions because any such lag would have had to persist for at least a decade to produce the pattern shown in the figure.

Third, and much more plausible than any farfetched time-lag hypothesis, is the possibility that questions about whether the treatment of criminals is too harsh or not harsh enough really only elicit responses which reflect general attitudes regarding crime and criminal justice. The more worried people are about crime, the more they are likely to attribute its incidence to the failure of the courts to control it by severe penalties. Under these circumstances, while public dissatisfaction might produce higher rates of imprisonment, higher rates of imprisonment would not in any direct fashion reduce levels of public dissatisfaction. Public attitudes regarding leniency would therefore reflect levels of fear of crime rather than being responsive to indices of penal severity. On this analysis the relationship between public opinion and rates of imprisonment is a one-way street.

But the explanation of high imprisonment rates or increased severity of punishment as a function of fear of crime and public dissatisfaction with the leniency of the courts is clearly deficient. If increased severity of punishment is always politically popular and the public will always be dissatisfied with rates of imprisonment as long as crime rates are unacceptably high, there remains the problem of explaining what it is that moderates or deflects that pressure in periods when rates of imprisonment are stable. The ad hoc reference to punitive public attitudes when prison population increases is analogous to the attribution of rainfall to the performance of a rain dance while conveniently overlooking all the occasions when the ceremony was not followed by rain but by prolonged periods of dry weather or drought.

The second effect to be tested is how variations in the salience of the crime issue in public opinion may affect rates of imprisonment. It may well be that the public always thinks that criminal offenders are treated too leniently. But this attitude is likely to be far more politically significant when crime is the number one or number two public concern than when chronic dissatisfaction with the operation of the criminal justice system is not a preeminent concern.

5.2.3 Demography and Imprisonment

Not all age groups participate equally in crime rates or in rates of imprisonment. Persons committed to prison are clustered in young adult age groups. One explanation of fluctuations in rates of imprisonment might be that they are a function of the expansion and contraction over time of particularly high-risk age groups as a proportion of the total population. As the proportion of the population in the young adult years increases, the rate of imprisonment per 100,000 population should increase as well. Since the age composition of the population can be predicted with accuracy over five-, ten-, and fifteen-year periods, changes

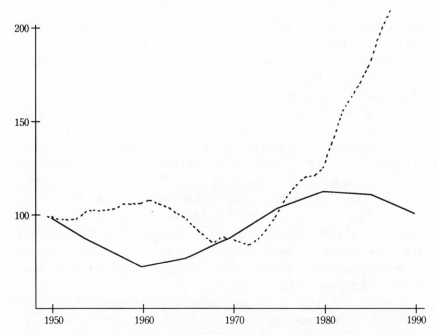

FIG. 5.5. Trends in young adult share of total population and rate of imprisonment per 100,000 in the United States, 1950–1990. Solid line: young adult share. Dashed line: imprisonment rate. 1950 = 100 (young adult share = 15.79%; imprisonment rate = 109). Sources: U.S. Department of Commerce, Bureau of Census, 1965–1988; and U.S. Department of Justice, Bureau of Justice Statistics, 1988c:486.

in the age composition of the population over time might both explain historical fluctuations in prison population and make possible the prediction of patterns of increase and decrease in prison population over future periods.

If the relationship between changes in the age composition of the population and the numbers in prison is a close one, the task of forecasting imprisonment numbers becomes straightforward and mechanical. But how close is it?

Figure 5.5 contrasts the proportion of the population in the age group with the highest risk of imprisonment, the twenty- to twenty-nine-year-olds, with aggregate prison population rate per 100,000 for each five-year period from 1950 through 1990.

The concentration of young adults in the U.S. population decreased in the 1950s, increased modestly in the 1960s and 1970s, and leveled off near its highest values through the 1980s.

There are two reasons why the variance in population concentration does not seem to be a major influence on rates of imprisonment. First, the concentration of the population varies less than half as much over the period as does the rate of imprisonment. There is not enough change in population concentration to account for the significant variations in rates of imprisonment.

Second, the fit between changes in population concentration and movements in rates of imprisonment is not close. The young adult share of total population drops 25 percent as the population expanded during the baby boom of the 1950s. During the 1960s, the young adult share of the total population increased by more than 20 percent, a change that should on this theory be paralleled by increasing rates of imprisonment; yet rates of imprisonment fell. During the 1970s, when the concentration of young adults increased by the same proportion as during the 1960s, the prison population turned upward. Then the 1980s boom in prison population occurred while the concentration of young adults in the population was flat.

The lack of a simple relationship between the young adult concentration and imprisonment does not mean that demographic factors are unrelated to prison populations. It just means that the relationship is more complex than a mechanical approach to the four decades from 1950 to 1990 would predict. In this respect, our findings on population trends parallel those reported on crime earlier in this chapter.

5.2.4 Economic Forces

A number of different theories have been advanced on the relationship between levels of imprisonment and the performance of the economic system over time. At the outset, it is important to distinguish between direct and indirect theories. There are, for example, theories that posit a relationship between unemployment and higher crime rates and thus indirectly to whatever higher rates of imprisonment might be produced by higher crime rates.

Direct theories predict that economic conditions affect the ways in which the system responds to crime in that imprisonment levels will be affected by macroeconomic conditions even if crime rates are not themselves affected by such conditions. One example of such a direct theory may be found in David Greenberg's 1977 article cited in chapter 1. He states there that "[w]hen the supply of labor is high relative to demand, this perspective would suggest that the rate of imprisonment would be increased, with the goal of taking excess labor off the market." As we

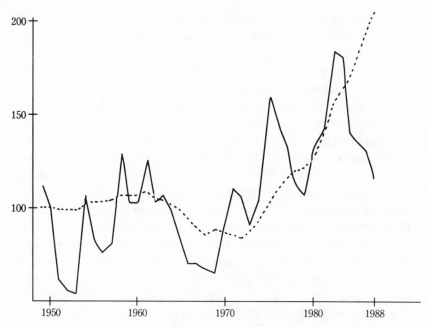

FIG. 5.6. Unemployment rate and rate of imprisonment per 100,000 in the United States, 1949–1988. Solid line: unemployment rate. Dashed line: imprisonment rate. 1950 = 100 (unemployment rate = 5.3; imprisonment rate = 109). Sources: U.S. Department of Labor, Bureau of Labor Statistics, 1988, 1985–1989; and U.S. Department of Justice, Bureau of Justice Statistics, 1988c:486.

noted, in support of his argument Greenberg cites a study showing that in the United States "for the period 1960–1972, the correlation between the unemployment rate and the rate of first admissions to federal prison was 0.91, and for first admissions to state, 0.86 . . . this was not a trend effect; prison admissions rose and fell with the unemployment rate" (1977:648–649).

Figure 5.6 compares rates of unemployment with rates of imprisonment in the United States over the forty-year span that is the focus of this chapter.

Inspection of figure 5.6 suggests what further statistical analysis corroborates. There is some relationship between levels of unemployment and movements in the rate of imprisonment but nowhere near the powerful association noted in Greenberg's 1977 study. Imprisonment rates are low and declining during the boom years of the early and middle 1960s. But imprisonment rates are high and increasing during the low-unemployment boom years of 1984 through 1988. Over the thirty-eight years from 1949 to 1988, the correlation between unemployment rate and rate of imprisonment is .59.

But a change in *this* year's unemployment rate is not strongly correlated with a change *this* year in the rate of imprisonment. The correlation between change in unemployment rate and change in imprisonment rate is only .21.

Unemployment is only one of several measures of macroeconomic performance we could use to test the relationship between imprisonment and the economy. But most of those measures of economic activity are highly correlated with each other and the explicit theoretical linkage is more substantial with employment and unemployment than with any other measure of economic growth and activity.

Our lack of positive conclusion on economic conditions as an explanation of rates of imprisonment parallels points we have made in relation to crime and demography. More refined measures and more complex theoretical formulations regarding economic performance and prison populations might well yield stronger results. It is the lack of a simple and direct relationship noted here that makes the case for the pursuit of complexity in later chapters and subsequent work.

5.2.5 Drugs and Imprisonment

One further influence on rates of imprisonment that deserves special attention is the relationship between levels of illicit drug use and those rates. Increasing use of illicit drugs might lead to higher levels of imprisonment for a variety of reasons. Some drug use is itself criminal so that increasing levels of use multiply the number of offenses occurring in the community. Further, some drugs are said to be criminogenic in that they increase the frequency and variety of criminal acts that users engage in, including those committed in order to obtain the resources necessary to purchase drugs.

Finally, high levels of drug abuse among offenders may diminish the prospects of correctional success for those affected in a community setting. So the drug-using offenders may be sent to prison more frequently than offenders not using drugs. Drug-using offenders may also recidivate more quickly and more frequently and more seriously, thus occasioning increasing reimprisonment.

One problem involved in testing the relationship between levels of drug abuse and rates of imprisonment is that of finding an appropriate measure of aggregate levels of illegal drug abuse in the United States

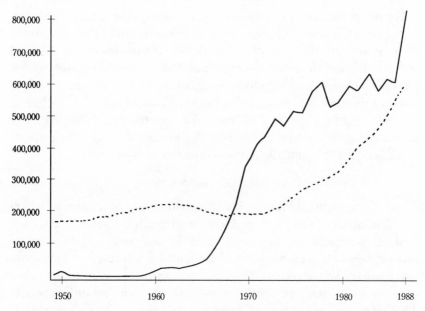

FIG. 5.7. Total number of drug arrests and total prison population in the United States, 1949–1988. Solid line: drug arrests. Dashed line: prison population. Sources: U.S. Department of Justice, 1950–1989; and U.S. Department of Justice, Bureau of Justice Statistics, 1988c:486 and 1989:2.

over time. Some survey research evidence on illicit drug use in the general population is available for roughly the twenty years from 1970 to 1990. But the only substantial illegal drug abuse indicator available over the full time period 1950–1989 is rates of drug arrests by police as reported by the FBI. Figure 5.7 contrasts trends in drug arrests with prison population over the period 1950–1988.

Drug arrests fluctuate without clear trend through the 1950s and then explode from 10,500 in 1959 to over 480,000 in 1973, a forty-seven-fold increase in fifteen years. The volume of drug arrests then fluctuates between 450,000 and 616,000 per year for the next decade before further significant increases after 1984.

The lack of fit between patterns of drug arrest and prison population trends is startling. As arrests increase at compound annual rates close to 30 percent, the aggregate prison population is stable. When prison population starts to increase, the volume of drug arrests stabilizes. It is only in the mid-1980s that drug arrests and prison populations grow together. By any standard, figure 5.7 celebrates the counterintuitive.

For many reasons, such statistics do not disprove a linkage either be- tween drug abuse and imprisonment or between drug law enforcement patterns and prison population movements. Drug arrests are a biased and incomplete measure of drug abuse. Such statistics mostly count possession charges and less serious drugs of abuse. In some settings, drug law enforcement is a critical element in prison population, including the federal prison system and many states in the late 1980s. But the relationships are contingent and complex in ways that belie the conven- tional wisdom regarding American correctional expansion.

5.3 THE LIMITS OF AGGREGATE ANALYSIS

There is in addition to the methodological difficulties to which we have already alluded a problem of overriding importance in the analysis of rates of imprisonment in the United States. The use of ag- gregate data of the kind employed in figures 5.1 through 5.7 assumes that there is a single community experiencing social and economic phe- nomena and a single political entity dispensing criminal justice policy. The heterogeneous nature of American society is of some importance when aggregating across very different communities a single measure of phenomena like drug abuse or crime rates.

Of special importance in the study of imprisonment policies is the fact that there are fifty-one different political units with very different rates of imprisonment and priorities in the administration of penal laws. This fact both limits the credibility of aggregate analysis of the kind deployed in this chapter and represents a research problem of consider- able dimensions. How do the fifty different state systems vary in rates of prison utilization? What are the apparent causes and effects?

The analysis in the preceding sections tells us that no set of simple relationships provides a satisfactory account of fluctuations in rates of imprisonment in the United States. But the disaggregated nature of cor- rectional policy in the United States suggests the investigation of state and regional variation as one strategy for illuminating the complex web of factors that produce changes in rates of imprisonment. The next chapter shows how substantially the American states vary in the use of imprisonment and identifies some of the principal correlates of state-to- state variations in imprisonment rates.

6 Fifty-One Different Countries: State and Regional Experience

The United States is simultaneously one nation and many different political and social subunits. In governmental structure, and in culture also, there is enormous diversity to be found in the American federal system. Yet national totals and aggregate trends are far from meaningless, even in areas like criminal justice where decentralized decision making is the controlling policy influence.

Indeed, one of the most puzzling features of recent decades is the way in which the many different political units that share power in the American criminal justice system altered their policies in a way that increased prison populations at the same time and with similar intensity. Whether the analogy is with a single organism having diverse organs or parts that function together, or with a group of autonomous units functioning independently but marching in the same direction, the puzzle is both genuine and a significant key to understanding the dynamics of American prison policy.

This chapter addresses state and regional patterns of prison policy. Section 6.1 discusses the allocation of power among the various levels and branches of government in the determination of prison policy in the United States. Section 6.2 deals with the concept of regional patterns of prison policy: examining the regional contrasts to be found in current American imprisonment practice and recent historical trends in prison population by region. Section 6.3 emphasizes the individual state as the unit of analysis, discussing the range of differences between states in contemporary practice. It deals also with some of the factors that have been used to explain interstate variations and the tendency for individual states to maintain relatively constant concentrations of prison population vis-à-vis other states over long periods of time.

At stake in the analysis that follows is the appropriate unit of analysis for imprisonment policy. To the extent that the United States is a single social system, approaches that view variations in imprisonment as an

137

outgrowth of social and economic processes would emphasize the national scale as a unit of analysis. This is consistent with the emphasis of the theorists discussed in chapters 1 and 2. To the extent that prison population is best viewed as an outcome of conscious governmental choice, as discussed in chapter 4, the most significant political power over imprisonment is exercised at the state level and the state should be the significant unit of analysis.

6.1 PRISON POLICY IN THE AMERICAN FEDERAL SYSTEM

Political scientists looking for a signal illustration of the complexities and ironies of American federalism could hardly do better than direct their attention to the political setting of American prisons and jails. Responsibility for the administration of prisons and jails is spread unevenly across the three significant levels of American government—federal, state, and local. Table 6.1 shows the distribution of persons in confinement under criminal justice auspices on December 31, 1986 (September 30, 1986, for federal statistics) by type of facility holding them and the responsible government agency administering the institution.

With respect to prisons, typically institutions housing persons sentenced to more than one year, responsibility is unevenly divided between the federal government and the states. The federal prison system, which houses persons imprisoned for violations of federal law, accounted for 38,685 of the 540,963 persons confined in American prisons, or 7 percent of them (U.S. Department of Justice, Federal Bureau of Prisons, 1986:17–19). The other 93 percent of the United States prison population, now numbering over half a million, is held in institutions under the budgetary and administrative responsibility of state governments.

TABLE 6.1 Criminal Justice Population in Confinement
by Level of Government, 1986

	Prison		Jail	
Federal	38,685	(7%)	2,827*	(1%)
State	502,251	(93%)	—	
Local	—		274,444	(99%)
	540,963	(100%)	277,271	(100%)

* Metropolitan Correctional Centers.
SOURCES: U.S. Department of Justice, Federal Bureau of Prisons, 1986; U.S. Department of Justice, Bureau of Justice Statistics, 1987a, 1987b.

By contrast, jails in the United States—institutions for pretrial detention and the serving of short-term sentences—are the responsibility of
local government at the county or municipal level. All but a small number of persons awaiting federal trial or serving short sentences for federal
crimes in metropolitan correctional centers serve jail sentences under
the jurisdiction of a county or city government. The great majority of
jails are operated by a county sheriff, usually an elected official, by a
city chief of police, or by their designees.

The principal explanation for this allocation of responsibility is historical. English jails (or gaols), originally conceived as places for the
detention of suspected or arrested offenders until they could be tried by
the courts, were the responsibility of local government. By the mid-
eighteenth century, they had merged with penal institutions variously
named workhouses or houses of correction (Fox, 1952:20–25). When
the early colonists came to America, they brought with them the institutions developed in the mother country and the American jail assumed
its combined function of detention and correction in the early nineteenth century (Barnes and Teeters, 1943:842–843).

During the late eighteenth and early nineteenth centuries new institutions known as penitentiaries or prisons developed to replace capital
and corporal punishment with imprisonment as the normal sentence
for felons. In England they were originally administered by the county
authorities, and then in 1877 all jails and prisons were taken over and
merged into one system by the central government (Fox, 1952:48). In
America the states assumed responsibility for prisons. A distinctive federal prison system did not come into existence until 1930 when President Hoover signed an Act of Congress creating the U.S. Bureau of
Prisons. At no time have federal institutions housed more than 10 percent of the U.S. prison population.

The power of historical precedent is evident in American prison
policy more than in any other sphere of public administration. Those
units of government originally in charge of the different types of institution have remained administratively responsible throughout the country. And those units of government with administrative responsibility in
these areas typically pay the lion's share of the costs of administering the
relevant programs and institutions.

Unlike education and highway building, where state administrative
responsibility has been accompanied by substantial federal financial aid,
insofar as the building, maintaining, and running of prisons is concerned state governments in the United States pay the overwhelming

majority of all bills (U.S. Department of Justice, National Institute of Justice, 1980:III.137). And while state aid to local jail authorities is not uncommon, the federal fiscal contribution is trivial. In fact, the major share of the costs associated with jailing comes out of the budget of the local sheriff's office or the police department.

One reason for the passive, almost fatalistic, attitude of correctional administrators to forecasting correctional populations (U.S. Department of Justice, National Institute of Justice, 1980:II.45), noted in chapter 3, is the passive role played by correctional administration, and the level of government that sustains it, in regard to the determination of prison and jail populations. From the standpoint of prison administration the problems are a mix of separation of powers and federalism. Even if jail policy is determined by units of local government, it is not the people who run the jails who fill the jails but rather the police and the judiciary. State prison populations are determined by state legislatures, state and local judges, and local prosecutors. Only rarely are those who administer prisons given any substantial authority to set the terms of imprisonment served by those in their custody.

It is likely that some tension is generated by the fact that the level of government that is responsible for paying the bills for the upkeep of prisons does not make decisions about the number of persons sent to prison or the length of their stay there. To judges and prosecutors imprisonment may seem to be available as a free good or service or at least may be viewed as the subject of major state government subsidy. This phenomenon, which we call the "correctional free lunch," is analyzed in some detail in chapter 9.

This political configuration has resulted in at least one attempted penal reform: the so-called probation subsidy program pioneered in California in the 1960s (Lerman, 1975). The rationale for the program was that by offering financial incentives that rewarded local government for not sending those convicted of less serious offenses to the state-funded prison system the tendency to regard prison as a free good would be countered.

What was remarkable about that enterprise was not the modest attempt to use the probation subsidy program in that way but rather the absence of change in the governmental and fiscal structures of imprisonment. Federal aid, now so important in education, welfare, and highway construction, pays a significant fraction of current state costs in these areas. But the federal prison system, rather than absorbing state prisoners or moving toward taking over state criminal law enforcement responsibility, has protected itself from expansion, over the past fifteen years of prison population growth, better than the state systems. While the current configuration of power and fiscal responsibility may have few articulate defenders, it has not needed any.

One reason why the existing pattern of fiscal responsibility went unaltered and unchallenged was that until recently the states were not overwhelmed with prisoners. In 1975 the number of sentenced prisoners in state institutions was 216,462 (U.S. Department of Justice, Bureau of Justice Statistics, 1988b:12). The budgetary appropriation for state prisons was $2.3 billion, or about 6 percent of the $38.7 billion the states spent for primary and secondary education (U.S. Department of Commerce, 1988:119). Yet, while the expansion of state prison population to over half a million has put considerable pressure on state governments, prison budgets are still a relatively small part of state expenditure: 3 percent in 1985. Prison construction, however, is now a major element in state-level allocations for new construction, which has grown from 7.7 percent of total correctional spending to 11.2 percent in 1985 (U.S. Department of Justice, Bureau of Justice Statistics, 1986a).

The substantial division of authority in determining prison population has one further implication of significance throughout this chapter. While we speak of state prison populations and state imprisonment policies, frequently the power to choose between imprisonment and alternative sanctions and to fix terms of imprisonment is decentralized to the county level. Different areas in some states may have sharply contrasting rates of use of state imprisonment facilities, so that state aggregate rates of imprisonment may represent an amalgam of diverse imprisonment policies. Frequently what is called a state's imprisonment policy may include elements beyond the short-term control of the executive and administrative powers of state government.

A major change in responsibility for prisons and jails by level of government has been the growing involvement since the 1960s of federal courts in setting standards for correctional administration in prisons and jails run by state and local authorities. This judicial intervention covering every aspect of the practices and conditions of prison programs became a major force in the 1970s (Jacobs, 1980). By the use of structural injunctions (see Fiss, 1978, 1979) and special masters (see, e.g., Nathan, 1979) federal judges have gone far beyond resolving limited conflicts and become involved in restructuring and reorganizing prisons. At one point in the late 1970s a survey by the ACLU's National Prison Project found that in sixteen states the prison system or the major institution was under a court decree on account of crowding or a "totality of conditions" which amounted to cruel or unusual punishment; and in twelve other states such suits were pending (Jacobs, 1980:445). By 1986, forty-six states and U.S. territories were either under court order or involved in litigation concerning prison conditions likely to result in court orders (American Civil Liberties Foundation, 1986).

It might be expected that such federal intervention would align all state and local agencies, administrators, and officials, animated by devotion to states' rights, in opposition to the federal behemoth. But the peculiar distribution of authority in state and local corrections suggests that the officials who run state prisons and local jails may often see themselves as being helped and encouraged rather than undermined or overruled by federal court orders and injunctions. This is in part because the agencies that run state prisons have no control over commitments to institutions, which are determined by other levels of government.

Thus, in some of the many cases in which overcrowding has been held unconstitutional (U.S. Department of Justice, National Institute of Justice, 1980:I.34–36), federally imposed limits set on the number of inmates who may be confined in an institution may well have been regarded as a blessing *without* disguise. To the extent that federal court orders require expenditure for staff and amenities and the provision of better facilities, or prohibit overcrowding, the federal judge who orders such reforms is the natural ally of correctional administrators. This latent function of federal court intervention in state and local confinement policies and practices deserves more sustained study than it has received to date.

6.2 REGIONAL PATTERNS

Differences in imprisonment policy across the United States are produced by social and cultural diversity as well as the exigencies of political structure. The clearest demonstration of this can be found by the examination of regional patterns, for, while states may be grouped into regional clusters in the United States, such groupings are sociocultural rather than governmental. If states within the same region show prison policy trends similar to each other and different from the patterns found in other regions, no explanation for this can be found in common governmental authority over prisons or criminal justice.

Yet the states within a region do tend to have prison population policies similar to other states within the region and different from those in other regions. Table 6.2 demonstrates this pattern. To construct this table, all states in the United States and the District of Columbia were

TABLE 6.2 Percentage Distribution of States by Prison Population and Region, 1980

	Northeast	North Central	South	West
Top third	11	25	71	8
Middle third	11	33	29	54
Bottom third	78	42	—	38
	100% (9)	100% (12)	100% (17)	100% (13)

SOURCE: Cahalan, 1986:30.

ranked in terms of their 1980 prison population per 100,000 adults. Calendar year 1980 was selected because it was the last decennial census year available. States were then assigned a numerical rank so that North Carolina with a commitment rate of 281 per 100,000 was number one and New Hampshire with a rate of 28 per 100,000 was number fifty-one. Table 6.2 shows how the states in each region clustered relative to level of prison population.

The most concentrated patterns are found in the southern and north-eastern regions. Sixty-five percent of all southern states were found in the top third of the national distribution by prison population. The other 29 percent of southern states are found in the middle third of that distribution. No southern state is found in the bottom third. The north-eastern region shows a similar degree of concentration but tending toward the bottom end of the national profile. Only one of the nine northeastern states is in the top third of the national imprisonment rate while 78 percent of the northeastern states are clustered in the bottom third of the national distribution. The western states in 1980 are found near the middle of the table, with only 1 percent of those states in the top third of the national distribution. Only the north central states seem to be spread in a pattern that displays the same pattern as the one that exists in the nation as a whole.

Why is regional location so strong a predictor? Obviously social and demographic circumstances associated with regional position produce cultural traditions and/or political structures that give rise to particular tendencies in prison policy. Examining how persistent the regional patterns are over time seems one natural approach to testing a theory like Alfred Blumstein's stability of punishment hypothesis. One good test of the persistence of regional tendencies over time is displayed in table 6.3, which tracks regional levels of prison population through seven observation points over the years 1930 through 1987.

The basic lesson of table 6.3 is that regional patterns do show some stability. A region tends to maintain the same general relation to im-

TABLE 6.3 Regional Prison Population by Rate per 100,000 and Rank Order, 1930–1987

	1930	1940	1950	1960	1970	1980	1987
Northeast	61 (4)	87 (4)	88 (4)	82 (4)	70 (4)	93 (4)	169 (4)
North Central	112 (2)	121 (2)	121 (2)	114 (3)	86 (3)	116 (2)	185 (3)
South	99 (3)	138 (1)	142 (1)	164 (1)	125 (1)	183 (1)	254 (1)
West	116 (1)	119 (3)	111 (3)	143 (2)	105 (2)	116 (2)	214 (2)

SOURCES: Cahalan, 1986; and U.S. Department of Justice, Bureau of Justice Statistics, 1987b.

prisonment rates in other regions over several decades, but this is far from invariable; and the exceptions shown in table 6.3 are as interesting to analyze as the general pattern. The northeastern states stay at the bottom of the national distribution throughout the fifty-seven years covered in table 6.3. The South after ranking third in prison population in 1930 rises to first place among the regions by 1940 and remains in that position consistently for the next half century. The West, by contrast, drops from first to third place between 1930 and 1940, then holds second position for the last four years in the survey.

These rough contrasts show that not all regions experience the same movement in prison population at the same time. Only three of the seven time periods covered in table 6.3 show a pronounced national trend, a period when all regions either dropped or increased prison population by over 10 percent. All the regions drop together between 1960 and 1970, and all regions of the country show a significant increase over the 1970–1980 term and between 1980 and 1987.

One further regional trend is worth noting. There is ambiguous evidence in table 6.3 of convergence in prison population. Regions with the lowest prison populations show higher-than-average percentage rates of growth, but the absolute increase is not higher. The Northeast, that region with the lowest prison population in 1970, increased its prison population at a lower rate during 1970–1980 than did the South and increased its prison population by 76 per 100,000 between 1980 and 1987 compared to a 73 per 100,000 increase in the South for the same period. The absolute increase in prison population of the latest period seems evenly spread over the four regions rather than concentrated in some more specific pattern.

A further potential use of the comparison of prison population movements over time on a within-region basis is as a method of testing the validity of the regional classification as a meaningful unit of analysis. For example, we can take the period 1950–1960, dividing states into four regions as in table 6.3, this time asking whether states within particular regions show a greater propensity to match trends in other states within the region than they do to match the generality of states in the nation. That inquiry is the subject of tables 6.4 and 6.5.

Table 6.4 deals with the decade 1960–1970, when the total United States prison population decreased. Table 6.5 relates to the decade 1970–1980, when total United States prison population increased. Both tables compare the imprisonment rate of each state per 100,000 population at the beginning of the decade with the imprisonment rate

Table 6.4 Regional and National Trends in Prison Population, 1960–1970

	Significant Increase	Stable	Significant Decrease
National (48 states)	10%	15%	75%
Regional			
Northeast (9 states)	33%	11%	56%
North Central (12 states)	8%	0%	92%
South (16 states)	6%	25%	69%
West* (11 states)	—	18%	82%

* Hawaii and Alaska, new states in 1959, are not included.

Table 6.5 Regional and National Trends in Prison Population, 1970–1980

	Significant Increase	Stable	Significant Decrease
National (50 states)	78%	18%	4%
Regional			
Northeast (9 states)	44%	33%	22%
North Central (12 states)	92%	8%	—
South (16 states)	81%	19%	—
West (12 states)	85%	15%	0%

of that state at the end of the decade. The states are classified in one of three categories: those that experience significant declines in prison population (10 percent or more); those that show a significant increase (10 percent or greater); and those with stable trends during the decade (rates of fluctuation of less than 10 percent).

The first important finding that comes from inspection of the tables is the existence of national trends of some significance during the two decades. During the 1960s imprisonment decreased in three-quarters of American states when measured against the standard population; and seven times as many states experienced significant decreases as experienced significant increases. During the decade of the 1970s, by contrast, three-quarters of American states experienced significant increases in prison population and ten times as many states experienced significant increases as experienced significant decreases.

This sharp turnaround is worthy of note. More important, however, is the fact that the majority of states trend in the same direction in recent years even though the decisional process that drives prison population is decentralized to the state and local level. The explanation for this phenomenon cannot be found in any interpretation that is based on the actions of the political powers that pass criminal laws and administer prison systems because recent trends push across conventional jurisdictional boundaries.

Regional patterns tend to be more homogeneous than the national aggregate. During the 1960s only one state outside the Northeast experienced an increase in imprisonment rate greater than 10 percent and in two regions of the country—the North Central and the West—more than 90 percent of jurisdictions showed decreasing rates of imprisonment. The addition of the region as the unit of analysis adds some clarity of focus even when only four regions are employed in the exercise.

The regional contrasts we have been discussing are subject to a number of qualifications. First, to the extent that prison population policy is the outcome of deliberate decisions, regional patterns are the product of an aggregate of individual instances of governmental activity. In the strict sense, regions do not have prison population policies or indeed prison populations.

Second, partly because the term "region" lacks governmental reference, what constitutes a region in the United States, and for what purposes, is to some extent arbitrary and is always open to question. In our analysis we denominate four regions—the grossest breakdown of the country used in regional discussions; other analyses specify six or even eight regions. But using any standard regional breakdown, the clustering pattern we described in considering prison policies seems to hold. There is no reason on the basis of currently available data to suggest that one pattern of regional classification would be better than another.

Third, to talk about regional similarities as if they reflect social and cultural conditions does not mean that only social and cultural factors can account for similarities in patterns of imprisonment or for the persistence of regional patterns over time. For example, one reason why a region with a relatively high imprisonment rate in 1950 might still have a relatively high imprisonment rate in 1980 might be that the prison facilities built in 1950 were still available in 1980 to house a higher number of prisoners without strain than in a region with lower historical rates of imprisonment.

Of course, the reasons why prisons were built in 1890 or in 1920 may well have been social and cultural. Thus, the availability of prison facilities may be a legacy not unrelated to social and cultural forces.

Moreover, those forces may have other kinds of impact on state government, and exercise an independent influence on policy and on the maintenance of high or low levels of prison population.

It may also be true that the states within some regions are more similar to each other in the age and racial composition of their populations than to states in other regions. To the extent that particular demographic patterns influence imprisonment rates, as discussed in chapter 2, this would produce more similarity within regions than across them.

Finally, whatever patterns are revealed by the analysis of regional-level data need to be confirmed by the examination of state-level data. While units within regions may exhibit some degree of social and cultural homogeneity, a regional group like "the West" is large enough to encompass both Hawaii and New Mexico. Computing regional imprisonment rates as we have done by comparing total regional population and total prison population may obscure divergent trends in smaller individual states by giving greater weight to data from the very large states.

6.3 PATTERNS AMONG STATES

Figure 6.1 reports on variations among the states of state prison population per 100,000 citizens for 1980. The most striking visual message of figure 6.1 is that of diversity. The rate of imprisonment in the state with the highest rate, North Carolina at 281 per 100,000, is ten times the rate reported for New Hampshire, the state with the lowest rate of imprisonment, 28 per 100,000. And large differences in rates of imprisonment are not confined to a few jurisdictions with extreme values on the chart.

The median rate of imprisonment reported in 1980 was 115 per 100,000. States such as New Jersey and Wisconsin, about three-quarters of the way down the distribution, show rates of imprisonment about half as large as the rates reported in Oklahoma and Louisiana, states about three-quarters of the way up the distribution.

The regional patterns discussed in the section 6.2 are evident in the distribution of individual states. Thus, southern states are clustered at the top of the distribution, including seven of the top ten and the District of Columbia, while four of the bottom five states in imprisonment rates are located in New England. But neither geography nor demography provide a complete explanation for the diversity displayed in figure 6.1.

Thus, southern states like Mississippi and Alabama report prison pop-

Ranked from top to bottom:

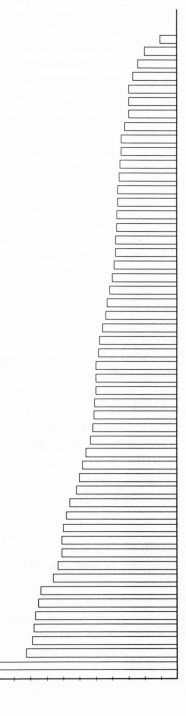

North Carolina	281	South Dakota	156	Washington	115	Nebraska	83
South Carolina	230	Michigan	153	West Virginia	115	Rhode Island	81
Delaware	223	Kentucky	146	Alaska	110	Montana	80
Washington, D.C.	219	Connecticut	143	Illinois	108	Pennsylvania	79
Texas	216	Tennessee	138	Oregon	104	Hawaii	76
Georgia	214	Arizona	136	Colorado	100	Minnesota	70
Kansas	209	Arkansas	129	Mississippi	96	Iowa	69
Nevada	190	New Mexico	125	Alabama	93	Vermont	69
Florida	183	Indiana	123	Utah	92	Maine	56
Maryland	177	Ohio	121	Idaho	90	North Dakota	49
Louisiana	176	California	120	Wyoming	90	Massachusetts	44
Oklahoma	170	New York	119	Wisconsin	86	New Hampshire	28
Virginia	161	Missouri	116	New Jersey	85		

FIG. 6.1. Rates of imprisonment in the United States, 1980 (per 100,000 population). Source: Cahalan, 1986:30.

150 CHAPTER SIX

TABLE 6.6 Number of Prisoners per 100,000 in Western European
Countries, 1977

Netherlands	27	Italy	56
Cyprus	33	Denmark	62
Greece	34	France	62
Iceland	34	Belgium	64
Portugal	39	Spain	64
Ireland	45	England and Wales	81
Norway	49	West Germany	83
Luxembourg	50	Turkey	100
Sweden	51	Austria	114
Switzerland	55	Finland	115

SOURCE: Kaiser, 1984:184.

ulations below the national median in 1980. Kansas is quite high in the ordinal scale of imprisonment rates in the American states, while neighboring Nebraska imprisons at proportionately less than half the rate of Kansas. Pennsylvania and Ohio are geographic neighbors and also demographically similar, but Ohio reports a rate of imprisonment one-half again as great as Pennsylvania.

There is in fact more diversity in rates of imprisonment among the cross section of American states than one finds when a comparison is drawn across the whole of Western Europe. As table 6.6 shows, the countries in Europe with the greatest diversity provide less contrast than the ten-to-one ratio noted in the United States. Finland, at the top of the distribution, imprisons at a rate 4.3 times that of the Netherlands. When twenty-fifth percentile and seventy-fifth percentile countries are compared, the results are similar to those in the United States. Portugal, at 39 per 100,000, imprisons at about half the rate of England and Wales, the same order of difference noted in figure 6.1.

6.4 VARIATION OVER TIME

There is also change over time in both the rate at which the states imprison and the relative ranking of the individual states, for the wide variation among the states of the United States is paralleled by substantial variations in rates of imprisonment within individual states over time. North Carolina, for example, ranks first in the rates of imprisonment shown in figure 6.1 because the measurement was taken at an opportune time. In 1960 North Carolina's rate of imprisonment was 242 per 100,000 but fell by 39 percent to 147 per 100,000 over the next ten years. Its rate subsequently rose to 281 per 100,000 in 1980 but then fell back by 11 percent between 1980 and 1987. Nor is North Carolina's history by any means unique in this respect.

Four patterns of variation in state prison population over time are worthy of special note by students of the political economy of imprisonment. First, while rates of imprisonment change dramatically in almost all states, there is a pronounced tendency for a particular state to maintain the same position relative to other states in imprisonment rate over time. To test this hypothesis, we rank-ordered all the American states at two time periods, 1950 and 1980. The rank-order correlation between the states' initial rank in rate of imprisonment and their final rank in rate of imprisonment was .68, suggesting that a state's 1950 rank is a fairly good indicator of its rank order thirty years later. While a state's inventory of prison space may account for some of the persistence in relative ranks, the rank-order correlation is just as high in periods of explosive change in imprisonment rates when states must expand the scale of imprisonment merely in order to retain their position relative to other jurisdictions. The rank-order correlations between the states when 1980 and 1987 ranks are compared was .77, and this occurred when rates of imprisonment increased by 70 percent.

The second pattern to be noted in the data is the tendency of a particularly sharp change in the rate of imprisonment over time to be followed by a tendency to move back toward the national trend in the subsequent time period. Table 6.7 shows the ten states with the greatest increases in rates of imprisonment over the period 1970 to 1980 and shows movement in imprisonment rates over the eight years 1980 to 1987.

TABLE 6.7 1980–1987 Movement in Rate of
Imprisonment for Ten Largest-Increase
States during Previous Decade

Delaware	+47
South Dakota	−1
South Carolina	+50
Hawaii	+86
North Carolina	−11
Texas	+7
Arkansas	+76
Utah	+21
Idaho	+66
Montana	+84

NOTE: Fifty-one jurisdiction averages. Median: 59%. Mean: 70%.

Table 6.7 shows that two of the states in the top ten states show a decline in prison population between 1980 and 1987, when the general prison population was expanding rapidly; and the mean change for the top ten states was 43 percent, compared with a mean change of 70 percent for all states during that period. So while there is some modest evidence that the kind of oscillation Blumstein and his associates wrote about partially explains movements in rates of imprisonment, there are also circumstances where above-average changes are compounded with the passage of additional time.

The third pattern which emerges from the analysis of individual state variations is a break out from apparently cyclical movements in rates of imprisonment that occurs between the mid-1970s and the mid-1980s. We have already seen that while three-quarters of the American states' rates of imprisonment increased between 1970 and 1980 this followed a decade in which three-quarters of the American states had experienced decreasing rates of imprisonment. So an argument could be made that much of the movement was an oscillation or cyclical fluctuation around an unchanging mean. As of 1980 only eleven states reported rates of imprisonment higher than at any previous point in the century.

But a cyclical hypothesis has been decisively disproved by prison population trends since 1980. Forty-six of the fifty states report rates of imprisonment between 1985 and 1987 which are the highest they have experienced in a century. While break-out patterns no doubt begin some time before 1980, it is not possible to locate a precise point of departure. Nevertheless, taking the experience of each state as a separate sample of penal policy overwhelmingly confirms a trend toward real increases in rates of imprisonment. The theory of the constancy of imprisonment, as discussed in chapter 1, has been put to a serious strain by the movements in rates of imprisonment in the 1980s.

It is also worth noting that long-term changes in some states are more dramatic than in others. Table 6.8 contrasts the fifteen states with the largest and the smallest one-decade movements in rates of imprisonment over the period 1960 to 1987. While the selection of any starting date for such a comparison is arbitrary and one could always argue that a longer time period would even out apparent differences, it is clear that rates of increase in rates of imprisonment have differed significantly.

The first lesson from table 6.8 is once again the enormous diversity of state-level experience since 1960. Concentrating on changes in the rate of imprisonment rather than absolute levels of prison population, the states are arrayed in a continuum from three jurisdictions with a net

TABLE 6.8 States with the Fifteen Highest and Lowest Net Percentage
Increases in Rate of Imprisonment, 1960–1987

Highest		Lowest	
1. Delaware	474%	1. Colorado	2.8%
2. Alaska	391%	2. North Carolina	3.3%
3. Washington, D.C.	292%	3. North Dakota	3.6%
4. New Hampshire	224%	4. Indiana	10.3%
5. Nevada	198%	5. Vermont	15.3%
6. Louisiana	196%	6. Iowa	21.7%
7. Mississippi	173%	7. Maine	23.2%
8. Oregon	163%	8. New Mexico	28.0%
9. Rhode Island	144%	9. Minnesota	29.4%
10. New Jersey	136%	10. Kentucky	32.4%
11. California	122%	11. Nebraska	36.7%
12. New York	120%	12. Massachusetts	43.2%
13. Arkansas	114%	13. Hawaii	65.9%
14. Illinois	114%	14. Maryland	67.9%
15. Pennsylvania	113%	15. Montana	69.0%

growth of less than 5 percent to eight states with recorded increases in excess of 150 percent.

There is no single simple explanation for these differences in growth rate. When using statistics based on growth rate, we would expect small jurisdictions with low base rates of imprisonment to assume extreme positions in the distribution, and to some extent table 6.8 bears this out. The five states with the highest growth rates in the table are quite small, and two of the five lowest-growth-rate jurisdictions, North Dakota and Vermont, can be counted among the micro-states in the American system.

But there are a number of large states at both ends of the distribution. Three middle-sized states—Mississippi, Oregon, and Louisiana—all report increases in excess of 150 percent. And four of the five largest states are among the fifteen highest-growth-rate jurisdictions. With respect to low-growth-rate states, Colorado, North Carolina, and Indiana are at the very bottom of the distribution, a substantial distance away from the average pattern of growth between 1960 and 1987. So it is clear that something more than jurisdictional size determines high- and low-growth status in the table.

If variations in rates of imprisonment among the states were more or less random fluctuations around a national mean, the states that have grown the least since 1960 would be expected to be those that had been

on the high end of these patterns of random fluctuation when the baseline measurement was taken. Thus, states like North Carolina that were
quite high, by their own historical standards, in 1960 would be expected
to show less of an increase in the subsequent period. States that were
below the level of imprisonment we would expect in 1960, on the other
hand, would tend to grow more rapidly from these artificially low base
values in subsequent years.

The data in table 6.8 lend only qualified support to this kind of hypothesis. Many of the states reported as high-growth-rate states since
1960 had imprisonment rates in 1960 that were below the average in
the region. We might therefore expect their prison populations to grow
faster from their low base rates while catching up with national trends.
But there is no strong evidence that high-baseline prison populations
are a driving force to explain those states that grow at less-than-average
rates. North Carolina and Indiana, two of the five lower-growth states,
do show concentrations of prisoners in 1960 higher than their regional
averages. But ten of the fifteen lowest-net-increase states already had
below-regional-average rates in 1960. Massachusetts, Minnesota, Ken-
tucky, and Nebraska all fall below the average prison population rates at
the beginning of the period and stay well into the low end of the growth
curve.

So more than regression toward a mean value is at work. Minnesota
and Massachusetts, two of the large-population states reporting small
prison population increases, also have a recent reputation for attempting
to control prison population. We shall deal with Minnesota in this regard in greater detail in chapter 7. For now it is important to note that
one way to test the impact of strategies designed to limit prison population is to compare aggregate data over a relatively long time period.

The contrasts in table 6.8 also discourage any tendency to regard
regional determinism as a uniform explanation. States in the Deep
South (Louisiana and Mississippi) appear as sixth and seventh in highest
net increase, but one southern state (North Carolina) is also reported as
second lowest. Maine and Vermont are among the seven lowest-growth
states while New Hampshire shows the third highest net increase. And
while the southern states' record can be largely explained in terms of
Louisiana and Mississippi's making up for all the below-average prison
populations of 1960, North Carolina stabilizes at rates well above the
1960 regional average (see figure 6.1).

The unexplained variations in pattern among the states should be
regarded as an invitation to do policy research at the individual state

TABLE 6.9 Largest One-Decade Percentage Changes in Rates of Imprisonment
in American States, 1960–1987

Increases			Decreases		
343%	Delaware	(1970–80)	−59%	Hawaii	(1960–70)
311%	Washington, DC	(1980–87)	−51%	Virginia	(1960–70)
230%	Alabama	(1980–87)	−46%	South Carolina	(1960–70)
208%	Alaska	(1980–87)	−45%	Montana	(1960–70)
189%	New Hampshire	(1980–87)	−44%	North Dakota	(1960–70)
169%	South Dakota	(1970–80)	−41%	West Virginia	(1960–70)
165%	Mississippi	(1980–87)	−40%	Alabama	(1960–70)
141%	Massachusetts	(1980–87)	−40%	Maine	(1960–70)
127%	Nevada	(1980–87)	−39%	North Carolina	(1960–70)
126%	Arizona	(1980–87)	−36%	Colorado	(1960–70)
123%	South Carolina	(1970–80)	−34%	Wyoming	(1960–70)
117%	Hawaii	(1970–80)	−33%	Arkansas	(1960–70)
117%	Wyoming	(1980–87)	−33%	West Virginia	(1980–87)
108%	New Jersey	(1980–87)	−33%	Minnesota	(1960–70)
97%	Louisiana	(1980–87)	−32%	Idaho	(1960–70)

SOURCE: Cahalan, 1986.

level. No doubt Nebraska and Massachusetts, which come so closely together in quarter-of-a-century time trends, have taken different paths to these results. The same must be true of any comparison between Oregon and Louisiana at the high end of the scale. But one useful way of identifying individual candidates for case study is the kind of preliminary exploration that table 6.8 reports.

The final table in this chapter underscores the convergence toward national trends in prison population movement. Table 6.9 isolates the fifteen largest one-decade movements in state-level prison population over the period 1950–1987. As Table 6.9 shows, all but one of the fifteen largest state-level decreases came from the decade 1960–1970, while eleven of the fifteen largest increases came from 1980–1987 and the other four came from 1970–1980. There is no regional pattern in either the dominant increases or the dominant decreases. Only time is clearly associated with extreme midterm population movements, and that association is very strong. The convergence of the states toward a single national trend is a fundamental shift that is not yet well explained. The message of table 6.9 is that even the extraordinary fluctuations in state prison population are now in the direction of dominant national trends.

7 Policy or Process?

The prison statistics reproduced in previous chapters are aggregate representations of a series of governmental decisions; and those decisions reflect governments' policies. For this reason, the natural way of thinking about the determinants of prison population is in programmatic terms. Thus, when prison populations increase, observers will look for specific programs or policies that explain the increase. By the same token, those who wish to moderate an increase in prison population or to diminish the size of that population will search for programs or policies designed to cut back the rate of increase or to reduce prison population.

This chapter and chapter 8 survey a number of criminal justice policies thought to affect prison population in the United States. The analysis here concerns not the relationship between social forces and prison population, as examined in chapters 1, 2, and 5, but the impact of government programs designed to influence the criminal justice system. To what extent are the fluctuations in recent years attributable to specific anticrime policies? Can designed programs reduce prison populations?

We begin this chapter by contrasting what we term mechanical and contingent theories of program impact and arguing for the adoption of a contingent perspective. We then survey four aspects of criminal justice policy thought to have contributed to recent increases in prison population in the United States, assessing the evidence that they have made a contribution and examining the extent of that contribution. The next chapter considers policies designed to reduce prison population or to offset pressures making for an increase in that population.

7.1 MECHANICAL VERSUS CONTINGENT APPROACHES

Underlying a mechanical approach to the relationship between criminal justice policies and prison population is the assumption that criminal justice policy and prison population are parts of a system that

156

works in a manner which is both predictable and relatively uncomplicated. Once a particular policy is put in place, the impact of that policy
will be more or less immediate and the extent of that impact will be of
similar proportions in any jurisdiction that adopts it.

Mandatory minimum sentencing, to take an example from the next
section, would be assumed to have an impact equivalent to the stated
terms in the legislation wherever it is introduced. And those who hold
a mechanical perspective would expect the same mandatory minimum
sentence for burglary to have the same effect on prison population in
Florida as in New York, and in 1985 as in 1975.

A contingent approach to the study of the impact of criminal justice
policy on prison population would emphasize the interaction of policies
with complex and changeable environments and thus the variable impact of policy changes on rates of imprisonment. At the outset we argue
for the adoption of a contingent perspective and demonstrate the need
for such an approach with two illustrations from recent literature.

7.1.1 Rehabilitation

The first illustration of the contingent approach concerns two
differential assessments of the impact of rehabilitative correctional justifications on prison population. It appears at first sight to represent a
difference of opinion, but it may not be a disagreement at all. The first
assessment comes from Alfred Blumstein's 1988 article "Prison Populations: A System Out of Control?" in which he considers, among other
things, factors contributing to prison population growth in the United
States since the early 1970s. He notes that, while incarceration rates in
the United States were relatively stable from the mid-1920s until the
early 1970s, they then started to climb so that by 1988 they had almost
tripled.

First among the factors contributing to that dramatic growth, Blumstein lists "the decline in faith in the effectiveness of rehabilitative correctional programs." Until the early 1970s, he says, "there was a
widespread consensus on punishment policy in the United States . . .
the consensus accepted offender rehabilitation as the primary objective
of imprisonment." During the 1970s, however, as a result of evaluations
summarized and publicized by Robert Martinson and others (Martinson, 1974; Lipton, Martinson, and Wilks, 1975; Sechrest, White, and
Brown, 1979) rehabilitative rationales lost their credibility. For those
evaluations "conveyed the impression that rehabilitation did not 'work'
[and] this impression became conventional wisdom."

Prior to this "it was the parole board that determined when prisoners were released [and] in most jurisdictions, at most times, parole release decision making was ad hoc and discretionary and, in theory, premised on rehabilitative considerations." Loss of faith in the rehabilitative rationale, however, led in some states to the abolition of parole release and in others to the adoption of parole guidelines and "more punitive release policies . . . to assure that offenders serve more time in prison." In addition, a move to determinate sentences led to pressure for raising those sentences and "consequently, prison populations grew" (Blumstein, 1988:237–241). The role of rehabilitation as a theory in this analysis was to keep prison stays and thus prison populations lower than would have been the case without the rehabilitative consensus?

Yet two decades earlier a very different view of the impact of the rehabilitative rationale on prison population in America had been advanced by a number of scholars working in the field of criminal justice. A categorical statement of that view appeared in *Struggle for Justice* (1971), "a report on crime and punishment in America" prepared for the American Friends Service Committee. The report focused on "the California correctional system, which has pushed further forward toward full implementation of the rehabilitative ideal than any other correctional system in the United States."

The passage from the report which deals with the most significant trends in appraising "the consequences of California's adoption of the rehabilitative ideal" runs as follows:

> First, the length of sentences has steadily increased. From 1959 to 1969 the median time served has risen from twenty-four to thirty-six months . . . Second, the number of persons incarcerated per 100,000 has continued to rise, from 65 in 1944 to 145 in 1965 . . . During a period when the treatment ideal was maximized, when vocational training programs, group and individual therapy programs, milieu therapy, and many other rehabilitative experiments were introduced, more than twice as many persons served twice as much time. (American Friends Service Committee, 1971:83, 91)

An analogous view of the consequences of the implementation of the rehabilitative ideal in penal practice may be found in Rupert Cross's *Punishment, Prison and the Public*, published the same year as the American report (1971). In that work Cross too sees the adoption rather than the abandonment of the rehabilitative ideal as the cause of a dramatic rise in the British imprisonment rate. Indeed, he refers specifically to "the baneful influence of the myth that prison could be reformative if only the authorities were given enough time" as the cause of "the vast increase in the average length of sentence which took place between 1938 and 1959" (Cross, 1971:98–99, 101).

Nor was Rupert Cross alone in interpreting developments in this way. Lionel Fox as chairman of the English Prison Commission wrote that "the prison system of 1950" represented "the natural growth of the seminal ideas of the years between the wars," the first and most basic of these ideas being that "the prison regime should be one of constructive training, moral, mental and vocational." He pointed out further that "the training that can be given will affect only those who are there long enough to profit by it . . . [P]enologists, prison administrators and informed opinion in general . . . unsparingly condemned the short sentence" (1952:113–114, 128).

English judges and magistrates were in fact advised to avoid imposing short prison sentences because they would not allow time for rehabilitative techniques to operate successfully. Moreover, from 1940 onward the United Kingdom imprisonment rate, which had been declining for nearly a decade, began to climb until by 1951 the daily average population of English prisons had reached the highest figure recorded since the records were begun in 1878: 22,500, double the prewar average. By this account, confidence in rehabilitation as a purpose of punishment increased the prison population by increasing the length of stay for convicted offenders sent to prison.

The different theories expressed about rehabilitation might reflect basic disagreement about the impact of confidence in rehabilitation on prison numbers, but this is not necessarily the case. What Blumstein says of the American states may be true when correctional and judicial elites are less enthusiastic than the general public about extensive use of imprisonment. Leaving prison terms to expert opinion in these circumstances may reduce both sentence lengths and prison populations whereas, when elite enthusiasm for prison programs is strong, a rehabilitative thrust may increase the use of imprisonment. We might expect this sort of effect near the beginning of periods when rehabilitation is relied on, and increased skepticism and therefore reductionist tendencies later on in a correctional epoch. In such circumstances it is the interaction of rehabilitation with other aspects of the decision-making environment that can produce either a positive or a negative effect.

7.1.2 The Tale of Two Sentencing Commissions

A stunning demonstration of contingency in the impact of criminal justice reform in recent American history concerns what we shall call "The Tale of Two Sentencing Commissions," one in Minnesota and the other in the federal criminal justice system. The sentencing commission is an agency designed to displace judicial discretion with guidelines carrying at least presumptive weight in the determination of sentences for individual offenders. In part designed to create centralized control over the allocation of prison space, the system which was enacted in 1978 went into effect in Minnesota in May 1980 and has been relatively rigorously evaluated in that setting (Minnesota Sentencing Guidelines Commission, 1984; Tonry, 1987a and b; Knapp, 1984 and 1987).

The impact of the sentencing commission on prison population trends has been rather dramatic in Minnesota in one respect. What had happened in every other state with a large metropolitan population in the United States has not happened in Minnesota. During the first seven years of the 1980s, while states experienced a median increase in imprisonment rate of 58 percent, the rate of imprisonment in Minnesota decreased by 14 percent. By 1987 the rate of imprisonment in Minnesota was reported at 60 prisoners per 100,000 population, the lowest of any American state with a significant metropolitan population. One might be tempted to conclude from the Minnesota experience that a sentencing commission that promulgates sentencing guidelines will tend to serve as a restraint on growth in prison population, particularly if, as in Minnesota, the avoidance of prison crowding is one of the responsibilities the legislature imposes on the commission.

Any mechanical notion that sentencing commissions and sentencing guidelines moderate growth in prison population has been disconfirmed by the early career of the U.S. Sentencing Commission, an agency established by the Criminal Justice Act of 1984 (18 USC 994). In many respects, the U.S. Sentencing Commission is a replication of the Minnesota experiment. The federal legislation that created a sentencing commission makes the commission responsible for the issuance of sentencing guidelines and charges the commission to pay attention to the impact of such guidelines on prison population and prison crowding.

In its early work, the commission took two steps that again suggest a parallel to Minnesota. First, the founding staff director of the Minnesota Sentencing Guidelines Commission was recruited as the first executive director of the U.S. Sentencing Commission, and, second, a study of the impact of federal sentencing guidelines on federal prison populations was a significant part of the early research of the commission staff.

But the discontinuities between the Minnesota and the federal experiences soon began to appear. Some months prior to the effective date of the first sentencing guidelines, the U.S. Sentencing Commission published its own projections of federal prison populations in the five to fifteen years after 1987 and the impact of sentencing guidelines on those populations (U.S. Sentencing Commission, 1987). As mentioned in chapter 3, the commission projects a ten-year growth in federal prison populations of 125 percent as the low estimate and 190 percent as the high estimate. In that climate of growth, the commission's guidelines were designed to add to the net prison population impacts of other factors. For the first five years of sentencing guidelines, the U.S. Sentencing Commission estimated that its changes in prescribed sentences over those meted out in 1985 would add 4,000–5,000 additional prisoners, approximately 10 percent of the 1987 prison total, to increases of at least 100 percent that were projected to be a result of other factors. Rather than being associated with declines in rates of imprisonment, as was the case in Minnesota, the federal sentencing commission plans to preside over more than a doubling of prison population in federal penal institutions in the first ten years in operation under sentencing guidelines.

It would be hard to imagine a more concrete example of similar mechanisms producing different impacts than these two versions of the sentencing commission and sentencing guidelines. There are, of course, many reasons for the differences in impact. But merely emphasizing the particular differences in sentencing commission personnel or political climate that produced these differences may miss the essential point of this subsection. That point is the highly contingent relationship that usually exists between a criminal justice reform and its impact on the size and character of prison population. Under these circumstances, predictions about the impact of reforms on prison population must be heavily qualified and studied in a variety of contexts.

The tale of the two sentencing commissions illustrates another advantage of the contingent analysis of penal reform. Discovering that the structure of a sentencing commission may produce either an increase or a decrease in prison population pushes the observer toward a more specific inquiry into the factors which may determine the direction of impact.

One cannot regard the mechanical approach as exhaustive in the search for causes once it is determined that there is no necessary or even close relationship between a policy change and its prison population outcome. From the methodological perspective, then, a contingent approach stands as a caution against taking inappropriate shortcuts in attempting to explain changes in imprisonment rates. As we review various hypotheses about the proximate causes of recent increases in prison population, the necessity for an element of caution becomes increasingly evident.

7.2 EXPLANATIONS OF INCREASE

There is commonly an ad hoc quality apparent in the search for changes in the criminal law that can account for shifts in the scale of imprisonment. Observers first note a movement in prison population—such as the decrease in rates in the 1960s or the sharp increases in the 1980s—and then look for changes in the penal law or the administration of criminal justice that occurred contemporaneously. The logic underlying this method of identifying candidates for causal attribution from the proximate time sequence of the presumed cause and the presumed effect is simple. Temporal proximity is taken to be an indication of a causal relationship.

In fact, there are at least three possible relationships to explain the proximity in time of changes in penal policy and shifts in the scale of imprisonment: causal, contributory, and coincidental. A change in policy might be the cause of a change in the scale of imprisonment in that the change in imprisonment rate would not have occurred at the level noted but for the policy change. There may be circumstances where a particular policy change is responsible for the *totality* of a change in the rate of imprisonment. Thus, if a move from discretionary to mandatory prison sentences for convicted burglars is followed by an increase in the rate of imprisonment, we might want to think of the legal change as the cause of that increase, assuming that all or substantially all of the increase in the rate of imprisonment could be attributed to the change in legal policy.

It might be, however, that that particular policy change was one of a number of events which played a part in producing the change in the imprisonment rate. The mandatory sentence for burglary may have increased the imprisonment rate for burglars, but other factors might be responsible for higher rates of imprisonment across the board. In such circumstances a change in penal law may not be the *but for* cause of a change in the rate of imprisonment, but may be making an independent contribution to a more general trend in imprisonment policy which is itself multiply determined.

There is the third possibility that, while the changes in penal policy and in imprisonment rate are temporarily contiguous, this is quite co-incidental in that the change in policy has no independent impact on the imprisonment rate. Thus, if the rate of prison commitment of burglars has changed no more than the rate of commitment of other offenders and the upward movement in sentences for burglars is no greater than that for robbers and automobile thieves, the relationship between the change in penal policy and the rate of imprisonment could be quite coincidental.

One particular type of coincidental rather than causal relationship deserves preliminary mention here: the phenomenon of the "third cause." Thus, it may be that widespread public disapproval of leniency in the treatment of offenders puts pressure on judges to sentence more severely and puts parallel pressure on legislators that induces them to pass mandatory minimum sentence legislation for burglars. It is in fact quite likely that both these developments would result from the same kind of public pressure; and one might expect them to occur together rather frequently. But the change in law may or may not be making an independent contribution to increasing rates of imprisonment since the same pressures that produce increasing rates of prison commitment frequently produce concurrent changes in criminal justice policy. Third-cause problems are thus recurrent when candidates for causation of increases in prison population are selected because of temporal proximity.

No single program is a credible candidate for the role of dominant cause of increases as widespread and substantial as state prisons have seen in the 1980s. But four programs have been frequently identified as important in the explanation of expansion trends in the decade: (1) new targets for penal emphasis; (2) mandatory minimum prison term legislation; (3) the displacement of indeterminate with determinate sentencing systems; and (4) the expansion of prison capacity as a cause of increasing reliance in prisons. Section 7.2.1 examines whether these programs have been contributory or coincidental to the recent increases in imprisonment rates.

7.2.1 New Penal Emphases

An almost universal part of explanations for increased imprisonment rates is played by social and legislative decisions to accord penal priority to a number of behaviors considered particularly harmful or threatening. Faced with the task of explaining increases in prison population, observers naturally direct attention to behaviors that, in the relevant period, have been increasingly viewed as deserving or requiring more severe punishment by the agencies that administer the criminal law. These are rarely new crimes. Commonly they are crimes previously subject to informal processing that are elevated to formal processing or jailable offenses that are escalated to imprisonable offenses.

A list of offenses that were singled out for this kind of increased penal emphasis during the 1980s would include many types of sex offenses, life-threatening and sexual abuse of children, drunken driving, domestic violence, and above all the possession and sale of hard drugs. In any discussion of expanding prison populations it is likely that new areas of penal priority will be prominently mentioned. And it will often be assumed that such changing patterns of emphasis are a large part of the explanation of observed increases in prison population.

One natural method of measuring the impact of changing patterns of penal priority over time is to trace changes in the proportional representation of particular offenses in the prison population. Thus, if the principal explanation of a significant increase in prison population is a new or renewed emphasis on drug offenses, then not only will the absolute number of convicted drug offenders have increased but also the proportion of drug offenders in the prison population should account for a major share of the increase in population.

Measured in this way, many of the new penal priorities in the criminal justice system have failed to have any significant impact on prison population. A greatly increased emphasis on the seriousness of domestic violence has resulted in a greater propensity to arrest but not in a much higher rate of long-term incarceration. Drunken drivers are flooding American jails but not prisons. The most significant impact on prison population of the greater priority awarded to drunk driving is that the jail space occupied by this group of offenders is not available for use in absorbing other types of offender who would otherwise be in prison but for crowding.

Judged by this rough yardstick of increased representation in the prison population, sex offenders are a considerably increased group and drug offenders are a very significantly increased group in most systems. Between 1974 and 1986 the state prison population grew from just under 300,000 to 527,000, an increase of over 70 percent. But the number of males imprisoned for drug offenses increased about twice as fast, from

TABLE 7.1 Five Most Frequent Offenses of State Prison Inmates in the United States, 1979 and 1986

	1979 Percent of Prisoners	1979 Rank	1986 Percent of Prisoners	1986 Rank
Robbery*	25	1	21	1
Burglary*	18	2	17	2
Murder and manslaughter*	16	3	14	3
Drug offenses	6.4	4	8.6	5
Rape and other sex offenses	6.3	5	8.7	4

* Rounded to nearest percent.
SOURCE: U.S. Department of Justice, Bureau of Justice Statistics, 1988b, at table 6-25, p. 494.

about 18,000 to over 44,000. Those imprisoned for rape and other sex assault crimes also more than doubled over this seven-year period, from about 20,000 to over 45,000. The increase in sex offenders was concentrated in the category of "other sexual assaults," which increased from about 6,000 to 25,000 prisoners (U.S. Department of Justice, Bureau of Justice Statistics, 1988c:493, 494).

Apart from the two categories of sex and drug offenders, the U.S. state prison population has been quite stable in terms of the offense that led to prison commitment. Table 7.1 shows the five leading offenses in the state prison population for prisoners in custody in 1979 and 1986.

The same five offenses occupy the top five ranks in 1979 and 1986, and the only shift in rank occurs when drug and sex offenses trade places. These five offenses together account for just over 72 percent of all prisoners in 1979 and for just over 68 percent of all prisoners in 1986. This stability in the face of a 70 percent expansion in prisoners is at least as remarkable as the modest changes noted.

Perhaps the most striking projection of the impact of new penal priorities can be found not in historical data but in the exercise in forecasting prison population carried out by the U.S. Sentencing Commission discussed in chapter 3. The commission, it will be recalled, considered among other things the likely impact of the Anti–Drug Abuse Act of 1986 on the aggregate projected population of federal prisons. According to the commission, half of the entire increase in the federal prison population, or 24,000 prisoners, would in the next ten years be added to the federal prison population as a result of this single piece of legislation. That increase represents more than half the total federal prison population as of the base year of 1987 in the commission's research (U.S. Sentencing Commission, 1987:71, 73).

While the measurement of increases in prison population attributable to particular offenses provides a straightforward method of estimating how significant new penal emphases are, there are logical problems involved in making the assumption that new evaluations of the seriousness of drug crime, for example, are a sufficient condition for increases in prison population. In chapter 5 we saw that there was no direct relationship between increases in drug arrests and increases in total prison population in the United States. One reason for this lack of obvious relationship is that increased concern about drugs (which may be reflected in increased arrest rates) need not result in increased prison commitments.

Drug arrests in the 1960s, like domestic violence arrests in the 1980s, reflected significant changes in criminal justice policy but were not accompanied by any substantial increase in the use of imprisonment. Only when there is a combination of a new penal emphasis with a belief that imprisonment is the appropriate sanction to use is there likely to be an increase in prison population. Moreover, the belief that drug offenders should be sent to prison may simply reflect a belief that large numbers of all types of offenders should go to prison. Rather than the crackdown on drug offenders increasing the aggregate use of imprisonment, the increasing belief that prison is the appropriate penal sanction may be responsible for the increased proportion of drug offenders in a prison population that is also inflated by more extensive commitment of many other types of offenders.

To test the independent contribution of a particular pattern of penal emphasis would require more sophisticated evaluation than has yet been attempted. Do prison populations increase more dramatically in jurisdictions with large drug problems? Are the states with the highest rates of increase in the use of imprisonment also the states in which significant new penal provisions have been introduced? Are metropolitan states with lower-than-average expansion in prison population also those with less law enforcement emphasis on drug offenses or other crimes recently upgraded in penal priority? Some of the raw material required for this kind of analysis may be found in the later sections of chapter 6. Only after such analyses are carried out can the impact of new penal emphases be rigorously evaluated.

7.2.2 Mandatory Minimum Prison Sentences

The second category of legislative change commonly mentioned when considering the explanation of increases in prison population is the provision of mandatory prison sentences upon conviction for the commission of particular offenses. These mandatory minimum provisions are in one sense a subset of the penal priorities discussed in section 7.2.1. But in another regard they are somewhat more abstract as a category and also have a fairly substantial history as a frequently invoked legislative measure: possibly the *most* frequent legislative crime control tool.

Thus, a review of legislative crime control programs reveals innumerable attempts to address gun crimes, crimes committed by repeat offenders and habitual criminals, and certain categories of drug crimes by abolishing the sentencing authorities' discretion to choose from among prison and other penal sanctions. Provisions for fixed minimum terms of imprisonment as the least severe sanction available on conviction for specific crimes that leave enhancements of the minimum possible term at the sentencing authorities' discretion have also been attempted.

Legislative initiatives of this kind are commonly directed at two quite different targets. On one hand, they are aimed at particular types of crime or criminal thought to represent a special threat or problem either for the community as a whole or for law enforcement agencies. On the other, not infrequently they are the product of power struggles and internecine conflict within the criminal justice system, as when the police, prosecutors, or legislators blame judges or parole and probation authorities for exercising their discretion in a manner which is seen as "coddling criminals" or being "conned" by offenders.

We are not clear how far back in the history of the criminal law such initiatives can be traced. The provision of the English Prevention of Crime Act of 1908 dealing with habitual criminals may be seen as a historical antecedent. That act provided for the imposition of sentences of "not less than five years" of preventive detention when an offender either admitted that he was, or was found to be, a habitual criminal. The imposition of such sentences was not, however, mandatory but discretionary (Morris, 1951:379).

Pressure for mandatory terms probably began shortly after authority to exercise discretion for a number of offenses was extended to the judiciary. The idea of responding to public discontent regarding discretionary leniency in this way is frequently encountered in recent history, and mandatory sentencing laws have been the subject of some attempts at evaluation (Tonry, 1987b:25–35).

We do not intend a comprehensive treatment of the impact of mandatory imprisonment legislation on the criminal justice system. Nor are we concerned here with the impact of such legislation on the nature and extent of crime. However, these initiatives feature prominently in discussion of the explanation of large increases in prison population when such increases occur, for one of the principal attractions of such laws for politicians and the public was the belief that they would result in more offenders going to prison for longer periods.

Both the difficulties of measurement mentioned in section 7.2.1 and the problems associated with the "third cause" phenomenon are encountered when mandatory minimum sentence legislation is invoked as explaining increases in prison population. Thus, the sorts of crimes that are popular candidates for mandatory minimum prison terms are commonly the crimes that led to long terms of imprisonment under the previous discretionary regime. And the imposition of such terms serves as an alternative to mandatory minimum legislation in other jurisdictions.

The detection of the unique contribution of this device to increases in prison population is a task of considerable difficulty. How many additional prison sentences occur as a result of the change from discretionary to mandatory prison sentences? It has to be remembered that the changes in public mood and political climate that lead to the passage of mandatory minimum legislation will also have been likely to increase both the number of prison sentences imposed and their length. This mood or climate change is, in this case, the "third cause" of both the new legislation and longer prison sentences, making it impossible to identify the specific effect of mandatory minimum legislation in any jurisdiction that enacts it.

There is some literature on the evaluation of mandatory minimum penal terms as an anticrime initiative. A review of the literature suggests that the unique contribution of these laws to recent increases in prison population is not great. Michael Tonry has summarized the findings of research on the operation of mandatory sentencing laws in Massachusetts, Michigan, and New York as follows:

> Discouraging findings appear in the evaluation of all three states'
> experience. The probability that a person who is arrested will be

imprisoned does not generally increase . . . To the extent that [mandatory sentence laws] prescribe sanctions more severe than lawyers and judges believe appropriate, they can be, and are circumvented. For serious criminal charges, the mandatory sentence laws are often redundant in that offenders are, in any case, likely to receive prison sentences longer than those mandated by statute. For less serious cases mandatory sentencing laws tend to . . . result in increased rates of dismissal or diversion of some defendants to avoid application of the statute. (1987b:34–35)

7.2.3 The Displacement of Indeterminate Sentencing

Another frequently invoked candidate for a causal role in the expansion of prison populations is the decline in the confidence in the rehabilitative ideal which had led to sentencing discretion, extended use of probation and parole, and indeterminate sentencing up to the 1970s. We have already made reference to this in section 7.1.1 of this chapter, but we postponed discussion of how much evidence exists to support this hypothesis and of the quality of that evidence.

At the outset we might distinguish between fixed price or determinate sentencing regimes of the kind discussed by Alfred Blumstein and the mandatory minimum legislation discussed in section 7.2.2. While mandatory minimum sentencing proposals are frequently labeled as "get tough" measures, they have little explicit philosophical content. They tend to represent a reflexive response to particular crimes or groups of crimes rather than to constitute an attempt to restructure the whole sentencing scheme; and they are usually focused on the discretion of the sentencing judge rather than the parole, or other correctional, authorities.

There are three elements in the determinate sentencing schemes introduced in the mid-1970s that might contribute to increasing imprisonment rates, although only one of the three is a structurally necessary element of determinacy in sentencing. In the first place, the adoption of determinate sentencing might result in more and longer prison sentences because it exposes the whole question of the use of imprisonment to the political process at a time when such a reopening of the question is likely to evoke a response tending in the direction of greater punitiveness.

A second possible contribution of such schemes to the increased use of imprisonment derives from the fact that they give more power over sentence fixing to the legislature than to sentencing commissions or judges or parole boards. The abandonment of indeterminate sentencing need not give more power to elected legislators, but the determinate sentencing schemes adopted in California, Indiana, and Maine did in fact concentrate more specific responsibility in the legislatures. Because legislators are more closely involved in popular politics, this reallocation of responsibility might tend to produce larger prison populations whenever and in whatever area it is attempted.

The third aspect of the decline of indeterminacy that might tend to produce larger prison populations is that it involved the removal of the power of parole boards to reduce large numbers of sentences toward the end of the offenders' terms and thus to use parole release as a prison population control mechanism or safety valve. On grounds of both dangerousness and desert the most acceptable candidates for release from prison are always those nearing the end of their sentences and furthest removed from the time when their crime was committed and perhaps also from the peak period of proclivity to commit crime. The power to shorten sentences at the "backdoor" is thus an attractive and relatively noncontroversial way of relieving prison population pressures. Any move toward strict determinacy necessarily reduces that power and may contribute to increasing prison population when other pressures are also operating to that end.

Measured most directly, the displacement of indeterminacy by determinate sentencing laws did not appear to make any significant contribution to the increase in prison population in those states which adopted determinate sentencing systems. California, which was the pioneer state in adopting this kind of sentencing reform, did not differentially increase its prison population after its determinate sentencing law took effect in 1977. Six years after the law took effect, the National Academy of Sciences Panel on Sentencing Research found that while prison use had increased that increase was best viewed as the continuation of preexisting trends in California toward increased prison use and not as the effect of the determinate sentencing law (Blumstein et al., 1983:206).

However, the movement toward determinacy may have had two delayed effects that contributed to increasing prison population in the 1980s. First, the reallocation of power to set prison terms to legislatures may over time result in more or larger upgrades in punishment than in states with sentencing commissions or nondeterminate sentencing systems. In a legislative body "it takes no more than an eraser to make a one-year 'presumptive sentence' into a six-year sentence for the same offense" (Zimring, 1984:273). Recurrent legislation authorizing the "aggravation" of offense by extending prison terms is a regular event in California. The impact of this on the growth in prison population has not been precisely measured.

Second, the parole board's release power with its safety valve function may not have been very significant in controlling prison population growth in the late 1970s and early 1980s. However, the lack of that power in the late 1980s when imprisonment rates reached an all-time high meant that the parole board's ability to react to fluctuations in prison population no longer existed at a time when it might have been employed. So the structural element in determinate sentencing that might have contributed to increased prison populations may not have become significant until nearly a decade later, when the entire prison population situation had changed dramatically.

7.2.4 Prison Construction

An explanation of increased imprisonment of a rather different character from those discussed above rests on a hypothesis about the relationship of prison population to prison capacity. Thus, some observers, noting the way in which any additional prison capacity provided quickly becomes filled, have asserted that something akin to Parkinson's law operates to ensure that prison population always expands to fill the available buildings. This appears to have been regarded as something approaching a law of nature by those who in the 1970s argued for a moratorium on prison construction (Nagel, 1977:154).

Thus, the National Council on Crime and Delinquency (NCCD) in a 1972 policy statement on institutional construction asserted dogmatically: "To allocate funds for institutions will increase rather than decrease institution populations" (NCCD, 1972:332). Harold Confer of the Friends Committee on National Legislation told the Congressional Committee on the Judiciary Hearings on Prison Construction that "just as the availability of guns facilitates armed robbery, the construction of new prisons tends to strengthen policies of incarceration" (U.S. Congress, 1975:11). And the NCCD's Milton Rector argued that judges who had in the past been reluctant to sentence offenders to imprisonment because of bad conditions in prisons would "send throngs of inmates" to any new ones that were constructed (Rector, 1977:17).

The "construction" hypothesis has been the subject of some inconclusive empirical work. A study of American prisons and jails by Abt Associates appeared to confirm the Parkinsonian hypothesis and demonstrate that available capacity did in fact influence prison population as had been suggested on an almost one-to-one basis (Mullen, Carlson, and Smith, 1980:56). This finding was derived from a relatively simple statistical model having prison population as the dependent variable with previous years' capacity and prison populations (and no other factors) as independent variables. It was nevertheless widely accepted. The National Institute of Corrections, for example, asserted: "Data strongly suggest that prison populations are driven by capacity and that criminal justice agencies will generally fill, and overfill, a state's facilities" (U.S. Department of Justice, National Institute of Corrections, 1981:14). However, a reanalysis in 1983 by Alfred Blumstein and associates of the data that gave rise to the conclusion demonstrated that the finding was the product of a mistake in the original statistical analysis of the data (Blumstein, Cohen, and Gooding, 1983:49–51).

Of course, as Blumstein has acknowledged, showing the incorrectness of the Abt "proof" of the influence of capacity on population does not demonstrate the contrary, that is, that population is unaffected by capacity (Blumstein, 1988:261). Indeed, it seems likely that in some criminal justice systems excess prison capacity does invite population and the provision of new capacity may make the difference between a stable and an increasing number of prisoners. As the existence of unused capacity in prisons may be associated with a lower marginal cost to the state of additional imprisonment, the creation of new space should lead to more prisoners.

But if capacity may sometimes lead, not follow, population this is certainly not an invariable law, for if it were there would rarely be any unused prison space. In fact, many jurisdictions had, at the time when the Abt survey was carried out and for years prior to that, an excess of capacity over population. Moreover, the Parkinsonian hypothesis seems largely irrelevant to the massive increase in U.S. prison population in the 1980s, when prison construction seems to have lagged far behind the demand for prison space. But that is not to say that additional capacity provided to solve today's crowding problem might not in the late 1990s come to lead population.

It is clear that the interaction between prison population and prison capacity is a much more complex issue than could be comprehended within the terms of the Abt model, which ignored a great variety of factors that could affect both prison construction and prison population. Most important, the phenomenon of the "third cause," referred to above, may well be in operation. Thus, the same kind of public or community pressures which lead legislatures to authorize and appropriate funds for the provision of additional prison capacity may also put pressure on prosecutors and judges to be harsher and increase their imposition of prison sentences. In that case, the relationship between capacity and population would not be one of cause and effect but rather one of two independent results of the same force or agency.

The general problem here is that the forces that lead to prison construction in those jurisdictions that expand capacity may also be producing other changes that increase prison population, and those jurisdictions that produce large new prison facilities may have been subject to special forces that produced larger changes in prison population. So even if larger increases in capacity are associated with especially large increases in population, the "third cause" explanation for the relationship may be the real explanation.

7.2.5 Conclusion

We began by suggesting that none of the legislative changes or specific criminal justice initiatives in the 1970s and 1980s was sufficiently widespread to provide a major part of the explanation of the unprecedentedly large increase in prison population in the United States that followed. A review of the evidence on this matter is consistent with this conclusion. Legislative changes may have contributed somewhat to increases in prison population in most states and had some differential impact in others. But since prison commitments have been a more important part of the increase than the length of sentences imposed, the role of legislation in increasing prison population was evidently limited. It seems likely that the political pressure which animated the adoption of the sentencing legislation was more important than the modest efforts of legislators to increase penalties. Prison construction, moreover, could not have been a major force in the 1970s and 1980s because there was relatively little prison construction.

Might there not be other changes in the structure of criminal justice processing which made a more impressive contribution to the growing numbers in prison than those we have reviewed here? That is not only possible but also probable. But the really significant changes are more likely to have been changes in mood and context rather than in the mechanical aspects of case processing and sentencing.

We believe, for example, that the information revolution in criminal case processing has increased accountability throughout the system and that this may lead to greater use of imprisonment. If prosecutors, judges, and sentencing commissions feel more visible in making decisions and are more conscious of the capacity of others in the system to tie them to their decisions and the results of those decisions, this is bound to affect their performance. Thus, the fact that information is cheaper, of better quality, and easier to retrieve will engender a feeling of accountability and will tend to produce a large number of "safe" decisions.

In many systems, the safe decision is likely to involve the continuation of prosecution rather than its abandonment; a sentence of imprisonment rather than probation; a decision to hold in prison rather than to release. It is difficult to estimate how large a force this element of accountability represents. But if this hypothesis is correct, major developments in information management and dissemination in criminal justice will be followed by upward pressures on prison and jail populations. Moreover, those states which have modernized their information systems will have larger-than-average prison population growth rates.

This, of course, is conjecture. Furthermore, as with the four hypotheses reviewed in this section, there is the possibility of the "third cause" phenomenon. Thus, the same pressure that led to the improvement of information systems and increased accountability may also have operated to increase prison population. There is, however, one wholly external force which has improved accountability but should not have generated pressure to increase prison population: the money and technical assistance provided by the Federal Law Enforcement Assistance Administration.

A second example of technology creating pressure toward increased prison population concerns drug testing and parole in California. Not using illegal drugs has always been a condition of parole release in California and other states. With the creation of inexpensive drug-testing methods, however, the means to verify drug use suddenly created pressure to return large numbers of California parolees to the prison system for violation of this condition. It now appears that as many prisoners are returned to California prisons each month for parole violations as are committed as a result of felony convictions. This additional pressure is one significant reason why California prisons grew dramatically in the mid-1980s. While the testing methods were not intended to have a major impact on prison population, they will continue to push the total population up until major adjustments are made in the system.

Finding that recent increases in U.S. imprisonment rates are not to any conspicuous extent the product of specific programs does not mean that increases in imprisonment in other times or other settings may not have been intimately linked with particular policy initiatives. Well-co-ordinated systems with fewer opportunities for the exercise of discretionary power probably function so that there are closer connections between program initiatives and major changes in levels of imprisonment. As we shall see in chapter 9, the decentralized and discretionary structure of state and local criminal justice in the United States involves a series of loose linkages which make it extremely difficult to ascribe responsibility for major changes or developments to specific actors or forces. We suspect that other Western nations may differ substantially in this respect.

The absence of a conspicuous programmatic explanation for the increase in prison population in the United States in the 1970s and 1980s leaves this pattern a compound mystery. As we saw in chapter 5, there is no simple set of social variables thought to be related to imprisonment that would explain the increase as a consequence of forces external to governmental criminal justice policy. To those who might be inclined to regard that finding as tantamount to a demonstration that the pattern was the product of variations in government policy, the absence of any plausible specific policy as a major causal agent is both perplexing and frustrating.

What appears instead is a broad pattern across the United States without a distinctive policy precursor. Seventy-five percent of the states had a significant increase in prison population during the 1970s, and 90 percent of the American states experienced further increases in the 1980s. To call this a "trend" or to say that it reflects a "mood" is singularly unhelpful. While many of us know what a public "mood" is not, in the sense that it is not a particular piece of legislation or a change in the age structure of the population, we have yet to encounter a clear positive definition or denotation of the essential elements of a public mood. And the term "trend" is usually defined vacuously as a general tendency manifest over some period of time without any specific reference to cause, character, or duration. The explanatory value of this nebulous notion is, of course, illusory.

8 Decarceration Policies and Their Impact

That the recent pattern of American imprisonment rates does not have any dominant programmatic causes does not imply that conscious human agency in the form of deliberately designed programs is irrelevant to the control of prison populations. Aspirin has been effective in providing relief for headaches even though the causes of many types of headache remain mysterious. So it is not inconsistent with the findings of the previous chapter to turn to an examination of the kind of policies and programs that have been proposed or put into practice to deal with the problem of prison crowding.

Of course, if an investigation had revealed that a particular policy initiative has been responsible for a particular pattern of sharp increase in imprisonment, then designing a policy to counteract the effects of that initiative is a simpler task. Once the "on" switch has been found in a lighted room it does not require great intelligence or ingenuity to figure out how to turn the lights off. But discovering ways of moderating prison population pressures without any clear sense of causal mechanism requires more substantial independent theory and more rigorous evaluation than does the reversal of identifiable policies with known effects.

Searching for the explanation of increases in prison population is largely a historical exercise, but looking for devices to reduce prison numbers must to some extent be a hypothetical matter. Ideally one would seek to identify mechanisms that restrict imprisonment rates by distinguishing states and localities with lower-than-average prison population growth rates and then attempt to determine what elements in their policies were associated with this patten. But there are neither many countertrend states to examine in recent years nor many obvious programs that unite those states with less substantial prison population growth.

A second and weaker method of identifying promising methods of prison population reduction is to study programs that have been de-signed for that purpose and try to determine whether and to what extent they have in fact reduced prison population. A third and still weaker method is to design a model program and attempt to estimate its effec-tiveness by means of simulation and speculation. As we shall see, this is by far the most frequently chosen approach in contemporary discus-sion of devices to reduce prison crowding.

In this chapter we discuss a number of the most commonly identified devices in contemporary literature on prison population. Section 8.1 deals with alternative correctional programs that attempt to reduce prison population by diverting convicted offenders from prison sen-tences to other programs that treat or punish outside prison walls. Four alternative programs are profiled: suspended sentences, probation and parole, community service orders, and community treatment orders. We then discuss why such alternative treatment programs so often fail to cut significantly into prison numbers even as they become the sanc-tion of choice for many, even most, offenders.

Section 8.2 deals with policies other than alternative treatments for offenders that are designed to reduce prison numbers or inhibit expan-sion of penal scale. Under this heading we profile decriminalization, amnesty programs, and other executive-level adjustments at the back end of prison sentences, limits on prison construction, intergovernmen-tal incentives to limit prison commitments, and the restructuring of sentencing authority to facilitate management of numbers committed to prison. The odds are against any of the strategies we discuss generat-ing significant limits on prison growth. But programs other than alter-native treatment seem to have had more success than new diversions into nonprison treatment in recent years.

8.1 ALTERNATIVE CORRECTIONAL PROGRAMS

Over half a century ago a leading American criminologist, Ed-win Sutherland, suggested that what was required in the United States, "where prison population has been increasing and where overcrowding of prisons is a chronic evil even though many huge prisons have been constructed," was some "changes in penal policies," notably "the sub-stitution of other measures for imprisonment" (1934:880, 898). Suth-erland, of course, was not the first to propose this solution to prison overcrowding; and he was certainly not the last, for since that time a considerable literature has developed in which "alternatives to incar-ceration" or "nonincarcerative options" have been canvassed as a means to deal with prison overcrowding and to "reduce our nation's reliance on incarceration" (Petersilia, 1987:iii).

In section 8.1.1 we review the research on the impact of four popular alternative programs. Section 8.1.2 discusses some reasons why alternative programs fail to displace prison, and section 8.1.3 deals with some conditions for programs that succeed in displacing prison.

8.1.1 Four Alternative Programs
8.1.1.1 Suspended Sentences

The suspended sentence was one of the first devices proposed as a means of limiting or reducing prison population. Introduced in England under the Criminal Justice Act of 1967, "it was hoped that it would reduce the mounting pressure on the prisons" (Radzinowicz, 1971:vi). But it began its career a century ago in Belgium and France and was in use in most Western European countries before World War I.

The essence of the suspended sentence is simply that a sentence is imposed but its "execution is suspended on condition that the offender does not commit a further offence" (Ancel, 1971:32). It is, because of its conditional nature, sometimes referred to as a "conditional sentence." In some countries the imposition of the sentence may be suspended and not merely its execution. It can be used as an alternative to probation or in addition to it.

Marc Ancel traces the origin of the suspended sentence to "nineteenth century penology in France," which "began to question the usefulness of punishment in general and in particular the penalty of loss of liberty." From discussions at various penitentiary congresses there emerged the conclusion that "prison more often than not had a detrimental effect on the offender, and that a remedy must be found for the injurious nature of imprisonment. Out of this arose firstly the idea of the 'alternative sentence' and secondly that of the conditional suspension of prison sentences" (Ancel, 1971:6).

The suspended sentence was introduced in Belgium in 1888 and in France in 1891 primarily as a means of avoiding the injurious effects of imprisonment and because it was believed that it would encourage rehabilitation and diminish recidivism. The question of its impact on prison population is nowhere mentioned in Ancel's study of the origins, historical development, and current use of the suspended sentence throughout the world. The subject of the effectiveness of the suspended sentence is dealt with solely in terms of "comparison of the rate of recidivism in respect of persons who have undergone their sentences and those whose sentences have been suspended" (1971:61–62).

In England, however, a critical examination by Anthony Bottoms of the use of the suspended sentence deals with it specifically in relation to the intention to reduce the reliance on imprisonment and its success in limiting prison population. This difference in evaluative approach is due to the fact that it appears that the principal object of the introduction of the suspended sentence in England was to reduce the prison population (Radzinowicz, 1971:vi; Bottoms, 1987:177). "The introduction of this new measure," says Richard Sparks, "was apparently motivated by a number of considerations. But one factor which was of obvious importance was the size of the prison population . . . it seems clear that one main objective of the suspended sentence was to reduce the numbers in prison" (1971:384–385).

In England the suspended sentence is a sentence of imprisonment of up to two years which is "held in suspense" during a period fixed by the court (minimum one year, maximum two years). It is, in fact, the only penal measure which is by statute specifically an "alternative to custody" because the statute provides that no suspended sentence shall be passed "unless the case appears to the court to be one in which a sentence of imprisonment would have been appropriate in the absence of any power to suspend such a sentence" (Bottoms, 1987:183). If the offender is reconvicted of an imprisonable offense during the operational period, the court is obliged not only to pass sentence for the fresh offense but also to implement the suspended term of imprisonment.

"The adoption of the suspended sentence in this country," wrote Radzinowicz, "was based more upon a pious hope than upon examination of hard evidence" (1971:vi). In fact, at that time no hard evidence was available on the effectiveness of the suspended sentence as a means of reducing the prison population. However, after suspended sentences had been available to the courts for three-and-a-half years, Richard Sparks reviewed the available evidence on its use and effectiveness. He concluded that the measure, far from reducing prison population, "has been counter-productive" and that "a measure which was intended (inter alia) to reduce the prison population has resulted in an increase in that population" (1971:385.)

When Anthony Bottoms reviewed the evidence some twenty years after the introduction of this measure into English law, he also reached a negative conclusion. The suspended sentence, he said, "had contributed little or nothing to reducing the prison population." He pointed out that "at the end of this twenty-year period the prison population in England stands at a record high level" and noted that "the courts' proportionate use of custody has been rising slowly but steadily since the mid-1970s" (1987:191, 198).

Both Sparks and Bottoms make the familiar point that many defendants receive the suspended sentence not in lieu of imprisonment but instead of other noncustodial penalties, and Bottoms adds that "those who then fail and are imprisoned will add to the prison population." Bottoms also notes the tendency of the courts "to pass longer sentences when suspending" than would have been the case if the sentence had been unconditional, which adds to the prison population if the sentence is subsequently activated (1987:190).

What these research studies demonstrate is not that the suspended sentence must inevitably fail in attaining the objective of limiting prison population but simply that measures designed as "alternatives to custody" are always liable to malfunction. As Norman Bishop puts it, "introducing new non-custodial alternatives can have unforeseen effects— effects which are by no means positively related to the original hopes and intentions" (1988:107).

8.1.1.2 Probation and Parole

Radzinowicz writes of "the virginal simplicity of the original suspended sentence" and refers to probation as "its more adventurous and adaptable sister." In the twentieth century the distinction between the two has become obscured because many countries have "permitted their courts to use one or more devices derived from probation . . . in addition to the suspended sentence" (Radzinowicz, 1971:vii). But there are significant differences between the two in both theory and practice.

The promoters of the original suspended sentence "put aside any idea of assistance to, or supervision of," the offender who was granted suspension. "The aim of the conditional [i.e., suspended] sentence was essentially to intimidate . . . by a precise and, in a sense, calculated threat" (Ancel, 1971:23–24). By contrast, the principal justification for the use of probation has, since the introduction of the first probation law in Massachusetts in 1878, always been the prospect of the offenders' reformation or rehabilitation; and assistance and supervision are essential elements of probation work.

Similarly, "what is now called parole was from its start tied to the concept of offender reformation." Both probation and parole were "originally intended as useful and humane alternatives to confinement" (Gottfredsen, 1983:1249, 1254). As with probation, supervision and the rehabilitation function are crucial constituents to the program. Indeed, probation and parole are virtually identical; and in many jurisdictions they are administered by a single agency.

In both cases, supervision was also intended to have a control function in relation to the individual offender. But in neither case was the control of prison populations a significant consideration. More recently, however, both probation and parole have been seen as having "latent functions" or unofficial goals among which the avoidance of the dangers and costs of prison overcrowding has been prominent.

Sutherland, moreover, saw the development of probation as one of the principal means of achieving a reduction in commitments to prison (1934:889–890). Probation and parole have been historically the most significant alternatives to imprisonment, and probation is today the most widely used nonincarcerative felony sentence. The number of persons on probation vastly exceeds the number in correctional facilities.

Of the more than 3.4 million adults under the care, custody, or supervision of a correctional agency in the United States, 3 out of 4 are not incarcerated. The 25 percent incarcerated is made up of 16 percent in prison and 9 percent in jail. The 75 percent not incarcerated is made up of 65 percent on probation and 10 percent on parole (U.S. Department of Justice, Bureau of Justice Statistics, 1988a:59).

These figures are of some significance when considering the possibility of diverting people to sentences other than prison as a means of reducing prison crowding, for it is evident that the great majority of convicted offenders are already serving sentences other than prison. Nor are they all "low-risk" offenders. In fact, "[t]oday, about half of those granted probation are convicted felons, many of them repeat offenders who would probably not have been considered for probation in the past" (Petersilia, 1987:3).

Both the issues relating to the impact of, and the skeptical conclusions of students of, suspended sentences can be found in the discussion of probation and parole. Each seems more a supplement than an alternative to imprisonment in systems where it has been studied. And this tendency not to displace prison has led some reformers to design interventions to fit between probation and prison. Two of these "in between" sanctions, community service orders and community treatment, round out our list of alternative treatment programs.

182   CHAPTER EIGHT

8.1.1.3 Community Service Orders

The Community Service Order (CSO) was introduced in England by the Criminal Justice Act in 1972. It has been described as "probably the most important penal measure introduced for adults since the probation order" (Young, 1979:x). It was at first applied only experimentally in six pilot areas, but in 1975 it was made generally available as a penalty and by the 1980s it was being used as frequently as probation for male offenders. Apart from one Australian state, Tasmania—which introduced a similar scheme in 1972—England was the first country to use the community service work order as a penal measure in itself. Similar legislation has since been introduced in Canada, New Zealand, and several states in the United States. But in England it has been used more intensively and over a longer period than anywhere else; and it is there that it has been most systematically examined (Young, 1979; Pease, 1985; Bottoms, 1987).

The CSO imposes on an offender the obligation to carry out supervised community work for a number of hours specified by the court between 40 (minimum) and 240 (maximum), the work to be carried out within one year of sentence. The statute provides that the CSO is only imposable for imprisonable offenses, and it was designed as an alternative to imprisonment for any offender aged seventeen or over convicted of any offense (other than murder). There is considerable evidence, however, that it "has not fulfilled the high hopes held of it as an 'alternative to custody'" (Bottoms, 1987:143).

In the first place, an analysis of court sentencing in the early years of the CSO carried out by Warren Young found that there was unmistakably an "over-all tendency for the community service order to be imposed upon offenders who could be classified as significantly less serious (in terms of previous record and prison characteristics) than those receiving imprisonment" (1979:116).

In the second place, there is a body of research which indicates that about half the community service order clientele are drawn from offenders who would not have been sentenced to imprisonment but to other noncustodial alternatives (Pease, 1985:60–64).

Third, a time-trend analysis of sentencing in England during the period of the expansion of the CSO to national coverage revealed no evidence of any drop in the proportion of offenders sent to prison; in fact, the reverse was true. Thus, "in 1985 some 21 percent of adult males and 22 percent of young adult males were given immediate custodial sentences; the corresponding figures in 1975 had been 16 percent and 17 percent" (Bottoms, 1987:184–187, 192).

Summing up the British research on the extent to which community service orders have replaced custody, Ken Pease states that "community service orders have shared the fate of other sentences introduced explicitly as alternatives to custody. They have been used in many, perhaps most cases to replace other noncustodial sentences" (1985:60). Elsewhere such evidence as is available confirms this conclusion. As A. T. Harland puts it, "The tendency of community service programs to deal predominantly or exclusively with offenders who are extremely unlikely to be incarcerated is reinforced by examination of a large majority of the programs that have been evaluated" (1981:444).

8.1.1.4 Community Treatment

The Community Treatment Project (CTP) was at one time "repeatedly cited by national crime commissions as a model program of substituting community-based treatment services for institutional confinement" (Ohlin, 1975:ix). The project, in contrast to preceding examples, did succeed in reducing commitments to prison. It did so, however, by using incarceration at the local level.

Paul Lerman's *Community Treatment and Social Control* (1975) contains a rigorous analysis of the correspondence between the intentions and the actual accomplishments of the California CTP. It focuses on the assumptions, choices, and consequences related to the implementation of this particular program, which was designed as an alternative to traditional institutional programs. The analysis is concerned with a wide range of relative advantages and disadvantages associated with the project.

The CTP was a research and action project, or experimental/demonstration program, designed to provide individually programmed intensive treatment services for young offenders in lieu of commitment to a California Youth Authority (CYA) institution. It was launched in 1961 with an experimental research design that randomly allocated eligible youth to the experimental or the traditional correctional programs. Control youths spent an average of eight months in an institution while experimentals were released to community placements under supervision. For deprivation of liberty was to be substituted individual treatment in the community for an eight-month period.

At the time when Lerman made his study, CTP research reports had evaluated the program as highly effective in reducing recidivism rates at a fiscal cost much lower per capita than the traditional CYA program of institutionalization and regular parole. Lerman, by contrast, found that reanalysis of CTP data provided "rather clear evidence that CTP did not have any measurable impact on youth behavior" and that it "demonstrated that it is possible for a community treatment alternative to be more expensive than a regular program on a per capita basis" (1975:95, 98).

In the context of our discussion, however, the most relevant finding is that the community treatment program itself included an appreciable amount of deprivation of liberty. As Lerman put it, "CTP was an organization that did not place youth in CYA's traditional program but instead imposed other living arrangements. These other living arrangements included foster homes, group homes, county detention facilities, the lockup facilities of a 'reception clinic' . . . It is misleading to term involuntary living arrangements as merely treatment." Lerman also found that "CTP youth spent more time in detention facilities than they did with their community treatment agents" (1975:7, 51).

Lerman concluded that the CTP delivered to its youth much more social control than treatment and that "*the primary program element* actually experienced by CTP wards *was short-term confinement* and not intensive treatment services" (1975:41; emphasis added). He did find, however, that "CTP youth spend fewer total days in an institutional setting than if they had experienced the traditional CYA program in its totality (i.e., institutionalization plus parole)" (1975:7).

It may seem paradoxical or ironic that the primary element in this "most highly prized example" (Lerman, 1975:16) of community treatment as an alternative to incarceration should have turned out to be incarceration, albeit described as "a tool in the rehabilitation process" and a "treatment technique" (Lerman, 1975:43). There are, of course, as Lerman acknowledges, "limitations regarding the generality of the findings" (1975:15), and the examination of one program in one state does not provide an adequate basis for generalization about all community treatment strategies. What it does provide, however, is striking evidence of the way in which "implementation measures or unintended consequences can subvert the accomplishments of project goals" (Ohlin, 1975:x); and that applies to *all* the programs considered in this chapter.

8.1.2 Explaining Nondisplacement

The nonincarceration alternative treatment programs just discussed show a pattern of consistently not displacing imprisonment even as they are successfully institutionalized as separate subsystems in criminal justice. This section examines the general characteristics of such programs that limit displacement.

8.1.2.1 Net Widening

One of the major problems associated with noncustodial alternatives to imprisonment is that they are not always, nor even commonly, used as substitutes for imprisonment. The prime candidates for community-based programs, says Joan Petersilia, are nonviolent and low-risk offenders—"the ones who are least likely to be sentenced to prison in the first place." Moreover, "as judges become more familiar with the programs, they may use them for defendants who would normally have been sentenced to probation with nominal supervision. Hence, rather than reducing crowding, the programs may in fact widen the net of social control" (Petersilia, 1987:x).

There is some evidence that this is in fact what has happened. "Most evaluations," according to Blumstein, "have found that the programs handled mostly individuals who would have been on probation ('widening the net of social control') rather than those who would have gone to prison" (Blumstein, 1988:255). A survey of the use of noncustodial sanctions in Europe also found that "when they are used [they] are too often substitutes for other non-custodial sanctions rather than imprisonment." The report on that survey by Norman Bishop concluded "that there is little hope of significantly reducing the size of the average prison population as non-custodial alternatives are currently used" (1988:8, 127).

Bishop also makes the point that "there is no necessary reason to think that a successful search for credible noncustodial sanctions would lead to a reduction of the prison population" (1988:127). In fact, not only does the greater use of alternatives to imprisonment not necessarily imply less frequent use of imprisonment, but there is often a positive correlation between the use of nonincarcerative sanctions and high incarceration rates. Bishop noted that "[a]mong the European countries which are expanding the number of places in the prison system are those which make extensive use of non-custodial alternatives" (1988:6). And in the United States it has been pointed out that "many of those states which most frequently employ penal confinement to deal with offenders also tend most frequently to employ probation" (Sherman and Hawkins, 1981:44).

One reason for this is that, when the development of noncustodial alternatives to imprisonment is designed as a means of reducing the size of the prison population, this will usually be in situations when prisons are overcrowded as a result of the court's extensive use of custodial sanctions. In such circumstances, however, courts provided with a new method of punishment are likely to see it, not as an alternative to imprisonment, but, rather, as a means of dealing, not with candidates for imprisonment, but with those of a lower level of seriousness in the scale of criminality, that is, with some of the 84 percent of offenders who currently escape imprisonment.

8.1.2.2 The Rejection of Unacceptable Alternatives for Prison

Another reason which had led observers to be skeptical about the likelihood that the use of noncustodial sanctions would reduce prison population relates to their acceptability as alternatives to imprisonment. In order to be regarded as acceptable they must in some measure be seen as serving the purposes of imprisonment.

Prisons are multipurpose institutions serving a variety of functions which can be divided into their practical or instrumental functions and their symbolic or expressive functions. In relation to at least one of those practical functions, and to the symbolic or expressive function generally, it is evident that noncustodial punishments are not seen by many as satisfactory or credible alternatives to imprisonment.

Incapacitation. The practical or instrumental function of imprisonment is, in this context, incapacitation or containment. This is implicit in the custodial process, for while the offender is incarcerated he cannot commit new offenses against the general public. This has been seen by some scholars as the "one primary task" of the prison system (e.g., Thomas, 1972:4); and it seems likely that in the eyes of the public one of the principal measures of the success or failure of the system is the degree to which this function can be achieved.

This preventive function of imprisonment is in fact its distinctive contribution to social order: the thing it can clearly do that other punishments cannot. The contribution of imprisonment to other functions of punishment such as general deterrence or rehabilitation may be problematic, but there is no doubt it can, at least while they are in custody, disable those regarded as posing a threat of harm to society or to the general public. Moreover, even the most committed critics of imprisonment see it as being necessary "for the offender who, if not confined, would be a serious danger to the public" (NCCD, 1973:449).

But standards of dangerousness vary considerably as do the grounds on which imprisonment is regarded as necessary. Thus, in European countries it was found that imprisonment was "considered to be necessary" for offenses "involving serious danger to life, health, and well-being, serious trafficking in drugs, aggravated thefts, gross fraud, serious economic crime, serious offences against the environment and offences which seriously endanger national security." In addition, certain kinds of offender were "deemed unsuitable for non-custodial sanctions" including "vagrants, habitual offenders, asocial persons and drug offenders as well as violent offenders [and] in some countries those who have served a previous prison sentence during some specified prior period" (Bishop, 1988:1)

There is no reason to believe that in this country, with its "traditional American fusion of punishment and incarceration" (Sherman and Hawkins, 1981:22), a comparable listing of offenses for which imprisonment was considered necessary and offenders for whom noncustodial sanctions were considered unsuitable would be any less inclusive. As John Conrad put it, "We have not managed to educate the public to accept anything less than a prison sentence" (1977a:28). But it is quite possible that no amount of "education" would persuade the public that noncustodial alternatives would provide the degree of protection for the community which is the great attraction of imprisonment for many citizens. In 1987 Joan Petersilia observed that "the public has become increasingly skeptical that anything other than prison constitutes real punishment" (1987:xi).

The expressive function. "Punishment," according to Joel Feinberg, "is a conventional device for the expression of attitudes of resentment and indignation, and of judgments of disapproval and reprobation, on the part either of the punishing authority or of those in whose name the punishment is inflicted. Punishment, in short, has symbolic significance" (1981:24). What is true of the institution of punishment applies, of course, to the various methods of punishment and in particular to imprisonment; it provides a symbolic affirmation of public disapproval and reprobation.

Indeed, one of the principal criticisms of imprisonment advanced by penal reformers in the past has always been that the stigmatization, the reduction in status, the reprobation, rejection, and exclusion from society involved in incarceration were psychologically and socially harmful in that they made rehabilitation and subsequent adjustment in society more difficult. One of the main reasons given for using noncustodial alternatives to imprisonment has always been that they do not have the stigmatic significance which attaches to imprisonment and thus do not hinder the offender's adjustment in society.

At the same time, one of the principal reasons for public dissatisfaction with noncustodial alternatives is that they are "inadequate to express the necessary degree of reprobation" (Bishop, 1988:119) in that they do not carry the necessary symbolic message. Offenders who are dealt with by being put on probation, for example, are seen as being dealt with too leniently and, in effect, let off or excused. In such cases the law-abiding citizen is likely to feel cheated by the granting of impunity to the lawbreaker (van den Haag, 1975:21). Far from adequately expressing disapproval or condemnation such lesser penalties seem to signal public tolerance.

Recognition of this symbolic or expressive function of imprisonment has somewhat ironically led some of those who want to see the link between punishment and incarceration broken to suggest that this could be facilitated if the prison's unequivocal message of reprobation, disavowal, and disapprobation were somehow attached to noncustodial alternatives. Thus, they argue that if noncustodial alternatives to imprisonment are to be made acceptable they must "be able to carry the necessary symbolic message" and that "the time is now ripe to transfer much of the reprobation expressed through custodial sanctions to noncustodial sanctions" (Bishop, 1988:5, 119). At the present time, however, this has not been achieved; nor is it at all clear how it could be achieved.

The noncentrality of prison displacement. There is one other reason we believe that alternative treatment programs often fail to make a dent in prison population. While many diversion and alternative programs have broad constituencies in the community, supporters of these programs can achieve most of their goals without decreasing prison populations. It is easier to fill program rosters with the many thousands of persons who would not be imprisoned than to attempt true diversion from prison. As long as the program can obtain lower-risk subjects, program staff and management may not worry about reduction in prison as a major goal. If many persons with strong personal stakes in alternative programs do not place large value on reducing prison numbers, alternative programs may soon cease to function as alternatives even as they create their own independent identity in the ecology of a local criminal justice system. This seems to have been the career of many diversion programs in the 1970s. It may be an important part of the system dynamic of net widening.

8.1.3 Conditions of Successful Displacement

How might a program of alternative treatments or sanctions be administered to reduce prison population? Four elements of program design seem significant: specific targeting of the subjects of the program, the selection of targets that are politically feasible candidates for nonprison, the creation of incentives in the administration of treatment programs for prison diversion, and the functional design of alternative programs.

It is obvious in a system where only a small proportion of criminal offenders are sent to prison that a treatment program needs to be designed to deal with that small group rather than other types of offenders. The natural way to establish this is to study sentencing patterns in a jurisdiction and focus the program on a group of offenders who are frequently sent to prison. This is not often a part of alternative planning at present because displacement is not a central goal for program stakeholders.

Does the selection of imprisoned target groups mean that an alternative program should focus on bank robbers with extensive conviction records and major dealers of hard narcotics? These groups do provide the raw material for displacement, but community pressures either would lead prosecutors and judges to reject the alternative program or would reshape the program to provide the incapacitation and punitive bite the community demanded for these groups. Instead, the preferred targets for an alternative program are groups that are near the margin as candidates for prison: burglars and nonviolent property offenders in most systems, and drug users with relatively minor involvements in dealing. With this target group, nonincarcerative drug treatment programs or short-stay community correctional programs can function without direct clash with high-intensity needs for incapacitation or condemnation. One way of discerning what categories of offenders are on the margin for imprisonment is to study which categories are disproportionately part of the new cohort in prison as rates of imprisonment rise.

There is a trade-off between selection of marginal categories of offender and the net displacement effect of nonprison programs. If a program targets a group of offenders near the margin on prison commitment, each 100 such subjects will provide a smaller number of persons headed for prison than if bank robbers were the target group. This is one reason why early release programs (where all the subjects are in prison) generate more displacement than programs that focus only on those at risk of commitment.

In all this, evaluation and incentives for displacement are necessary if an alternative treatment program is to function as a displacement. Program administrators have natural tendencies to seek out subjects with low failure risks. The lower the risk of the treatment group, the higher the apparent success rate of the treatment program. These are usually the same groups with small chances of prison commitment in rational systems. It requires a strong commitment to displacement and good evaluation data to countermand this nearly gravitational pull toward low-risk groups.

Functional design. The key to the design of alternative programs that effectively displace imprisonment for specific offender groups is the creation of alternatives that respond to the reason why imprisonment is felt to be necessary for the target group. If imprisonment is required for a particular group of offenders because only imprisonment seems to match the moral gravity of the offense, the stigma conveyed by the alternative must be substantial or the alternative will not be acceptable. If imprisonment is felt to be necessary because the offender is defined as dangerous, then the alternative program must respond to the felt need for public protection if displacement is to occur. Thus, the successful functional design of alternatives to imprisonment depends first on identifying the dominant motive for applying the prison sanction and then on responding to that motive in creating the elements of the alternative sanction.

If, as we believe, the comparative advantage of imprisonment is usually its ability to incapacitate those believed dangerous, then the critical element in the design of alternative programs will be the creation of alternative means of controlling dangerousness. Two recent programs seem to reflect this design logic. Programs of intensive supervision in probation for high-risk probationers feature extensive face-to-face contact with probation officers, drug tests, and house arrest, with or without electronic monitoring. These programs substitute a monitoring approach to the control of dangerousness for an incapacitative approach (vide Petersilia, 1987). To the extent that the controls are credible, programs of this nature can appeal as genuine alternatives to imprisonment for offenders deemed too serious for routine probation, those convicted of felonies in the middle range of seriousness and regarded as at some risk of reoffending.

A second class of alternative programs, community treatment programs designed to control drug abuse, may be regarded as an acceptable alternative to imprisonment for offenders when the greatest danger presented by the offender is seen as the continued use of drugs. Indeed, an effective drug abuse treatment program might be seen as not simply a substitute for imprisonment but rather as superior to it when prison does not produce acceptable rates of drug abstinence in the subsequent community setting.

Drug treatment programs, however, will be acceptable alternatives to imprisonment if the dominant reason for imprisonment is the fear of drug recidivism. If either deterrence or reprobation is the dominant rationale for incarceration, then there will be no functional fit between the reason for requiring the imprisonment of the offender and the components of the alternative program. In such cases drug treatment might meet the offender's needs but not those of the community.

Such a functional approach to the design of alternative programs suggests both a method of designing such programs and criteria for evaluating the likely success of programs already in operation and competing for correctional resources.

The problem of net displacement. Even if alternative programs succeed in diverting from prison groups of offenders who would otherwise be incarcerated, there is no guarantee that a decline in the prison population of the same magnitude as the numbers diverted would result. Making prison space available by those means may simply mean that accommodation is provided for an assortment of other types of offender. But this kind of substitution phenomenon is not necessarily a bad thing. Indeed, the benefits of the reallocation of prison space may be quite substantial. This possibility, however, represents a significant qualification in the assessment of the effectiveness of alternative programs and in the identification of the nature and magnitude of their benefits.

8.2 DECARCERATION POLICIES

There are a wide variety of policies other than alternative treatments that have been designed to reduce prison population. In this section, we examine five of the more important contemporary governmental policies aimed at reduction of prison numbers: decriminalization, executive-level amnesties and early release programs, limits on prison construction, intergovernmental incentive programs designed to reduce prison commitments, and the restructuring of sentencing power. This list, while not exhaustive, includes the major governmental policies discussed in the United States over the 1970s and 1980s.

8.2.1 Decriminalization

Since prison functions as a criminal sanction, one obvious strategy for reducing the use of imprisonment would be a reduction in the scope of the criminal law. When behaviors that lead to imprisonment are removed from the penal codes and the people who committed these behaviors are released from prison, both the number of persons in prison and the demand for prison space are reduced. While the theoretical connection between decriminalization and reduction in prison numbers is direct, the practical impact of decriminalization as a method of decarceration has been quite small in recent years, even though the pace of decriminalization, particularly in so-called victimless crime, has been an important feature of the recent history of the criminal law.

One reason why most decriminalization does not lead to a radical reduction in prison population is that, at the historical point when decriminalization of a particular behavior becomes politically acceptable, it is unlikely that prisons are still being filled with those convicted of the offense. The same social and political forces that push toward decriminalization usually reduce the share of a prison population committed for the candidate offense many years before formal decriminalization occurs.

This pattern is confirmed by a review of the active candidates for decriminalization in Western industrial nations over the 1970s and 1980s. Most prominently discussed have been commercialized sex and various other sexual behaviors, pornography, gambling, public drunkenness, and vagrancy. Many offenses in these categories generate substantial arrest records and produce multiple impacts on the criminal justice system. Their contribution to the overloading of police resources and the courts may be considerable, but their present contribution to prison populations in the United States is inconsequential. The very forces that make them candidates for decriminalization have already downgraded the social evaluation of the harm associated with the conduct and thus reduced prison admissions.

There is, however, one striking exception to this pattern in the contemporary dialogue about decriminalization. Drugs are simultaneously an important part of the debate about decriminalization and a major contributor to prison population in the state and federal systems in the

United States. It is in the area of drug control that claims are made that a significant decarcerative impact would be achieved if decriminalization policies were pursued.

One way of obtaining perspective on the issues involved in decriminalization of drugs and decarceration is to examine the best historical precedent in the United States for the likely impact of major decriminalization in the drug control area. That precedent is the oft-invoked period of alcohol prohibition, in this case the impact of the repeal of Prohibition on prison population. A brief review of available statistics from that period suggests that the issue is not as clear-cut as many have imagined.

The repeal of the National Prohibition Act of 1920 (the Volstead Act) in 1933 provides something of a test case for the impact of drug decriminalization. The passage of that act had resulted in a large increase in the number of prisoners received in federal penal institutions. By the 1930s the largest group of offenders in those institutions was liquor law violators. During the year 1932, when the enforcement of the liquor law was at its height, nearly 50 percent of those committed to a federal institution were sent there for liquor law violations (5,045 out of 10,496). This is a larger concentration than the percentage of drug cases in new federal prison referrals in the 1980s.

The repeal of Prohibition resulted in an immediate decrease in the total number of persons convicted of liquor law violations, and in 1934 the proportion of those committed to federal institutions for such violations had fallen to about 28 percent (2,208 out of 8,007). This decline did not continue, however, and by 1935 the trend had been reversed and the proportion had climbed back to 42 percent (4,615 out of 11,000). In his report for 1934–1935 the director of the Federal Bureau of Prisons, Sanford Bates, declared "[t]he relief which we expected to come from the repeal of Prohibition has not materialized."

He reported in relation to "this unexpected failure to reduce the number of liquor violators" that "penitentiary commitments for liquor are substantially the same as they were during Prohibition days." Hence, far from reducing the federal prison population, the repeal of Prohibition resulted in a "sharp increase in our federal institution population." The Bureau of Prisons had been "almost frantically attempting to secure appropriation for new institution facilities" (U.S. Department of Justice, Bureau of Prisons, 1936:1–3).

The failure of this dramatic example of decriminalization to reduce prison population and the demand for prison space was due principally to the fact that the "enforcement of other liquor law violations continued under revenue laws" (U.S. Department of Justice, Bureau of Justice Statistics, 1986c:151). This failure is, of course, directly relevant to current proposals regarding the decriminalization of the possession, use, sale, and manufacture of the so-called hard drugs, for those who support decriminalization do not advocate complete decontrol or total deregulation but the substitution of other means of control, such as administrative regulations and licensing, for our present absolute prohibitions (President's Commission, 1968:98). And such regulatory efforts would have to be, as in the case of alcohol, backed up by criminal sanctions.

The principal lesson of the repeal of the prohibition of alcohol in relation to decriminalization as a means of reducing prison population is that it is very unlikely, except possibly for a brief initial period, to achieve any significant reduction. As noted above, by 1935 the proportion of federal prisoners committed to prison for liquor law violations was at 42 percent, up to Prohibition levels again; and as a percent of the total this category continued to be high for years thereafter. In 1940 it was at 44 percent, still higher than the average for the five-year period 1929–1934, which was 43.4 percent.

There is direct relevance to the debate about drug decriminalization of the failure of the repeal of what John Kaplan called "the nation's most ambitious effort at drug control" (1970:1) to have any significant impact on prison population. It is only if prison sentences are felt inappropriate to the enforcement of regulations after repeal that substantial decarceration will occur.

8.2.2 Executive Adjustments

Some European countries have a political tradition of granting periodic amnesties or general pardons which may result in major reductions in prison population, and some U.S. states have experimented with early release programs to relieve prison crowding. There is no doubt that releasing prisoners creates an immediate decarcerative impact. The significant question is how long that effect will last and at what cost.

Two examples from foreign experience set the issue in perspective. The striking effect of these executive interventions on prison population figures for Italy over the ten-year period 1977–1986 is shown in table 8.1. Similarly in Poland, as David Greenberg has pointed out, some major reductions in prison population have occurred during the past half-century as a result of governmental amnesties, as shown in figure 8.1.

Governmental amnesties were issued in Poland in the years 1932,

TABLE 8.1 Italy: The Effect of Amnesties on
Year-End Prison Population, 1977–1986

1977	33,176
Amnesty, August 4, 1978	
1978	25,708
1979	29,058
1980	30,373
Amnesty, December 18, 1981	
1981	29,399
1982	35,043
1983	40,225
1984	42,795
1985	41,536
Amnesty, December 16, 1986	
1986	33,609

SOURCE: *Annuario Statistico Italiano,* 1977–1986.

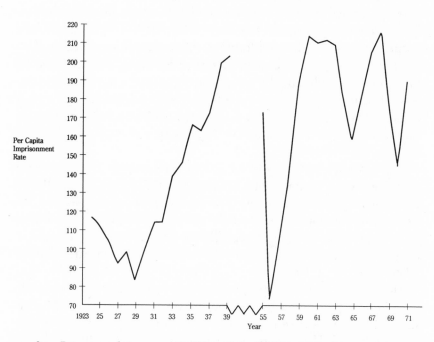

FIG. 8.1. Prison population per 100,000 in Poland, 1924–1971. (Note: information about imprisonment during the years 1940–1954 not available.) Source: Greenberg, 1980:197.

1936, 1956, 1964, and 1969. The effect of the amnesties of 1932 and 1936 on prison populations seems to have been relatively slight. The amnesties of 1956, 1964, and 1969, however, appear to have had a substantial impact, and major reductions in prison population seem to have occurred as a result of them.

Yet both in Italy and in Poland the reductions in prison population achieved by this method appear to have been short-lived. Thus, in Italy the 8,118 fall in population brought about by the 1978 amnesty is followed by two years in which the population increases by 5,315 and appears to be climbing back to the 1977 level until it is halted by the 1981 amnesty. Then the 1981 amnesty is followed the next year by an increase in population fives times greater than the fall produced by the amnesty.

In Poland the pattern is even more clearly marked. The rate of imprisonment per 100,000 falls from 172.5 in 1955 to 72 in 1956 after the amnesty but then rises to 214 by 1960. It falls again to 158 in 1965 after the 1964 amnesty, but by 1968 it has risen to 216. It falls in 1970 to 144 after the 1969 amnesty but then rises again to 191 in 1971.

In the United States the full extent of early release is unknown. The Bureau of Justice Statistics reported that in 1984 7,365 inmates were formally released early from fourteen states other than by parole (U.S. Department of Justice, Bureau of Justice Statistics, 1984). These figures, however, substantially understate the actual amount of early release, because several states use informal early release policies such as enhanced good time credits or accelerated parole board hearings in response to prison overcrowding but do not officially designate these programs as early release.

The most detailed study of the use of early release to relieve prison crowding in the United States is James Austin's report on the Illinois early release program, which he described, in 1986, as representing "the nation's most ambitious early release effort to date." Under the Illinois program, from 1980 to 1983 over 21,000 inmates, making up approximately 60 percent of all prison releases, were released early (Austin, 1986:406).

The primary object of the program was "to reduce temporarily the rate of prison population growth." Austin poses the question of what the size of the Illinois prison population would have been if early release had not existed. He answers the question by calculating the product of two figures: the number of early releases per year and the length of time reduced per released inmate. He concludes that, "[i]f the total averted prison years and the average population from 1980–1983 are pooled, the estimate is that early release reduced the population by over ten percent" (1986:447, 452).

Rigorous evaluation of such early release programs, however, would be difficult. It is, of course, a matter of simple arithmetic to multiply the number of affected offenders by the length of time sentences were reduced to arrive at an estimate of the number of prisons years avoided. But the conclusion that, had the program not existed, the prison population figures would have been 10 percent higher than were actually experienced involves an assumption that may well be mistaken.

Thus, if the early release practice is a known discount in the system, other actors may react to the discount by increasing nominal sentences through the earlier stages of the criminal justice process, so that the net effect of the early release program would be much less than appeared to be the case. It would not be the first time in the history of commerce that retail prices were raised to facilitate a later, dramatic price reduction. This is a particular problem that inevitably arises when a fixed discount operates in a system over a sustained period of time.

The relatively quick recovery of prison populations after amnesty or early release policies may understate the total decarcerative impact of a release program. If sharp upward pressure on prison populations is the motive for an administrative release, the return to pre-amnesty levels may still be significantly less than it would have been without the release program.

Another advantage of administrative release programs is that they allow the selection of offenders and do so near the end of a prison sentence, when an offender is presumably less dangerous than earlier. Even if administrative release generates no long-term savings in prison space, the turnover of space may be a policy tool of no small importance.

We suggest that the impact of administrative release programs in the United States would be highly contingent on the way in which such programs were administered. If linked with monitoring systems (which, however, increase the return rate of violators), such programs could become an important response to short-term crowding problems. But there is no evidence that such programs have promise as an independent long-term response to increasing rates of imprisonment.

8.2.3 Prison Expansion Limits

We argue in chapter 7 that the Parkinsonian hypothesis, according to which prison population always expands to fill the available prison space, is mistaken and is certainly not an invariable law. That is not to say, however, that the unavailability of prison space may not operate as a constraint upon the expansion of prison population. Indeed, at some point it will inevitably act as a constraint.

Thus, the possibility that capacity may invite population may *sometimes* be realized, but it does not invariably do so. On the other hand, the extent of the population that can be accommodated in existing buildings is *always* finite. Moreover, the refusal of federal judges to tolerate high levels of crowding may mean that the lack of prison space would impose a firm brake upon prison population.

To that extent, therefore, the policy of the National Moratorium on Prison Construction represented a rational attempt to limit prison population (National Moratorium, 1978). For even if the National Moratorium was mistaken in maintaining that additional prison capacity would inevitably generate an increased number of prisoners, there is no doubt that the capacity of existing facilities is limited and a moratorium on new prison construction would eventually stem the tide of prison commitments.

Nevertheless, what may in theory be tactically sound may also be both politically unrealistic and morally unacceptable. The moratorium policy has been criticized as being both. It is unrealistic, said James Q. Wilson, because "society clearly wishes its criminal laws more effectively enforced [and] this means rising prison populations, perhaps for a long period" (1977a:22). It is immoral, said John Conrad, because to oppose prison construction means "increased misery, violence, and murder" in prisons as they are today and "will cause inevitable suffering by men, women, and children whose consent cannot be solicited or obtained" (1977b:6, 12). On this view, the moratorium on prison construction represents the pursuit of a humane objective by immoral means.

We are not aware of detailed historical accounts of how nonconstruction has been used as a policy tool or with what effects on the conditions of incarceration in nonbuilding states. It is not clear that prison conditions vary systematically as a function of new prison construction. The decision not to build new prison space may be a policy gamble, but it does not inevitably generate crowding and substandard conditions. How important the absence of building is to stability in state prison population and how often a nonbuilding policy results in serious crowding are not currently known.

8.2.4 Intergovernmental Incentives

We noted in chapter 6 that, whereas prisons in the United States are paid for at the state level of government, prison populations are determined by the number of prisoners referred, and the length of sentences imposed, at the local level. Clearly, one means of reducing state prison population would be for the state somehow to induce local authorities to reduce commitments to state institutions. An attempt to do this was made when, in 1965, California enacted legislation empowering the state to provide subsidies to county probation departments if they reduced commitments to state adult and juvenile institutions. By 1972 three other states—Oregon, Washington, and Nevada—had adopted similar subsidy programs. But California's probation subsidy program provided the model for diverting offenders from state correctional institutions and is the only one to have been subjected to detailed critical evaluation.

California's Special Probation Supervision Subsidy Program, introduced in 1965, was described some years later as "a quiet revolution of significant proportions [that] has changed the nature of corrections" (Smith, 1972:1). It was presented as a community treatment program that would substitute for institutionalization at the state level. It was claimed that, "[a]s a result of reduced commitments, some institutions have been closed or are currently being phased out. And two new institutions have remained unopened" (Gemignani, 1972:iii).

The program was designed to encourage county probation departments to reduce their rate of commitments to state correctional agencies in return for a financial reward commensurate to the degree of reduction achieved. Funds were authorized for distribution to a county from general state revenues on condition that a county reduce its actual first commitments to state correctional facilities below its expected rate of commitments. It was estimated that the state could afford to pay the necessary subsidies out of the savings generated by receiving fewer offenders.

Paul Lerman subjected this program to the same kind of critical analysis as he had applied to the Community Treatment Project discussed earlier and made a detailed study of both the fiscal and the social costs of the scheme. A large part of Lerman's study deals with the fiscal impact of the project and with official claims of savings due to the probation subsidy. State officials had claimed that over $50 million had been saved in operating expenses, that millions of additional dollars had been saved by closing down institutions, by not using recently built units, and by deferring construction. According to Lerman, "upon close and detailed analysis none of these claims were substantiated"; on the contrary, there had been substantially increased fiscal costs at both state and county levels (1975:182–183).

Lerman acknowledged, however, that the probation subsidy did accomplish one of its principal explicit goals: the reduction of first commitments to state institutions. As he put it,

> Fewer youths and adults were institutionalized by the state from
> 1966 to 1972. Even if it is difficult to establish absolutely
> whether this would have occurred in the absence of subsidy payments, the evidence is fairly persuasive—particularly at the
> youth level—that persistent reductions in state commitments in
> the magnitude of 25 to 44 percent per year were an uncommon
> occurrence. In the presubsidy years of 1955–1965 the trendlines
> of youth commitment had been in the opposite direction. Subsidy legislation did appear to have a substantial impact not only
> in reversing this trend but in being associated with fewer initial
> commitments to the CYA. (1975:126)

In the light of this achievement it is not altogether surprising that George Saleeby, one of the architects of the program, in an article entitled "Five Years of Probation Subsidy," described it as "one of the truly amazing stories of our time" (1971:3). Yet the reduction in the commitment of persons to state institutions was not the only thing that happened during those five years, 1966–1971, for while fewer individuals were been deprived of their liberty at the state level many more were being detained at the county level.

The evidence, says Lerman, "clearly indicates that many more youth were locked up at a local level in 1970 than in 1965 or in 1960. This occurred while fewer youth were being locked up at a state level . . . the amount of local youth lock ups more than compensated for the fewer state lock ups." Using institutional days as an indicator, it appears that the net amount of statewide institutionalization when state and county figures were combined had not decreased but increased (Lerman, 1975:209).

When such unintended systemic consequences are taken into account, the California probation subsidy program seems not to have constituted a radical break with the old correctional strategy of reliance on institutionalization at all. Indeed, what Lerman calls this "highly prized example of the new correctional policy" (1975:16) did not represent a revolutionary innovation in correctional programming but rather a political and organizational restructuring which left the core of that strategy unaffected. Certainly commitments to state institutions were reduced. But a disinterested observer might well see the whole exercise as more like a sleight of hand than a novel correctional experiment. Still, if this program had occurred during a period of acute crowding at the state level, the results of the policy could be regarded as successful.

8.2.5 Restructuring Sentencing Power

Many jurisdictions, both in the United States and elsewhere, have been experiencing sharp rises in prison populations. The result has been prison overcrowding, with its attendant evils of deteriorating living conditions. If crowding is endemic and serious, the conventional palliatives offer little hope . . . Crowding can be effectively prevented only by controlling the inflow into the prisons and the length of stay there. Inflow and length of stay can be influenced through sentencing guidelines. Minnesota again provides the model. (von Hirsch, 1987b:12)

Professor von Hirsch is correct in identifying the shift toward centralized power in prison administration and release as important in controlling prison population. Insofar as the impact of commissions is concerned, however the example of Minnesota may be misleading. It is true that the establishment of a sentencing commission, an independent, expert rule-making agency to write guidelines for criminal sentencing which will regulate judge's decisions whether or not to imprison offenders, can have an influence on prison population. But as we have indicated in section 7.1.2 of the previous chapter, the nature of that influence is unlikely to be uniform in all cases.

As a matter of fact in Minnesota "the guidelines have successfully ensured that prison commitments would not exceed capacity" (Knapp, 1987:132). On the other hand, the U.S. Sentencing Commission anticipated that its guidelines would have the effect of more than doubling of the federal prison population in ten years (U.S. Sentencing Commission, 1987:71, 73). It is evident that the influence of a sentencing commission on prison inflow may be extremely variable. Why is this?

The Minnesota example is instructive. In the first place, as Michael Tonry has pointed out, "the commission chose to interpret an ambiguous statutory injunction that it take correctional resources into 'substantial consideration' as a mandate that its guidelines not increase prison populations beyond existing capacity constraints" (1987a:19). In the second place, Minnesota historically has had one of the lowest per capita rates of confinement in state prisons among American states so that the political acceptability of a firm capacity constraint would be likely to be much greater than in a state with a different tradition of punishment.

As to the first point, the sentencing commission experience in other states differs from Minnesota in a variety of ways. In Pennsylvania, for instance, the enabling statute was silent on the capacity question; as a result "some members of Pennsylvania's sentencing commission questioned that body's power to consider space availability—and the commission chose to skirt the prison-population issue in writing its guidelines" (von Hirsch, 1987a:69). In New York, the State Committee on Sentencing Guidelines "decided not to treat available prison capacity as a constraint on its policy recommendations" (Tonry, 1987a:22). In Washington state, the legislation provided that the commission should project whether its proposed guidelines exceeded available prison capacity (Washington Sentencing Reform Act, sec. 4(b)); the commission was not, however, explicitly required to ensure that its guidelines were consistent with available capacity. It is clear that differences of this nature are likely to be reflected in considerable variation in the impact of guidelines on prison population.

This brings up the second point, which is that local legal and political cultures are likely to determine both the character of the statutory directives given to sentencing commissions and the way in which the commissions interpret such directives. So that, while von Hirsch is correct in saying that when guidelines are drafted "prison overcrowding can be alleviated by regulating prison commitments and durations with capacity constraints in mind" (1987c:69), it by no means follows that all sentencing commissions will take such constraints into account.

This point about the importance of differences in the local culture and in the environments in which commissions work is well brought out by Michael Tonry. As he puts it,

> Minnesota and Washington, for example, are both relatively homogeneous states with reform traditions. In neither state were criminal justice issues highly politicized. New York and Pennsylvania, by contrast, are heterogeneous states in which criminal justice issues are highly politicized and law-and-order sentiment is powerful . . . the potential and effectiveness of a sentencing commission will depend on how it addresses and accommodates constraints imposed by the local culture. (1987a:26)

Because of differences such as these it is impossible to generalize about the effect of sentencing commissions on prison population. In a state with historically high rates of imprisonment in which law-and-order sentiment is powerful and the sentencing commission decides not to treat prison capacity as a constraint it might well be that the impact of commission guidelines will take the form of substantially increased prison commitments over existing levels, necessitating the provision of additional prison space. On the other hand, in a state with a penal reform tradition and little law-and-order pressure where the sentencing commission takes available capacity as a major factor in determining guideline severity levels it is conceivable that the implementation of guidelines might result in below-capacity prison populations.

There is, however, a further and more substantive point to be made. The use of available capacity as a measure of, and a limit on, the use of imprisonment is essentially arbitrary and unprincipled although these terms are used in a descriptive and not a pejorative sense. The question of the aggregate use of imprisonment, the question, that is, of "how much, apart from the availability of resources, the state ought to rely upon the prison sanction" (von Hirsch, 1987c:94), is ignored when the problem is treated as one of simply allocating existing prison space. The crucial importance of that question, the fundamental character of that issue, is something we deal with in the next chapter.

8.3 A NOTE ON THE VARIABILITY OF POLITICAL CONTEXT

The political setting in which reductions in imprisonment are attempted at the state level is both a fixed and a variable characteristic. The politics of "law and order" are a permanent feature of the administrative and legislative process at the state level, so that pressures against decarceration are a chronic condition in all regions of the United States at all times.

A significant variable in different states at different times may be the degree to which decreasing imprisonment rates is an important policy agenda item for influential groups in the administrative and legislative process. In one respect the history of decarceration policies discussed in this section may underestimate the potential of such policies, particularly at the administrative level. The reason for this is that the reduction or restriction of prison population has rarely been a significant priority at any level of state government outside the narrow policy confines of departments of corrections. The success of policy initiatives in Minnesota and Washington was in large part attributable to an executive branch constituency that regarded stability in prison population as desirable. By contrast, in the federal system through the mid-1980s stability in prison population was not regarded as a desideratum at any level of government including the Bureau of Prisons.

We would predict that the prospect of a decarceration policy having a significant impact on prison population would be substantially increased when decarceration had supporters throughout the administrative wing of state government, within the state legislature, and among those private and public sector lobbies that are an integral part of the state administrative and legislative process. There will always be strong countervailing pressures at every level of state and local government to contend with, but it seems likely that stability in prison population and restriction of the scale of imprisonment will be a more salient issue in many states in the 1990s than it was in the 1980s. And the same prediction can be made for the federal system as it rounds the corner from projections to the experience of substantial prison system expansion.

9 Toward a Political Economy of Imprisonment

This last chapter is designed to provide a strategic context for thinking about the scale of imprisonment. Section 9.1 shows the necessary relationship between notions about the scale of imprisonment and appropriate responses to prison crowding. Section 9.2 puts forward two modest contributions to what we call the political economy of imprisonment in the United States. In calling these analyses political economy, we have in mind Thomas Schelling's definition: "economics in a context of policy, where the policy is more than economics but the 'more' cannot be separated from the economics" (1984:vii). Section 9.3 discusses a variety of research issues that should be explored in this relatively novel subtopic of criminal justice studies. And section 9.4 sets forth some of the substantive findings of this study.

9.1 THE ISSUE BEHIND THE PROBLEM

There is no doubt that prison crowding is a serious problem in several American states and a substantial one in most American states and the federal system. This is true however crowding is measured and taking account of all the qualifications necessary when dealing with ambiguous and value-laden categories. Not only are very many American prisons crowded but the problem has intensified from year to year.

The problem of prison crowding is a peculiar one in that it admits of two opposite but logically equivalent solutions. If there are too many prisoners for existing prison facilities, the difficulty can be addressed by either reducing the number of prisoners or increasing the available facilities. For those with a single-minded concern about crowding it should be a matter of indifference which solution is chosen. This holds because a concern with crowding is not necessarily connected with any particular belief about the proper number to be imprisoned or the proper number of prison spaces that should be available. It is only the ratio that counts.

What we call the issue behind the problem is that of correctional scale. It arises whenever choices have to be made between reducing the number of prisoners and increasing the number of prison spaces. Here the decision maker's belief as to the appropriate level of imprisonment in a particular jurisdiction will prove decisive.

In our experience most participants in policy debates about prison crowding have a strong preference for one of these two remedies for crowding to the detriment of the other. And in the ideological division which is pervasive in the field of crime control, conservatives favor the construction of more prisons while liberals favor policies designed to reduce the number of prisoners. So implicit assumptions about the appropriate scale of imprisonment have played a major role in policy debates about prison construction. However, explicit references to the appropriate scale of the prison enterprise or to the criteria that should inform judgment on that matter are quite rare.

Commonly liberals appear to infer from the fact that prisons are crowded that there are too many persons in prisons. Conservatives, on the other hand, seem to infer from the same factual base that prison cells are in insufficient supply. Parties to this kind of dispute may well not even be aware of the significance of the assumptions about the scale of imprisonment which are implicit in the policies they endorse or reject. Because these assumptions about scale are implicit rather than explicit in contemporary dialogue, there is little to suggest how decisions about an appropriate penal scale might be derived. The dominant tone of the debate is the expression of strong feelings rather than the statement of particular value premises.

In fact, there are two aspects of the issue of penal scale in the late twentieth-century context that make it a very problematic subject for political debate. In the first place, what separates even the most extreme positions in debate about penal scale is not a clear-cut policy cleavage over the treatment of criminal offenders but rather a question of emphasis. Thus, when David Downes compared Great Britain, with its high and still rising prison population, with the Netherlands, which had achieved the most sustained decarceration of the post–World War II era, he found that, while 14 percent of British criminal cases resulted in prison terms, in the Netherlands the figure was 8.5 percent (1988:51).

Obviously in both countries there are a large number of possible responses to criminal cases and substantial discretion is associated with decisions in both criminal justice systems. Equally obviously this marginal difference in sentencing practice makes for a substantial difference in the size of the two prison populations. But a difference between 14 percent and 8.5 percent in prison terms imposed is an inconvenient subject for translation into the language of political values. Indeed, it is scarcely possible to accommodate this difference in the traditional terms of debate about penal policy.

Thus, punishment hardliners can far more easily call for the imprisonment of all felons or all serious offenders than defend a system that produces imprisonment for 14 percent of all criminal cases. Liberals by contrast are more likely to propagate a misleading impression of the proportion of offenders sent to prison than to assert in a public forum that 14 percent is too high. So it is much easier for conservatives to defend a presumptive imprisonment regime that does not exist and for liberals to attack it as if it did than it is for either party to conduct a principled debate within the statistical field of choice that exists for imprisonment policy in the United States.

It should be added that the statistical marginality of imprisonment as a criminal justice policy holds as well in the United States as in Europe. While the proportion of felony convictions leading to imprisonment increased through the 1980s, it nowhere represented a majority of criminal convictions on felony charges. Texas, with one of the highest rates of imprisonment in America, also reports one of the highest rates of felony probation.

A second difficulty that inhibits dialogue about the proper scale of imprisonment is that intuitions about an appropriate scale may derive from very different foundations. Moreover, parties to the debate on this subject are rarely attuned to their own premises on the matter, let alone those of the other side. We have found it helpful to distinguish between supply-based and demand-based foundations for judgments about scale. A supply-based theory of appropriate imprisonment scale derives its conception of the number of prisoners a system should accommodate by making a judgment about how many prisoners existing facilities should be permitted to hold. On this basis, crowded conditions at any given time are evidence that too many prisoners are being held. However, if new prison facilities are constructed, supply-based notions of scale are adjusted upward in parallel with the increase in capacity.

A demand-based theory of appropriate scale begins with questions about the special function of imprisonment as a criminal sanction and the types of offender who should go to prison. The supply of prison space is not the independent variable but is always a dependent variable—changing over time with the nature of the population at risk.

The supply-based approach is closest in its intellectual roots to the theory of the constancy of imprisonment discussed in chapter 1, while the demand-based approach is closer to the prescriptive programs dealt with in chapter 4. On occasion, the demand-based and supply-based approaches may be mixed either deliberately or inadvertently. An example of such a mixed approach may be found in Sherman and Hawkins's *Imprisonment in America: Choosing the Future* (1981). In that work, a sentencing scheme that specified relatively heavy sentences for a particular classification of violent offender was also advocated on the ground that such a policy could be implemented without exceeding the then-current prison capacity in 1980 (1981:99–122). As is usual in the advocacy of such a mixed approach, the Sherman and Hawkins scheme did not indicate whether a demand or a supply perspective should dominate if the number of prisoners called for in their demand criteria should come to exceed existing capacity.

The supply-based/demand-based dichotomy is not coterminous with the contrast between liberal and conservative policies. A supply-based perspective is far too unrestrictive for liberals in permitting the maintenance of large prison populations in periods of relative stability or periods of decline in rates of imprisonment, such as occurred in the United States in the early 1970s. Demand-based presumptions regarding optimal prison population can mean the provision of too few prison cells if highly restrictive criteria are used and stringently applied. Thus, the National Council on Crime and Delinquency (NCCD) in 1972 argued that only "dangerous" offenders should be imprisoned, and by its standard of dangerousness only small percentages of those in prison really required incarceration. "In any state," the NCCD declared, "no more than one hundred prisoners would have to be confined in a single maximum security institution" (NCCD, 1972:332). This type of demand-based assessment would not find sympathy among crime control conservatives, who subscribe to a very different theory of how much prison space is required.

In theory a demand-based approach to the optimal scale of imprisonment is the only principled approach to the criminal law of imprisonment. Yet one cannot derive prescriptive statements about the number of persons who should be confined in prison from sentencing principles that make a sentence of imprisonment one choice among many upon conviction for crime.

Perhaps the most useful feature of the distinction between supply-based and demand-based analysis is that it reflects the antithesis between pragmatists and theorists rather than that between liberals and conservatives. A demand-based analysis of the scale of imprisonment calls for a sense of the purpose of the prison and of the sufficient conditions for its use that is far more specific than anything in the current jurisprudence of criminal law.

In the United States a supply-based analysis of appropriate imprisonment scale in any jurisdiction has the signal virtue of providing a determinable benchmark. The capacity that New Jersey should have is a function of the prison capacity (however defined) that New Jersey does have. The problem is that the benchmark varies so dramatically from state to state that it is impossible even to pretend that the capacity of a state prison system at any given time is the outcome of a rational decision-making process.

While we suspect that any confrontation between a supply-based and demand-based conception of scale would rehearse many of the themes outlined above, we do not know this, because discussion of different approaches to the issue of appropriate scale is infrequent and episodic. This is unfortunate because decisions about the appropriate scale of the prison enterprise are a basic requirement for the resolution of any crowding condition regarded as problematic.

The question of penal scale is a significant one at any time in the operation of a prison system. But it can remain in a state of latency for extended periods of time only as long as choices between prison construction and decarceration need not be faced. However, when prison populations reach the level at which prison crowding is seen as a problem, explicit or implicit decisions about the appropriate scale of imprisonment cannot be avoided. In the United States of the 1990s, almost every jurisdiction seems at, or close to, that point.

9.2 Two Economic Excursions

In calling for a political economy of imprisonment, we do not mean to imply that either economic analysis or the economist's perspective possesses any unique problem-solving properties. We do think, however, that the economist's perspective can, as economist Thomas Schelling put it, sometimes "bring a little insight that . . . helps in finding a solution or in facing an issue" (1984:vii). In particular, it can prove helpful in the restatement of problems and it can illuminate key variables in the policy analysis of correctional problems. In this section, we attempt to restate in simple economic terms questions about the relationship between prison capacity and prison population, and some aspects of the current intergovernmental distribution of authority regarding prison population.

9.2.1 Is Crowding Equilibrium?

Assume for the moment that a single policy actor or a coordinated governmental office makes decisions both on whether additional prison facilities should be provided and on the number of convicted offenders to be sent to prison. For purposes of exposition, also assume that the definition of crowding is external to this actor, so that the point at which the choice has to be made between providing more prison capacity or turning away prospective prisoners is for him arbitrary.

For this decision maker the marginal cost of the first additional prisoner for whom new prison space must be provided is quite large and considerably greater than the marginal cost of committing the last prisoner who can be accommodated within existing state capital imprisonment resources. This sharp discontinuity in marginal cost would usually create circumstances in which the decision maker would pause before committing the necessary resources for new prison construction. There might also be a tendency to fill existing prison capacity to the point just before additional capital investment was required.

Is this set of commonplace propositions the equivalent of asserting that the existence of prison capacity automatically leads to levels of imprisonment that fill that capacity? Our answer is that it is not. In the first place, as long as the marginal costs of extra prisoners are not zero the rational decision maker may not wish to fill existing space. The decision maker may judge that the marginal benefit of additional imprisonment however measured is not worth the marginal cost of the additional prison commitment.

However, there is one set of circumstances where prison capacity and prison population are closely and positively related. When the decision-making body wishes to incur the substantial capital cost of providing new prison capacity, that decision reflects a judgment that more prison capacity is needed in that the expected benefits will outweigh the substantial capital investment required. If the decision to build more prison space was rational when made, then the tendency to fill it will be pronounced in the short term.

But time passes and circumstances change, and there is no inevitable pressure to keep prisons full. The capital costs of additional prison space are not the only constraint on the use of imprisonment; the noncapital costs of imprisonment may prove substantial enough to limit prison population.

This mode of analysis has three tactical implications for participants in the debate about the scale of imprisonment. First, the provision of additional capacity is a significant step in the determination of public policy regarding prison population, and opposition to prison construction is a rational attempt to limit prison population, as was discussed in the previous chapter.

Second, the economic perspective indicates that raising the costs associated with imprisonment, both fixed and variable, should be an effective way of limiting prison population. This is no more than a public choice variation of the first law of demand, which predicts that at a higher price a smaller quantity of any commodity will be consumed. In fact, it provides an illuminating way of reconceptualizing some of the aims of those using the federal courts to impose minimum standards on prison authorities that raise the effective cost per prisoner of incarceration.

The third point is that the rational operation of the system outlined in this section depends on the agency that is to incur the cost of imprisonment also having the power to determine the extent of imprisonment. Violation of this assumption can result in patterns of imprisonment that are anything but cost-effective across all levels of government. Yet the current distribution of prosecutorial, sentencing, and correctional authority in all states violates that assumption to an exorbitant degree. This introduces the second set of issues that we think arise when the problem is looked at from the viewpoint of the economist.

9.2.2 The Correctional Free Lunch

When Chicago school economists announce "there is no such thing as a free lunch," they are not denying the possibility of hospitality but merely pointing out that someone has to pay the bill when scarce resources are consumed (Lederer, 1989). The guest on such an occasion may order as though lunch was free, as indeed it is for him, but someone else has to pay the check. And the heedless ordering of a perpetual lunch guest will result in the misallocation of resources.

The parable of the free lunch is relevant to the discussion of prison population because prisons in the United States are, as we noted in chapter 6, paid for at the state level of government out of state correctional budgets, but prison populations are determined by the number of prisoners referred by local officials and the lengths of sentences imposed at the local level. Since localities do not contribute to central state correctional budgets, the marginal cost of an extra prisoner may be zero at the local level of government, where the decision to confine is made.

Thus, a perceived marginal benefit from imprisonment in excess of zero is likely to result in a decision to imprison, even though the total marginal cost to all levels of government far exceeds the perceived benefit of imprisonment. This is the phenomenon of the correctional free lunch.

This kind of misallocation of resources is liable to occur whenever the unit of government that makes decisions about prison population is separate and distinct from that which pays the cost involved in imprisonment. To the extent that this free lunch pattern misdirects resources into additional imprisonment, there are two ways of correcting this problem. The system can be restructured to centralize the power to make decisions about prison commitment and prison sentences; or the system can be restructured so that the cost consequences of imprisonment are in some fashion decentralized. Popular models of correctional reform can be thought of as representing attempts to restructure along both these lines.

Thus, creating a sentencing commission to displace or delimit the discretion of local judges by means of sentencing guidelines is an attempt to centralize authority over one major determinant of prison population and hold some power at the same level of government that pays the cost of imprisonment. The attempt to institute what were called probation subsidies in California was an effort to decentralize sensitivity to the cost consequences of additional imprisonment by offering monetary incentives to local government to restrict the commitment of offenders to state prisons. Much the same effect would be achieved if the state government were to surcharge units of local government for additional offenders referred to state prisons, but we know of no American jurisdiction where this has been seriously proposed or considered.

Viewed from this perspective, some recent sentencing reforms seem more likely to exacerbate than to correct the problem of the correctional free lunch. Under indeterminate sentence regimes, while local governments made decisions about how many offenders were sent to prison, a centralized unit of state government could decide how long each prisoner stayed in prison and in this way exercise some authority over the size of the state prison population. Eliminating or reducing the power of parole boards over the release of prisoners removed a significant means of controlling prison population from that level of government responsible for the cost of the prison system.

It is difficult to determine how important the phenomenon of the correctional free lunch has been in relation to the great expansion of prison population that has taken place over the years 1975–1990. The kind of perverse distribution of power and responsibility involved goes back many years before the current upward surge in prison population and was in place during past periods of both stability and decrease in rates of imprisonment. So it is clear that free lunch arrangements cannot be a sufficient condition of contemporary pressure on prison population.

Yet there is circumstantial evidence implicating such arrangements as a contributory cause of the present increase in the scale of imprisonment. There are, first, the high rates of imprisonment among American states when subjected to the inexact but inevitable comparison with other Western nations. This should be regarded as weak independent evidence because of all the other differences between U.S. states and other Western nations.

There is, second, an interesting contrast between fluctuations in prison population and fluctuations in jail population that provides a stronger indictment of the free lunch as a contributory cause of state prison population expansion. Local criminal justice officials make commitment decisions that regulate the population of local jails, but the cost of jailing is borne substantially and often exclusively by the local governments. During the period 1970–1987, when state prison populations increased from 196,000 to 562,000, or 192 percent, the increase in local jail populations was 83 percent, or less than half the rate of increase in prison populations (see U.S. Department of Justice, Bureau of Justice Statistics, 1988a). It might be asserted that this difference was merely coincidental, but that is a proposition that an economist would view with extreme skepticism.

Two further aspects of the correctional free lunch deserve emphasis. First, there is the relatively powerless and passive position of state government as a whole, and more particularly of state prison administrators. The director of a state prison system is a person who has no control over the number of persons placed in his custody, over whom they are or over how long they stay. Budgetary constraints on supply are imposed by the legislative branch at the state level of government, and the demand for the service the state prison director provides (a demand he *must* meet) is determined by local officials totally outside his sphere of influence.

Possessing power over neither the supply of prison space nor the demand for that space, it is his task to ensure that the two are always in harmonious balance. To hold him responsible for failure in these circumstances is as unwarranted as it would be to hold the weatherman responsible for a snowstorm he accurately predicts.

Under these circumstances, correctional administrators may have much to gain when they can convince a public and legislative constituency that their institutions are under crowded conditions. Those who run prisons can speak with some authority on conditions of confinement and in particular on what constitutes crowding. They are in a unique position when it comes to defining minimum standards. And they may be able to regain some power over the prison system by putting forward credible claims that no more than x prisoners can be accommodated until y prison space is constructed.

One of the developments that has lent credibility and force to such claims in the United States of the 1980s was the willingness of the federal courts to listen to lawsuits about prison conditions and minimum standards of correctional confinement. As we suggested in chapter 6, correctional administrators may have much to gain by being a party to lawsuits relating to prison practices and conditions. The power over the administration of prisons which is being assumed by the federal courts is not that of the correctional administrator, which is minimal, but that of prosecutors, judges, and legislators. And since the definition of crowding and the generation of minimum standards are seen as matters on which correctional professionals possess the necessary expertise, litigation regarding prison conditions may result in an accession of power to them.

The limits of the free lunch analysis. A literal interpretation of free lunch analysis proves too much in that it implies that the demand for prison space would be invariably incessant. That this has not been a permanent feature of twentieth-century experience suggests significant limits on an account of the political economy of imprisonment that defines units of local government simply as consumers of prison space considered as a costless commodity.

One reason for the inadequacy of this oversimplified analysis is that units of government are not individual organisms that regard prison space as a commodity. Local decision makers such as prosecutors and judges each have their own individual views of the value of imprisonment. And in the case of the judiciary those views might very well be not only complex but also sensitive to governmental costs. Those who hold power in local government are also citizens of the state government.

Another important point to note is that those responsible for making decisions about imprisonment do not necessarily regard the monetary cost of prison space as the only negative aspect of committing offenders to prison. Local decision makers who also deal on a personal level with criminal offenders are not unaware of the human costs of imprisonment. And they frequently acknowledge the influence of such nonpecuniary considerations on their actions.

We suspect also that the lack of a formal cost-accounting arrangement does not mean that there is no way in which local government can be held accountable for prison commitments. To resort again to the language of public choice, there is a strong incentive present at the state level to discourage the unlimited use of imprisonment. It seems likely that those at the center of state government have some influence in these matters on local officials.

In the aggregate those qualifications on the force of the free lunch analysis are of considerable significance. They do not, however, detract from the importance of the central point which that analysis makes. It would be foolish to ignore the evident limits of a simple public choice explanation relating to the use of imprisonment. At the same time, it would be irrational to ignore altogether its relevance to the explanation of patterns of imprisonment.

What is required here is empirical and theoretical work which will both complicate and enrich the public choice model with special reference to decisions about imprisonment. At present the index of the *Journal of Political Economy* lacks any reference to articles on the determinants of the scale of imprisonment. Credible contextual studies of the political economy of imprisonment will be both difficult and complex. But the investment of the necessary effort and resources in a balanced program of research into the determinants of the scale of imprisonment promises a return of more than merely academic or theoretical interest.

9.3 ELEMENTS OF A RESEARCH AGENDA

We reach the end of this preliminary inquiry with significant questions whose answers are shrouded in mystery. Are the forces that determine the scale of imprisonment over time the same as those that explain cross-sectional differences in the use of imprisonment? Why do large numbers of political entities exercising independent power tend to move in the same direction at the same time? Are there cycles analogous to the business cycle or the demographic cycle that underlie or influence fluctuations in rates of imprisonment? And if so, why?

Writing near the beginning of a sequence of studies, we believe it is important that attention be paid to the methods of study available and to the degree of rigor we can expect from empirical soundings in imprisonment policy. We begin with a discouraging word. Controlled experiment is not available as a method of investigation when the unit of analysis is a political state. While some of the effects of changes in imprisonment policy might be studied experimentally, penal policies themselves can only be studied as they naturally occur. We have to rely on the normal processes of social and political change to provide opportunities to investigate nonexperimentally the nature, incidence, and impact of such changes.

We discuss here three different types of research that can contribute to a balanced agenda of research on the scale of imprisonment: investigation of general variations in levels of imprisonment in the United States; comparative studies of policy and experience in selected U.S. states and in other Western industrial countries; and detailed studies that focus on the origin and impact of discrete changes in imprisonment policy. This emphasis is not a denial of the value of other sorts of research but only a plea for inclusion.

9.3.1 Variations in Levels of Imprisonment

Much needs to be known about the variations in levels of imprisonment over time and cross-sectionally in order to place recent movements in rates of imprisonment in the United States in an appropriate context. How extensive has the growth of imprisonment been in the 1970s and 1980s, and is there historical precedent for this degree of expansion? Are there discernible cycles in the past experience of American states, and, if so, how long is growth sustained? What usually follows the expansion phase in a correctional population cycle if there are in fact such cycles? Are there leading indicators of changes of trend to be discovered in the past history of prison population movement?

As the second decade of extraordinary growth in correctional populations comes to a close, we may be coming close to a shift in trend that would be of substantial value for the study of the range of variation in levels of imprisonment in the United States. An uninterrupted upward movement in prison population provides a far from ideal set of conditions for the investigation of the forces that determine rates of imprisonment, just as an uninterrupted stock market boom provides inadequate information for the historical study of the determinants of the movement of prices quoted on stocks and bonds.

The most informative studies of general variations in levels of imprisonment will separately analyze data from states and regions of America in the style of the analysis presented in chapter 6 rather than aggregating those values into a single national figure in the style of chapter 5. We also hope to see three further types of data dealt with in future studies.

First, it will be desirable to have a long-term time series of annual imprisonment figures for each state. Second, jail population figures will be required both to add to prison population for some analytic purposes and also for contrast. Jails in the United States are both alternatives and supplements to prison. They also hold discrete populations not at risk of imprisonment. There is no doubt that analysis of state-level problems of incarceration will be the richer for the inclusion of jail data, although this addition will frequently not be possible.

A third data set that might prove valuable would provide trends in rates of institutional confinement across the range of public facilities removing citizens from the community to settings of custodial security. For most of the twentieth century, state governments confined as large a number of citizens in public mental hospitals as in prisons. And local jails accommodate large numbers of persons at risk of both kinds of institutional commitment. In recent decades public mental hospital confinement rates have declined substantially, and this could have had two kinds of influence on rates of imprisonment. Deinstitutionalization in the mental health system may have put increasing pressure on prisons by increasing the number of high-risk persons in community settings. At the same time, the reduction in resources required for the confinement of other populations may have produced greater willingness on the part of state governments to expand prison population.

A cursory review of recent trends provides more support for the second hypothesis than for the first. Most of the population traditionally confined in state mental hospitals does not resemble in demography or behavior the groups most substantially at risk of imprisonment. The socially inadequate, mentally deficient, psychotically disordered, and disoriented geriatric citizens who make up the flotsam and jetsam returned to the community by deinstitutionalization have far more impact on local jails than on prison populations. But the notion that a decline in the level of resources committed to the custodial care of the population might increase willingness to devote more resources to the confinement of convicted offenders in prison is a hypothesis which merits sustained investigation.

9.3.2 Comparative Studies

The kinds of study referred to in the section 9.3.1 involve simultaneous analysis of fifty states in a statistical search for significant patterns in imprisonment policy. There is also substantial value in comparative studies that focus on a small number of political jurisdictions over time in an effort to illuminate the evolution and impact of penal policy. In the United States this approach might involve paying special attention to those jurisdictions with metropolitan populations that have recently experienced much less growth in prison population than the average. It might also be useful to compare otherwise similar jurisdictions with different imprisonment trends to discover what could account for any differences in policy and for the impact of those policies on prison population.

Less formal comparative studies might involve a more extensive international sample of jurisdictions. The nations of Western Europe have proved fertile ground for students of comparative government. The experience with prison population management of other Western democracies might provide examples of practices which could be evaluated in their native setting and considered as candidates for transplantation. Furthermore, historical statistics on rates of imprisonment in individual foreign countries could be used in investigating the possibility of cycles in correctional population trends.

9.3.3 Policy Studies

The third kind of research that will be needed is a series of detailed policy studies dealing with situations in which the precursory circumstances and the impact of particular policy changes are the primary focus of attention. Such studies would be much more specific in their focus than the examination of state or national experience over time. And they would not rely on aggregate statistics as a basis for inference, as do multistate studies of variations in levels of imprisonment. One way of demonstrating some dimensions of such studies is to provide examples of the kind of topics that could be pursued by these methods together with reasons why inquiries depending on aggregate statistics are inadequate.

There are a variety of reasons why microlevel studies of prison construction policies and programs in several different jurisdictions would be of value. In the first place, it is necessary to investigate where the demand for expanded prison capacity originated; how long a lead time there was between the adoption of plans for new construction and the availability of the increased prison space; and what impact both the short- and mid-term availability of new prison facilities had on aggregate prison population.

Without this kind of detail, there is no way to tell, when expanded capacity is followed by the expansion of prison population, whether the expansion of prison plant is an independent cause of higher levels of imprisonment or whether it is itself the result of the same set of conditions that are causing prison populations to expand. Of interest also in this connection would be an investigation of what happens after serious proposals for the expansion of prison capacity are rejected. Studies of this kind represent the best hope of disentangling the kind of third-cause conundrums generated by the statistics on construction and prison population discussed in chapter 7.

A second topic worthy of detailed policy studies relates to the scale of imprisonment as a political issue in American state governments. What Professor Jacobs calls "the politics of prison expansion" is something about which, he says, "we know very little" (1983–1984:209), in large part because it has long been ignored both by political scientists and by criminologists specializing in corrections.

Yet another group of detailed policy studies should focus on experimental programs designed to reduce population pressures. If, as seems likely, there will be a second generation of attempts to create programs designed to reduce prison population, rigorous evaluation of program impact should be a precondition of public funding.

Particularly useful would be an assessment of what we have called functionally designed alternative treatment programs and in particular the comparative assessment of alternative treatment programs and nontreatment-oriented decarceration policies, such as nonconstruction and the restructuring of economic incentives, for even if functionally designed alternative treatment regimes can reduce prison populations it is not clear that they can do so in a cost-effective way.

Our final example of useful policy evaluation research may reflect a bias deriving from our own background in legal studies. But it is undeniable that an important element in the design of systems to control prison population is the applicable criminal law, in particular, the criminal law of sentencing. On occasion, relatively simple legal revision would seem to be a promising means of coping with prison population pressures.

Thus, when California finds that drug testing increases the proportion of individuals returned to prison while under parole supervision, one way to reduce the prison population pressure generated by this new policy would be to subtract the expected years of prison time involved in parole revocation from the initial determinate sentence. If this were done, the initial term served by all offenders would be somewhat shorter because of the anticipated parole revocation prison time. By redistributing prison bed space from parolees who do not fail drug tests (who are released earlier and stay out) to parolees who fail drug tests (who are released earlier but returned), this program might also make more effective use of prison space as an instrument of incapacitation. This is only one example of how the substantive criminal law might be used in experiments designed to produce a better fit between available prison resources and the aims of the criminal law.

The need for empirical evaluation of such experiments is so obvious that insistence on the necessity for it may appear to be trite and redundant. But the absence of such policy studies during a period of substantial social and political change is one of the most striking features of the 1970s and 1980s in the United States so that emphasis on the importance and value of research in this area seems justified.

9.4 Some Conclusions

It may be helpful to rehearse some of the findings of this study in order to provide a context for further research on the scale of imprisonment.

In the first instance, it seems clear that levels of imprisonment in the United States vary widely both over time and from state to state. It is evident also that these variations are largely independent of variations in either crime rates or the provisions of penal codes.

Second, as seen in chapter 6, trends in rates of imprisonment over the period 1960–1990 have been much broader than the boundaries of political responsibility for imprisonment policy. Imprisonment policy decisions are made by state and local governments. But prison population has trended initially downward in the 1960s and then upward in the 1970s and 1980s on a national scale. We do not know whether the homogenization of American society is creating more uniform conditions of influence on imprisonment trends. We cannot determine this in part because we do not know what the social forces that produce changes in levels of imprisonment are.

Third, the evidence that interstate and interregional differences in rates of imprisonment may have been evening out over the past few decades is equivocal. A proponent of the evening-out hypothesis would point out that the percentage gains in prison population in the high-imprisonment states over the 1970s and 1980s are smaller than the percentage gains experienced in regions with smaller base levels of incarceration. But the absolute growth in the rate of imprisonment per 100,000 of population has been as great in high-imprisonment regions such as the South as in the low-imprisonment states of the Northeast. If a person three feet, two inches tall and a person six feet, four inches tall both grow an inch in height, the shorter man's growth rate is twice that of the taller man. But the shorter man is no closer to parity at the end of that growth cycle than at the beginning. This is approximately the situation with respect to rates of imprisonment in the United States as we head into the 1990s.

The lesson of chapter 5 is that there is no automatic linkage between rates of imprisonment and social indicators such as crime rates, unemployment, the age structure of the population, and trends in drug arrests. Using rates of imprisonment for the United States as a whole, none of these factors is a strong explanation of rates of imprisonment since 1950.

Nor have specific legislative programs played a major role in producing the significant upturn in imprisonment in the United States since the early 1970s, as discussed in chapter 7. New punitive emphasis on offenses involving drugs and sexual exploitation has contributed to increased rates of imprisonment, and changes in specific laws and the structure of sentencing have been associated with rising rates of incarceration. But these legislative acts are probably more reactions to the same forces that are increasing rates of imprisonment than they are independent causes of the increase.

If legislative programs have not played a significant part in the recent increase in rates of imprisonment, there is also little evidence that such programs have had a major influence in moderating the growth of prison populations. Nonprison treatment programs rarely displace prison as a criminal sanction. A variety of other techniques ranging from early release programs to restructuring have the potential to reduce prison populations, but few such programs had significant impact during the 1980s.

One reason for the muted impact of decarceration policies in recent years is that reducing prison populations was not a significant political priority in most states during the 1980s. State departments of corrections, where prison population is an important issue, are not a power center in state government. If the reduction of prison populations were to become a more widely adopted goal, some of the devices designed for this purpose might have a more significant impact.

There seem to be incentives toward crowding and toward overconfinement in the cost structure of imprisonment and in the current allocation of fiscal responsibility for prisons to levels of government that do not decide on levels of imprisonment.

Amidst these general conclusions, two significant elements of the 1990s as a historical moment deserve special emphasis. The first of these is the sense of the scale of imprisonment as a phenomenon subject to significant variation over the short term. While the variations in rates of imprisonment between jurisdictions and over long periods of time have been acknowledged, the confirmation of wide variations of rate over short time periods has captured fresh attention. Variations in imprisonment scale could usually be attributed to fundamental differences in the character of a society over long time periods or significant differences in society or government among a cross-section of jurisdictions with divergent rates of imprisonment. When a number of American states double prison populations within a decade without experiencing fundamental change in social or governmental character, a sense of this variability of rates of imprisonment will produce more interest in social sciences in examining variations in rates of confinement.

In this connection, the contrast between what we have called supplybased versus what we have called demand-based approaches to levels of imprisonment is sharply drawn. The arbitrary quality of supply-based accounts of scale of imprisonment is much more evident during periods when political decisions will be taken that have lasting impact on prison facilities.

The absence of a principled basis for determining the appropriate scale of imprisonment is thus never more apparent than during rapid and unplanned changes. Fundamental questions about the size of the prison system come quickly to the surface of debates about crowding or construction. Thus, whatever else might be said about imprisonment during the 1980s, the swift changes in rates of imprisonment have had a definite and salutary effect on scholarly interest in the rate of imprisonment in American democracy.

References

American Assembly. 1973. *Prisoners in America*. New York: American Assembly, Columbia University.

American Civil Liberties Foundation. 1986. *Status Report—The Courts and Prisons*. Mimeo. National Prison Project.

American Friends Service Committee. 1971. *Struggle for Justice: A Report on Crime and Punishment in America*. New York: Hill & Wang.

Ancel, Marc. 1971. *Suspended Sentence*. London: Heinemann.

Anderson, Kurt. 1982. "What Are Prisons For?" *Time*, September 13, 1982, pp. 38–41.

Austin, James. 1986. "Using Early Release to Relieve Prison Crowding." *Crime and Delinquency* 32:404–502.

Austin, James, and Barry Krisberg. 1982. "The Unmet Promise of Alternatives to Incarceration." *Crime and Delinquency* 28:374–409.

Barnes, Harry Elmer, and Negley K. Teeters. 1943. *New Horizons in Criminology*. New York: Prentice-Hall.

Barnett, Arnold. 1987. "Prison Population: A Projection Model." *Operations Research* 35(1):18–34.

Beaumont, Gustave de, and Alexis de Tocqueville. 1964. Trans. Francis Lieber. *On the Penitentiary System in the United States and Its Application in France*. Carbondale: Southern Illinois University Press.

Beccaria, Cesare. [1764] 1963. Trans. H. Paolucci. *On Crimes and Punishments*. Indianapolis: Bobbs-Merrill.

Becker, Gary S. 1968. "Crime and Punishment: An Economic Approach." *Journal of Political Economy* 76:169–217.

Bentham, Jeremy. 1791. "Panopticon; or, The Inspection House." In J. Bowring, ed., *Works*, vol. 4, pp. 37–172. London: Simpkin, Marshall & Co.

———. 1802a. "Panopticon versus New South Wales." In J. Bowring, ed., *Works*, vol. 4, pp. 173–248. London: Simpkin, Marshall & Co.

———. 1802b. "Principles of Penal Law." In J. Bowring, ed., *Works*, vol. 1, pp. 365–580. London: Simpkin, Marshall & Co. (1843–1859).

Berk, Richard A., David Rauma, Sheldon L. Messinger, and Thomas F. Cooley. 1981. "A Test of the Stability of Punishment Hypothesis: The Case of California, 1851–1970." *American Sociological Review* 46:805–829.

Bishop, Norman. 1988. *Non-Custodial Alternatives in Europe*. Helsinki: Institute for Crime Prevention and Control.

Bittner, Egon. 1974. "Florence Nightingale in Pursuit of Willie Sutton: A Theory of the Police." In Herbert Jacobs, ed., *The Potential for the Reform of Criminal Justice*, pp. 17–44. Beverly Hills, CA: Sage Publications.

————. 1982. "Emerging Police Issues." In Bernard L. Garmire, ed., *Local Government*, pp. 1–12. Washington: International City Management Association.

Blumstein, Alfred. 1982. "On the Racial Disproportionality of United States' Prison Populations." *Journal of Criminal Law and Criminology* 73: 1259–1281.

————. 1988. "Prison Populations: A System out of Control." In Michael Tonry and Norval Morris, eds., *Crime and Justice: A Review of Research*, vol. 10. Chicago: University of Chicago Press.

Blumstein, Alfred, and Jacqueline Cohen. 1973. "A Theory of the Stability of Punishment." *Journal of Criminal Law and Criminology* 64:198–207.

Blumstein, Alfred, Jacqueline Cohen, and William Gooding. 1983. "The Influence of Capacity on Prison Population: A Critical Review of Some Recent Evidence." *Crime and Delinquency* 29:1–51.

Blumstein, Alfred, Jacqueline Cohen, Susan E. Martin, and Michael Tonry, eds. 1983. *Research on Sentencing: The Search for Reform*, vol. 1. Washington: National Academy of Sciences.

Blumstein, Alfred, Jacqueline Cohen, Soumyo Moitra, and Daniel Nagin. 1981. "On Testing the Stability of Punishment Hypothesis: A Reply." *Journal of Criminal Law and Criminology* 72(4):1799–1808.

Blumstein, Alfred, Jacqueline Cohen, and Daniel Nagin. 1976. "The Dynamics of a Homeostatic Punishment Process." *Journal of Criminal Law and Criminology* 67:317–334.

Blumstein, Alfred, Jacqueline Cohen, Jeffrey A. Roth, and Christy A. Visher, eds. 1986. *Criminal Careers and "Career Criminals,"* vols. 1 and 2. Washington: National Academy Press.

Blumstein, Alfred, and Soumyo Moitra. 1979. "An Analysis of Time Series of the Imprisonment Rate in the States of the United States: A Further Test of the Stability of Punishment Hypothesis." *Journal of Criminal Law and Criminology* 70:376–390.

————. 1980. "Growing or Stable Incarceration Rates: A Comment on Cahalan's 'Trends in Incarcerations Rates in the United States since 1880.'" *Crime and Delinquency* 26:91–94.

Bottomley, Keith, and Ken Pease. 1986. *Crime and Punishment: Interpreting the Data*. Philadelphia: Open University Press.

Bottoms, Anthony E. 1983. "Neglected Features of Contemporary Penal Systems." In David Garland and Peter Young, eds., *The Power to Punish: Contemporary Penality and Social Analysis*. London: Heinemann Educational Books.

————. 1987. "Limiting Prison Use: Experience in England and Wales." *Howard Journal* 26:177–202.

Braithwaite, John. 1980. "The Political Economy of Punishment." In E. L. Wheelright and Ken Buckley, eds., *Essays in the Political Economy of Australian Capitalism*, vol. 4. Sydney: ANZ Books.

Bythell, Duncan. 1980. "Book Review: Michael Ignatieff's A *Just Measure of Pain.*" *English Historical Review* 95:432–433.

Cahalan, Margaret. 1979. "Trends in Incarceration in the United States since 1880." *Crime and Delinquency* 25:9–41.

———. 1986. *Historical Corrections Statistics in the United States, 1850–1984.* U.S. Department of Justice, Bureau of Criminal Statistics, NCJ-102529. Washington: Government Printing Office.

Carter, J. A., and G. F. Cole. 1979. "The Use of Fines in England: Could the Idea Work Here?" *Judicature* 63:154–161.

Cohen, Jacqueline. 1978. "The Incapacitative Effect of Imprisonment: A Critical Review of the Literature." In Alfred Blumstein et al., eds., *Deterrence and Incapacitation: Estimating the Effects of Criminal Sanction on Crime Rates.* Washington: National Academy of Sciences.

———. 1986. "Research on Criminal Careers." Appendix B to A. Blumstein, J. Cohen, J. A. Roth, and C. A. Visher, eds., *Criminal Careers and "Career Criminals,"* vol. 1. Washington: National Academy Press.

Cohen, Stanley. 1985. *Visions of Social Control: Crime, Punishment, and Classification.* Cambridge: Polity Press.

Confer, Harold. 1975. In *Prison Construction Plans and Policy.* U.S. Congress, House Committee on the Judiciary Hearings, 94th Congress.

Conrad, John P. 1977a. "Response to Milton G. Rector." In Matthew Matlin, ed., *Should We Build More Prisons?* Hackensack, NJ: National Council on Crime and Delinquency.

———. 1977b. "Which Way to the Revolution?" In Matthew Matlin, ed., *Should We Build More Prisons?* Hackensack, NJ: National Council on Crime and Delinquency.

Cross, Rupert. 1971. *Punishment, Prison and the Public.* London: Stevens & Sons.

Downes, David. 1988. *Contrasts in Tolerance: Post-War Penal Policy in the Netherlands and England and Wales.* Oxford: Clarendon Press.

Durkheim, Emile. [1893] 1964. *The Division of Labor in Society.* New York: Free Press.

———. [1895] 1938. *The Rules of Sociological Method.* Chicago: University of Chicago Press.

———. [1900] 1973. Trans. T. A. Jones and A. T. Scull. "Two Laws of Penal Evolution." *Economy and Society* 12(3):285–308.

———. [1900] 1983. "The Evolution of Punishment." In S. Lukes and A. Scull, eds., *Durkheim and the Law.* New York: St. Martin's Press.

Ehrlich, Isaac. 1972. "The Deterrent Effect of Criminal Law Enforcement." *Journal of Legal Studies* 1:259–276.

Erikson, Kai T. 1966. *Wayward Puritans: A Study in Sociology of Deviance.* New York: Wiley.

Feinberg, Joel. 1981. "The Expressive Function of Punishment." In H. Goss and Andrew von Hirsch, eds., *Sentencing*. New York and Oxford: Oxford University Press.

Fischer, D. R. 1983. "Better Public Protection with Fewer Inmates?" *Corrections Today* (December): 16–20.

———. 1984. "Prediction and Incapacitation: Issues and Answers." Paper presented at American Society of Criminology Annual Meeting. Des Moines, IA: Statistical Analysis Center.

Fiss, Owen. 1978. *The Civil Rights Injunction*. Bloomington: Indiana University Press.

———. 1979. "The Forms of Justice." *Harvard Law Review* 93:1–58.

Florida Department of Rehabilitation, Bureau of Planning, Research, and Statistics. 1977. "Research Findings." Document No. 77-R-065. Cited in U.S. Department of Justice, National Institute of Justice. 1980. *American Prisons and Jails*, vol. 2, at 58.

Foucault, Michel. 1977. *Discipline and Punish: The Birth of the Prison*. New York: Pantheon Books.

Fox, Lionel W. 1934. *The Modern English Prison*. London: Routledge & Sons.

———. 1952. *The English Prison and Borstal Systems*. London: Routledge & Kegan Paul.

Garland, David. 1986. "Foucault's *Discipline and Punish*: An Exposition and Critique." *American Bar Foundation Research Journal*, Fall 1986, pp. 847–879.

Garland, David, and Peter Young. 1983. "Towards a Social Analysis of Penality." In David Garland and Peter Young, eds., *The Power to Punish: Contemporary Penality and Social Analysis*. London: Heinemann Educational Books.

Gemignani, Robert J. 1972. Foreword to Robert L. Smith, *A Quiet Revolution*. Washington: Government Printing Office.

Gottfredsen, Don M. 1983. "Probation and Parole: Release and Revocation." In Sanford H. Kadish, ed., *Encyclopedia of Crime and Justice*, vol. 3, pp. 1247–1255. New York: Free Press.

Grabosky, Peter N. 1984. "The Variability of Punishment." In Donald Black, ed., *Toward a General Theory of Social Control*, vol. 1. Orlando, FL: Academic Press.

Great Britain, Home Office. 1978. *The Sentence of the Court*. 3d ed. London: Her Majesty's Stationary Office.

Greenberg, David F. 1975. "The Incapacitative Effect of Imprisonment: Some Estimates." *Law and Society Review* 9(4):541–580.

———. 1977. "The Dynamics of Oscillatory Punishment Processes." *Journal of Criminal Law and Criminology* 68:643–651.

———. 1980. "Penal Sanctions in Poland: A Test of Alternative Models." *Social Problems* 28:194–204.

———. 1981. *Crime and Capitalism: Readings in Marxist Criminology*. Palo Alto, CA: Mayfield Publishing Co.

Greenwood, P. W., with A. Abrahamse. 1982. *Selective Incapacitation*, report R-2815-NIJ. Santa Monica, CA: Rand Corporation.

Grunhut, Max. 1948. *Penal Reform: A Comparative Study*. Oxford: Clarendon Press.

Harland, A. T. 1981. "Court-ordered Community Service in Criminal Law: The Continuing Tyranny of Benevolence." *Buffalo Law Review* 29:425–486.

Hart, H. L. A. 1957. "Murder and the Principles of Punishment: England and the United States." *Northwestern University Law Review* 52:446–467.

Hay, Douglas. 1980. "Crime and Justice in Eighteenth- and Nineteenth-Century England." In Norval Morris and Michael Tonry, eds., *Crime and Justice: An Annual Review of Research*, vol. 2, pp. 45–84. Chicago: University of Chicago Press.

Hirsch, Adam J. 1982. "From Pillory to Penitentiary: The Rise of Criminal Incarceration in Early Massachusetts." *Michigan Law Review* 80:1179–1269.

Hirst, Paul Q. 1972. "Marx and Engels on Law, Crime, and Morality." *Economy and Society* 1:28–56.

Hoffman, P. B. 1983. "Screening for Risk: A Revised Salient Factor Score (SFS81)." *Journal of Criminal Justice* 11:539–547.

Hoffman, P. B., and J. L. Beck. 1974. "Parole Decision-making: A Salient Factor Score." *Journal of Criminal Justice* 2:195–206.

Ignatieff, Michael. 1978. *A Just Measure of Pain: The Penitentiary in the Industrial Revolution, 1750–1850.* New York: Columbia University Press.

———. 1981. "State, Civil Society, and Total Institutions: A Critique of Recent Social Histories of Punishment." In Michael Tonry and Norval Morris, eds., *Crime and Justice: An Annual Review of Research*, vol. 3. Chicago: University of Chicago Press.

Jacobs, James B. 1977. "Macrosociology and Imprisonment." In David F. Greenberg, ed., *Corrections and Punishment.* Beverly Hills, CA: Sage Publications.

———. 1980. "The Prisoners' Rights Movement and Its Impact." In Norval Morris and Michael Tonry, eds., *Crime and Justice: An Annual Review of Research*, vol. 2, pp. 429–470. Chicago: University of Chicago Press.

———. 1983–1984. "The Politics of Prison Expansion." *New York University Review of Law and Social Change* 12:209–241.

Jacoby, Joseph E., and Christopher S. Dunn. 1987. "National Survey on Punishment for Criminal Offenses, Executive Summary." Paper presented at meeting of the National Conference on Punishment for Criminal Offenses, Ann Arbor, MI, November.

Jankovic, Ivan. 1977. "Labor Market and Imprisonment." *Crime and Social Justice* 8:17–31.

Jones, T. Anthony, and Andrew T. Scull. 1973. "Durkheim's 'Two Laws of Penal Evolution': An Introduction." *Economy and Society* 12(3):278–284.

Kaiser, Günter. 1984. *Prison Systems and Correctional Laws: Europe, the United States, and Japan. A Comparative Analysis.* New York: Transnational Publishers.

Kaplan, John. 1970. *Marijuana—The New Prohibition.* New York and Cleveland: World Publishing Co.

Knapp, Kay A. 1984. "What Sentencing Reform in Minnesota Has and Has Not Accomplished." *Judicature* 68:181–189.

———. 1987. "Implementation of the Minnesota Guidelines: Can the Innovative Spirit Be Preserved?" In Andrew von Hirsch, Kay A. Knapp, and Michael Tonry, *The Sentencing Commission and Its Guidelines*. Boston: Northeastern University Press.

Landes, William M. 1971. "An Economic Analysis of the Courts." *Journal of Law and Economics* 14:61–107.

———. 1973. "The Bail System: An Economic Approach." *Journal of Legal Studies* 2:79.

Lederer, Richard. 1989. "On Language." *New York Times Magazine*, September 3, 1989, p. 14.

Lerman, Paul. 1975. *Community Treatment and Social Control*. Chicago: University of Chicago Press.

Lipton, Dugan, Robert Martinson, and Judith Wilks. 1975. *The Effectiveness of Correctional Treatment: A Survey of Treatment Evaluation Studies*. New York: Praeger.

Mannheim, Hermann. 1939. *The Dilemma of Penal Reform*. London: Allen & Unwin.

Martin, J. P. 1965. "The Cost of Crime: Some Research Problems." *International Review of Criminal Policy* 23:57–63.

Martin, J. P., and J. Bradley. 1963–1964. "Design of a Study of the Cost of Crime." *British Journal of Criminology* 4:591–603.

Martinson, Robert M. 1974. "What Works? Questions and Answers about Prison Reform." *Public Interest* 35:22–54.

Melossi, Dario. 1977. "The Penal Question in Capital." *Crime and Social Justice* 6:26–33.

———. 1978. "Georg Rusche and Otto Kirchheimer: Punishment and Social Structure." *Crime and Social Justice* 9:73–85.

———. 1979. "Institutions of Social Control and Capitalist Organization of Work." In B. Fine et al., eds., *Capitalism and the Rule of Law*. London: Hutchinson.

Melossi, Dario, and Massimo Pavarini. [1977] Trans. 1981. *The Prison and the Factory: Origins of the Penitentiary System*. Totowa, NJ: Barnes & Noble.

Milovanovic, Dragan. 1981. "Book Review: *Discipline and Punish: The Birth of the Prison* by Michel Foucault." *International Journal of Comparative and Applied Criminal Justice* 5:125–127.

Minnesota Sentencing Guidelines Commission. 1984. *The Impact of the Minnesota Sentencing Guidelines: Three Year Evaluation*. St. Paul: Minnesota Sentencing Guidelines Commission.

Moore, Mark H. 1986. "Purblind Justice: Normative Issues in the Use of Prediction in the Criminal Justice System." In Alfred Blumstein et al., eds., *Criminal Careers and "Career Criminals,"* 2:314–315. Washington: National Academy Press.

Morris, Norval. 1951. *The Habitual Criminal*. Cambridge, MA: Harvard University Press.

————. 1974. *The Future of Imprisonment*. Chicago: University of Chicago Press.

Mullen, Joan, Kenneth Carlson, and Bradford Smith. 1980. *American Prisons and Jails*. Vol. 2, *Population Trends and Perspectives*. Washington: Government Printing Office.

Nagel, William G. 1977. "On Behalf of a Moratorium on Prison Construction." *Crime and Delinquency* 2:154–172.

Nathan, V. M. 1979. "The Use of Masters in Institutional Reform Litigation." *University of Toledo Law Review* 10:419–464.

National Advisory Commission on Criminal Justice Standards and Goals. 1973. *Task Force Report on Corrections*. Washington: Government Printing Office.

National Commission on Law Observance and Enforcement. 1931a. *The Cost of Crime*, vol. 12. Washington: Government Printing Office.

National Commission on Law Observance and Enforcement (Wickersham Commission). 1931b. *Report on Penal Institutions, Probation and Parole*, vol. 9. Washington: Government Printing Office.

National Council on Crime and Delinquency (NCCD). 1972. "Institutional Construction: A Policy Statement." *Crime and Delinquency* 18:331–332.

————. 1973. "The Nondangerous Offender Should Not Be Imprisoned: A Policy Statement." *Crime and Delinquency* 19:449–456.

National Moratorium on Prison Construction. 1978. *The Moratorium on Prison Construction: Some Questions and Answers*. Boston: Unitarian Universalist Service Committee.

Niederhoffer, Arthur. 1969. *Behind the Shield: The Police in Urban Society*. New York: Doubleday Anchor.

NORC. 1972–1989. *General Social Survey Trends*. Chicago: NORC.

Nozick, Robert. 1981. *Philosophical Explanations*. Cambridge, MA: Harvard University Press.

Ohlin, Lloyd E. 1975. Foreword to Paul Lerman, *Community Treatment and Social Control*. Chicago: University of Chicago Press.

Parkinson, C. Northcote. 1957. *Parkinson's Law and Other Studies in Administration*. Cambridge, MA: Houghton Mifflin.

Pease, Ken. 1985. "Community Service Orders." In Michael Tonry and Norval Morris, eds., *Crime and Justice: An Annual Review of Research*, vol. 6. Chicago: University of Chicago Press.

Petersilia, Joan. 1987. *Expanding Options for Criminal Sentencing*. Santa Monica, CA: Rand Corporation.

Petersilia, Joan, and Peter W. Greenwood. 1978. "Mandatory Prison Sentences: Their Projected Effects on Crime and Prison Populations." *Journal of Criminal Law and Criminology* 69(4):604–615.

Philips, David. 1983. "A Just Measure of Crime, Authority, Hunters, and Blue Locusts: The 'Revisionist' Social History of Crime and the Law in Britain, 1780–1850." In Stanley Cohen and Andrew Scull, eds., *Social Control and the State*, pp. 50–74. New York: St. Martin's Press.

Polinsky, A. Mitchell, and Daniel L. Rubinfeld. 1986. *A Note on Optimal*

Public Enforcement with Settlements and Litigation Costs. Working Paper No. 2114. Cambridge, MA: National Bureau of Economic Research.

Posner, Richard A. 1970. "A Statistical Study of Antitrust Enforcement." *Journal of Law and Economics* 13:365–419.

———. 1972. *Economic Analysis of Law.* Boston: Little, Brown & Co.

President's Commission on Law Enforcement and Administration of Justice. 1967a. *The Challenge of Crime in a Free Society.* Washington: Government Printing Office.

———. 1967b. *Task Force Report: Corrections.* Washington: Government Printing Office.

———. 1968. *Task Force Report: The Courts.* Washington: U.S. Department of Justice.

Quinney, Richard. 1977. *Class, State and Crime: On the Theory and Practice of Criminal Justice.* New York: David McKay.

Radzinowicz, Sir Leon. 1971. Foreword to Mark Ancel, *Suspended Sentence.* London: Heinemann.

Ramsay, Malcolm. 1982. "Two Centuries of Imprisonment." *Home Office Research Bulletin* 14:45–47.

Rauma, David. 1981a. "A Concluding Note on the Stability of Punishment: Reply to Blumstein, Cohen, Moitra, and Nagin." *Journal of Criminal Law and Criminology* 72(4):1809–1812.

———. 1981b. "Crime and Punishment Reconsidered: Some Comments on Blumstein's Stability of Punishment Hypothesis." *Journal of Criminal Law and Criminology* 72(4):1772–1798.

Reckless, Walter C. 1961. *The Crime Problem.* 3d ed. New York: Appleton-Century-Crofts.

Rector, Milton G. 1977. "Are More Prisons Needed Now?" In Matthew Matlin, ed. *Should We Build More Prisons?* Hackensack, NJ: National Council on Crime and Delinquency.

Rhodes, W., H. Tyson, J. Weekley, C. Conly, and G. Powell. 1982. *Developing Criteria for Identifying Career Criminals.* Washington: U.S. Department of Justice.

Roberts, Andrew. 1974. "Book Review: *The Discovery of the Asylum* by David Rothman." *British Journal of Criminology* 14:304–305.

Rothman, David J. 1971. *The Discovery of the Asylum: Social Order and Disorder in the New Republic.* Boston: Little, Brown & Co.

Rusche, Georg, and Otto Kirchheimer. 1939. *Punishment and Social Structure.* New York: Columbia University Press.

Saleeby, George. 1971. "Five Years of Probation Subsidy." *California Youth Authority Quarterly* 5:3–13.

Schelling, Thomas. 1984. *Choice and Consequences.* Cambridge, MA: Harvard University Press.

Scull, Andrew T. 1977. *Decarceration: Community Treatment and the Deviant—A Radical View.* Englewood Cliffs, NJ: Prentice-Hall.

Sechrest, Lee, Susan O. White, and Elizabeth D. Brown, eds. 1979. *The Rehabilitation of Criminal Offenders: Problems and Prospects.* Washington: National Academy of Sciences.

Sellin, J. Thorsten. 1976. *Slavery and the Penal System.* New York: Elsevier.
Sherman, Michael, and Gordon Hawkins. 1981. *Imprisonment in America: Choosing the Future.* Chicago: University of Chicago Press.
Shinnar, Shlomo, and Reuel Shinnar. 1975. "The Effects of the Criminal Justice System on the Control of Crime: A Quantitative Approach." *Law and Society Review* 9:581–611.
Singer, Richard. 1979. "Book Review: *Discipline and Punish: The Birth of the Prison* by Michel Foucault." *Crime and Delinquency* 25:376–379.
Smith, Robert L. 1972. *A Quiet Revolution: Probation Subsidy.* U.S. Department of Health, Education, and Welfare Publication No. (SRS)72–26011. Washington: Government Printing Office.
Sorokin, Pitirim A. 1937. *Social and Cultural Dynamics,* vol. 2. New York: American Book Co.
Sparks, Richard F. 1971. "The Use of Suspended Sentences." *Criminal Law Review* 384–401.
Spierenburg, Pieter. 1984. *The Spectacle of Suffering.* Cambridge: Cambridge University Press.
Stigler, George J. 1970. "The Optimum Enforcement of Law." *Journal of Political Economy* 78:526–536.
Sutherland, Edwin H. 1934. "The Decreasing Prison Population of England." *Journal of Criminal Law and Criminology* 24:880–900.
———. 1939. *Principles of Criminology.* 3d ed. Philadelphia: J. B. Lippincott.
———. 1947. *Principles of Criminology.* 4th ed. Philadelphia: J. B. Lippincott.
Thomas, J. E. 1972. *The English Prison Office since 1850: A Study in Conflict.* London and Boston: Routledge & Kegan Paul.
Tomlinson, Heather. 1980. "Book Review: *A Just Measure of Pain* by Michael Ignatieff." *British Journal of Criminology* 20:74–75.
Tonry, Michael. 1987a. "Sentencing Guidelines and Their Effects." In Andrew von Hirsch, Kay A. Knapp, and Michael Tonry, *The Sentencing Commission and Its Guidelines,* pp. 16–43. Boston: Northeastern University Press.
———. 1987b. *Sentencing Reform Impacts.* Washington: National Institute of Justice.
U.S. Congress, House Committee on the Judiciary Hearings. 1975. *Prison Construction Plans and Policy.* 94th Congress.
U.S. Congressional Research Service. 1974. *Prison Population and Costs—Illustrative Projections to 1980.* Washington: Library of Congress.
U.S. Department of Commerce, Bureau of Census. 1965–1988. *Current Population Reports.* Washington: Government Printing Office.
———. 1988. *Statistical Abstract of the USA.* Washington: Government Printing Office.
U.S. Department of Justice. 1950–1989. *Uniform Crime Reports.* Washington: Government Printing Office.
U.S. Department of Justice, Bureau of Justice Statistics. 1972–1989. *Sourcebook of Criminal Justice Statistics.* Washington: Government Printing Office.

————. 1983. Bulletin. *Prisoners at Midyear 1983.* Washington: U.S. Department of Justice.

————. 1984. Special Report. *Returning to Prison.* Washington: U.S. Department of Justice.

————. 1986a. "The Cost of Crime." *Bureau of Justice Statistics Data Report.* Washington: Government Printing Office.

————. 1986b. *Criminal Victimization 1985.* Washington: Government Printing Office.

————. 1986c. *Historical Corrections Statistics in the United States, 1850–1984* by Margaret Cahalan. Washington: U.S. Department of Justice.

————. 1987a. "Jail Inmates 1986." *Bureau of Justice Statistics Bulletin.* Washington: Government Printing Office.

————. 1987b. "Prisoners in 1986." *Bureau of Justice Statistics Bulletin.* Washington: Government Printing Office.

————. 1987c. *Sourcebook of Criminal Justice Statistics 1986.* Washington: Government Printing Office.

————. 1988a. *Data Report 1988.* Washington: U.S. Department of Justice.

————. 1988b. *Historical Statistics on Prisoners in State and Federal Institutions, Yearend 1925–86.* Washington: Government Printing Office.

————. 1988c. *Sourcebook of Criminal Justice Statistics—1987.* Washington: Government Printing Office.

————. 1988d. Special Report. *Federal Offenses and Offenders: Drug Law Violators, 1980–1986.* Washington: U.S. Department of Justice.

————. 1988e. Special Report. *Profile of State Prison Inmates, 1986.* Washington: U.S. Department of Justice.

————. 1989. Bulletin. *Prisoners in 1988.* Washington: U.S. Department of Justice.

U.S. Department of Justice, Bureau of Prisons. 1936. *Federal Offenders 1934–1935.* Fort Leavenworth, KS: Federal Prison Industries Inc. Press.

U.S. Department of Justice, Federal Bureau of Prisons. 1986. *Statistical Report Fiscal Year 1986.* Washington: Government Printing Office.

U.S. Department of Justice, Law Enforcement Assistance Administration, National Institute of Law Enforcement and Criminal Justice. 1978. *The National Manpower Survey of the Criminal Justice System.* Vol. 3, *Corrections,* by the National Planning Association. Washington: Government Printing Office.

U.S. Department of Justice, National Institute of Corrections. 1981. *Request for Proposals, Fiscal Year 1982.* Washington: U.S. Department of Justice.

U.S. Department of Justice, National Institute of Justice. 1980. *American Prisons and Jails.* Vol. 1, *Summary Findings and Policy Implications of a National Survey;* vol. 2, *Population Trends and Projections;* and vol. 3, *Conditions and Costs of Confinement.* Washington: Government Printing Office.

U.S. Department of Labor, Bureau of Labor Statistics. 1985–1989. *Employment and Earnings.* Washington: Government Printing Office.

————. 1988. *Handbook of Labor Statistics*. Washington: Government Printing Office.

U.S. Sentencing Commission. 1987. *Supplementary Report on the Initial Sentencing Guidelines and Policy Statements*. Washington: U.S. Sentencing Commission.

van den Haag, Ernst. 1975. *Punishing Criminals*. New York: Basic Books.

Vold, George Bryan. 1958. *Theoretical Criminology*. New York: Oxford University Press.

Voltaire, François-Marie Arouet. [1751] 1962. *The Age of Louis XIV*. New York: Dutton.

von Hirsch, Andrew. 1987a. "The Enabling Legislation." In Andrew von Hirsch, Kay A. Knapp, and Michael Tonry, eds., *The Sentencing Commission and Its Guidelines*. Boston: Northeastern University Press.

————. 1987b. "The Sentencing Commission's Functions." In Andrew von Hirsch, Kay A. Knapp, and Michael Tonry, eds., *The Sentencing Commission and Its Guidelines*. Boston: Northeastern University Press.

————. 1987c. "Structure and Rationale: Minnesota's Critical Choices." In Andrew von Hirsch, Kay A. Knapp, and Michael Tonry, eds., *The Sentencing Commission and Its Guidelines*. Boston: Northeastern University Press.

Waller, Irwin, and Janet Chan. 1974. "Prison Use: A Canadian and International Comparison." *Criminal Law Quarterly* 17:47–71.

Weisser, Michael R. 1982. *Crime and Punishment in Early Modern Europe*. 2d ed. Brighton, England: Harvester Press.

Williams, Bernard. 1982. "Cosmic Philosopher." *New York Review of Books* 29(2):32 (February 18, 1982).

Wilson, James Q. [1975] 1977. *Thinking about Crime*. New York: Vintage Books.

————. 1977a. Cited in Rob Wilson, "U.S. Prison Population Again Hits New High." *Corrections Magazine* 3:1–22.

————. 1977b. "The Political Feasibility of Punishment." In J. B. Cederblom and William L. Blizen, eds., *Justice and Punishment*. Cambridge, MA: Ballinger Publishing Co.

Wolfgang, Marvin, Robert M. Figlio, Paul E. Tracy, and Simon E. Singer. 1985. *The National Survey of Crime Severity*. Washington: Government Printing Office.

Wright, Gordon. 1983. *Between the Guillotine and Liberty: Two Centuries of the Crime Problem in France*. New York and Oxford: Oxford University Press.

Young, Peter. 1983. "Sociology, the State and Penal Relations." In David Garland and Peter Young, eds., *The Power to Punish: Contemporary Penality and Social Analysis*. London: Heinemann Educational Books.

Young, Warren. 1979. *Community Service Orders: The Development and Use of a New Penal Measure*. London: Heinemann.

Zedlewski, Edwin W. 1987. "Making Confinement Decisions." *National Institute of Justice, Research in Brief*. Washington: National Institute of Justice.

Zeisel, Hans. 1982. *The Limits of Law Enforcement.* Chicago: University of Chicago Press.

Zimring, Franklin E. 1984. "Making the Punishment Fit the Crime: A Consumer's Guide to Sentencing Reform." In Gordon Hawkins and Franklin E. Zimring, eds., *The Pursuit of Criminal Justice: Essays from the Chicago Center,* pp. 267–275. Chicago: University of Chicago Press; Midway reprint edition 1986.

Zimring, Franklin E., and Gordon Hawkins. 1973. *Deterrence: The Legal Threat in Crime Control.* Chicago: University of Chicago Press.

Index

(page references to graphs and tables are followed by *t*).

President's Commission on Law Enforcement and Justice, 64
President's Commission Task Force on Corrections, 67
Prevention, 86; costs of, 98; through incapacitation, 94–95 (*see also* Incapacitation); programs, productivity of, 101; security goods and services, costs of, 93, 101–2
Prevention of Crime Act of 1908 (England), 167
Preventive detention, 88, 90, 169. *See also* Selective Incapacitation
Prison Commission (England), 159
"Prison Populations: A System Out of Control?" (Blumstein), 157–58
Prisons, state and federal, 16; Auburn system, 11, 40; capacity of, 79, 80–81, 87, 90, 171–73, 203, 209, 210, 219; conditions in, 198 (*see also* Judicial intervention); construction of, 171–73, 177, 197–98, 211, 219; costs of, 93; correctional forecasting (*see* Correctional forecasting); crime control function of, 89–90; criminologists' studies of, 1, 3–37; expressive function of, 187–88; federal policies toward, 138–42; historians of, 38–60; incapacitative function (*see* Incapacitation); net stay in, 105; overcrowding in (*see* Overcrowding); Pennsylvania system, 11, 33; population in (*see* Population, prison); riots within, 40, 46, 78; in Victorian England, 48. *See also* Houses of Correction; Jails; Penitentiary; Reform school
Probation, 8, 65, 95, 180–82, 190, 207
Probation subsidy program, California, 140, 199–201, 212
Productivity relations, 4
Prohibition, 193–94
Prostitution, 51
Public danger, 187. *See also* Safety crime
Public facilities for custodial security, 217. *See also* Alternative correctional programs
Public opinion 125–30, 129t, 167, 189
Punishable behavior, 15, 164
Punishment: capital, 43, 52, 139; changes in emphasis of, 163–67; corporal, 139; "desert theorists," xii; dynamics of, through historical shift in types, 58;

expected, as cost of criminal enterprise, 91; imprisonment (*see* Imprisonment; Prisons); stability of, 14–29 passim; theories of, 4–37, 85–88, 187–88; time-series measures of, 23–24; torture, as public spectacle, 46; transportation to colonies, 6, 7, 51, 52. *See also* Fines; Galley slavery; Imprisonment; Sentence
Punishment and Social Structure (Rusche and Kirchheimer), 3–14, 30, 34
Punishment, Prison, and the Public (Cross), 158–59

Qualitative analyses of imprisonment, 58, 59–60
Quinney, Richard, 30

Race of offender, 73, 74t
Radzinowicz, Sir Leon, 179, 180
Ramsay, Malcolm, 53
Rand Corporation cost-benefit study, 93, 98, 99, 99t
Rape, 43, 106, 165t
Rauma, David, 23, 24–25
Recidivism, 47; among drug users, 134, 174; juvenile, 184
Reclassification, 78
Records of offenders, 109. *See also* Information management
Rector, Milton, 77, 171
Reductionism, 53
Reform, 91. *See also* Rehabilitation
Reformatory, 49
Reform school, xiii
Region: prison population by, 143t, 144t, 146t; as unit of analysis, 142–48, 221
Rehabilitation, 89, 157–60, 181; versus custody, 42
Release costs, 93
Repeat offenders, 88, 167. *See also* Career criminals
Report on Penal Institutions, Probation and Parole (Wickersham Commission), 63
Report on the Prisons (Wines and White), 43
Retribution, 85, 86, 91
Revenue laws, liquor, 193–94
Rhode Island, adopts Pennsylvania system, 11
Riots, prison, 40, 46, 78
Robbery, 43, 99, 105, 106, 107, 165t